CONTEMPORARY ISSUES IN LEARNING AND TEACHING

re

Education at SAGE

SAGE is a leading international publisher of journals, books, and electronic media for academic, educational, and professional markets.

Our education publishing includes:

- accessible and comprehensive texts for aspiring education professionals and practitioners looking to further their careers through continuing professional development

- inspirational advice and guidance for the classroom

- authoritative state of the art reference from the leading authors in the field

Find out more at: **www.sagepub.co.uk/education**

CONTEMPORARY ISSUES IN LEARNING AND TEACHING

Edited by
Margery McMahon, Christine Forde
and Margaret Martin

SAGE

Los Angeles | London | New Delhi
Singapore | Washington DC

First published 2011

SAGE Publications Ltd
1 Oliver's Yard
55 City Road
London EC1Y 1SP

SAGE Publications Inc.
2455 Teller Road
Thousand Oaks, California 91320

SAGE Publications India Pvt Ltd
B 1/I 1 Mohan Cooperative Industrial Area
Mathura Road
New Delhi 110 044

SAGE Publications Asia-Pacific Pte Ltd
33 Pekin Street #02-01
Far East Square
Singapore 048763

Library of Congress Control Number: 2010926544

British Library Cataloguing in Publication data

A catalogue record for this book is available from the British Library

ISBN 978-1-84920-127-8
ISBN 978-1-84920-128-5 (pbk)

Typeset by C&M Digitals (P) Ltd, Chennai, India
Printed in Great Britain by MPG Books Group Bodmin, Cornwall
Printed on paper from sustainable resources

Mixed Sources
Product group from well-managed forests and other controlled sources
www.fsc.org Cert no. SA-COC-1565
© 1996 Forest Stewardship Council
FSC

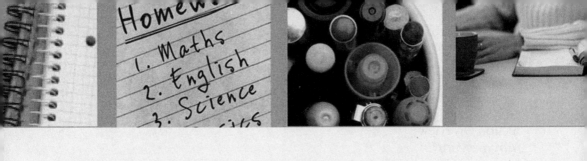

CONTENTS

PREFACE

This book grew partly from recognition of the range of research and professional interests of a group of colleagues working together and partly from a common standpoint of the importance of developing a critical stance in the education of teachers. Each of the authors contributes to programmes for initial and continuing teacher education where, in our view, an important task is to build a critical awareness of the contested nature of education. Education in the UK, as in many other countries, is a key element of social and economic policy and so not only is there an increasingly centralized decision-making process, but policy statements and guidelines have proliferated. Such material is designed to direct practice and there is only limited exploration of the issues associated with particular areas. Often we have found ourselves writing material which not only provided an overview of a particular area of practice, but also helped the students to ask questions about the underpinning purposes and assumptions in particular areas of policy and practice.

The book is designed to be used as a course text and has been structured to allow for group discussion as well as individual reflection. The book is divided into three sections – policy, learning and practice – and though each section and chapter is self-standing, we see as an important issue the interconnection between policy processes, the changing professional context of the teacher and learning and teaching in the classroom. Each chapter examines critically the central concepts related to the specific topic and highlights some of the key issues. Through each chapter there is a series of questions designed to enable the reader, individually or working together, to respond to these key issues. Given the range of topics covered in the book, each chapter provides an overview of the main issues but a series of questions and further reading is suggested at the end of each chapter in order that specific issues can be subsequently explored in greater depth.

ACKNOWLEDGEMENTS

We would like to thank our editors at Sage, particularly Jude Bowen who was very supportive of the original idea for a book of collected essays reflecting the interests of a group of colleagues. We would also like to thank Matthew Waters whose guidance in the subsequent shaping of the pedagogic focus of the book has proved invaluable.

We are very grateful to our colleagues in the Department of Educational Studies who contributed to the book and worked with good humour and enthusiasm to meet the deadlines we imposed.

We would also like to acknowledge the contribution of others and particularly Jamilla Razzaq whose work in preparing the final manuscript was invaluable. We would also like to thank the students and serving teachers on the various programmes we teach whose many questions and observations have challenged our thinking and helped to refine our ideas.

Margery McMahon
Christine Forde
Margaret Martin

ABOUT THE EDITORS AND CONTRIBUTORS

Dr Mike Carroll

Mike Carroll is a lecturer in the Faculty of Education at the University of Glasgow. Mike contributes to a range of Initial Teacher Education programmes including the BEd and PGDE programmes. Mike is Course Leader of PGDE Understanding Learning and Teaching and Course Leader of PGDE (Primary) School Experience. He has also been involved in programmes for serving teachers, with a particular interest in the development of leaders at all levels in the school; this work has including contributions to the Chartered Teacher Programme, courses for middle leaders and the Scottish Qualification for Headship. Mike has published a number of articles on his area of research interest including the development of collaborative enquiry, accomplished teaching and science education.

Robert Doherty

Robert Doherty teaches in the Department of Educational Studies at the University of Glasgow. After a career in shipbuilding and heavy engineering Robert taught technical subjects in secondary schools, with responsibilities for pastoral care and pupil support. His main research interests are around education policy, the politics of education, the sociology of education and teacher education. Robert currently leads the Education Policy Course within the Faculty's Ed D programme.

Professor Penny Enslin

Chair of Education in the Department of Educational Studies, Penny Enslin is Director of the Ed D programme. Until July 2006 she was a Professor in the School of Education at the University of the Witwatersrand, Johannesburg, where she now holds the position of Professor Emeritus. Her research and teaching interests lie in the area of political theory and education, with particular interests in citizenship education. Rated as an internationally acclaimed researcher by the National Research Foundation in South Africa, she has published internationally on higher education, globalisation and internationalisation, public reason and education, liberalism, gender and feminist theory, nation building, and African philosophy of education.

Dr Cathy Fagan

Cathy Fagan is a lecturer in the Department of Educational Studies at the University of Glasgow. She teaches on the Chartered Teacher Programme and on undergraduate and postgraduate initial teacher education programmes. Her main research focus is the social, cultural and policy contexts of work-related education, and her doctoral studies examined education and work in the contexts of a global knowledge economy, enterprise culture and entrepreneurship. Her current research is on values-based approaches to financial education programmes. She is chair of the International Association for Citizenship, Social and Economics Education (IACSEE) and is editor of that Association's international peer-reviewed journal of the same name (CSEE).

Professor Christine Forde

Christine Forde is Professor of Leadership and Professional Learning in the Faculty of Education at Glasgow University. During her career she has worked as a primary teacher and tutor in initial teacher education. She now mainly works in the area of leadership development and in teacher professional development and learning including Programme Leader for the Scottish Qualification for Headship (SQH). She has published several books and articles on teacher professional development including a number of books with colleagues, including *Professional Development, Reflection and Enquiry* (Paul Chapman, 2006) and *Putting Together Professional Portfolios* (Sage, 2009). She is involved in a number of projects on leadership development. In addition she has published books in the area of gender and feminist perspectives in education, including *Feminist Utopianism and Education* (Sense, 2007).

Dr George Head

George Head is a Senior Lecturer in the Department of Educational Studies at Gasgow University. He teaches, researches and publishes in Support for Learning and Inclusive Education. Within this area he has a special interest in the learning of children and young people with Social, Emotional and Behavioural Difficulties (SEBD). He teaches on undergraduate courses in initial teacher education, and on taught postgraduate courses leading to Certificate, Diploma and MEd in Inclusive Education. He is the author of

Better Learning, Better Behaviour (Dunedin Academic Press, 2007). George has played a key role in the development of Moving Image Education in Scotland.

Margaret Martin

Margaret Martin is Senior Lecturer in the Department of Educational Studies at Glasgow University. She has held a range of posts from head teacher to education officer and has a background in leadership and personal development. She has taught on post-graduate and undergraduate teacher education programmes, as well as middle leadership certificate programmes, but now concentrates on the professional development of head teachers in Glasgow, through the delivery of the Post Graduate Diploma in School Leadership and Management (Scottish Qualification for Headship). She also teaches on the Critical Reflection course of the Ed D online programme. Currently Margaret is working with a large Glasgow secondary school on the development of a professional learning community, providing support for the head teacher and professional development for the middle managers in the school.

Dr Margaret McCulloch

Margaret McCulloch teaches in the Department of Educational Studies in the University of Glasgow, where she works both with student teachers and with experienced teachers returning to postgraduate study. Originally trained and employed for many years as a primary teacher, she subsequently worked as a peripatetic Support for Learning teacher in both primary and secondary schools. During her time as coordinator of a team of support teachers and as an Inclusion Development Officer she gained valuable experience of working collaboratively with parents, teachers and colleagues from other professions. Her particular interests are in developing reading comprehension and in encouraging inclusive thinking and practice.

Dr Margery McMahon

Margery McMahon is Senior Lecturer and Head of the Department of Educational Studies, University of Glasgow. She is also Programme Director of the Chartered Teacher Programme – a Masters programme for experienced classroom practitioners. She is a member of the Board of the International Council for Education for Teaching (ICET). Formerly a teacher of History and Politics, Margery teaches on a range of courses relating to professional learning and leadership. Together with colleagues in the Department of Educational Studies she co-authored *Professional Development, Reflection and Enquiry* (Paul Chapman, 2006) and with Christine Forde and Jenny Reeves, *Putting Together Professional Portfolios* (Sage, 2009). She was instrumental in introducing International Educational courses into the Chartered Teacher programme at University of Glasgow and is currently working on a new publication on International Education. Her research focuses on teachers' professional development and learning and she has been involved in a number of research projects relating to this.

Dr Alastair McPhee
Alastair McPhee has worked as a Senior Lecturer in the Department of Educational Studies at the University of Glasgow. He has mainly been concerned with initial and continuing teacher development, and has worked extensively in the fields of access to teacher education, the development of teachers of music and teacher professional development. He has been the author of a number of papers in academic journals in these areas. He has particularly been engaged with Glasgow City Council in a successful project to widen the applicant pool to teacher education.

Dr Fiona Patrick
Fiona Patrick is a lecturer in the Faculty of Education at the University of Glasgow. She teaches on a variety of courses in initial teacher education and undergraduate education programmes. She is currently involved in the development of assessment processes and the use of feedback in undergraduate programmes. Her main research interest is in teacher professionalism and development but she has a background in the history of education which informs her other interests (the early development of educational psychology; the growth of educational provision in Britain and Europe).

Dr Niamh Stack
Niamh Stack is a lecturer in Developmental Psychology in the Faculty of Education at the University of Glasgow. She is also the Development Officer for the Scottish Network for Able Pupils (SNAP). As part of SNAP Niamh works with schools and education authorities across Scotland as they seek to make learning meaningful for highly able pupils through in-service events, subject development days and consultation activities. SNAP is also actively engaged in research activities related to gifted and talented education including a recent EPPI funded systematic review of interventions aimed at improving the educational achievement of pupils identified as gifted and talented. She is a member of the World Council for Gifted and Talented Children and the European Council for High Ability and has presented papers at national and international conferences on gifted and talented education.

Margaret Sutherland
Margaret Sutherland is the project leader for the Scottish Network for Able Pupils (SNAP) and lectures at the University of Glasgow in Additional Support for Learning and coordinates the Masters in Inclusive Education. She has 28 years' teaching experience in mainstream primary schools, behaviour support

and latterly in higher education. She has written articles in the field of gifted education and is the author of *Gifted and Talented in the Early Years: A Practical Guide for 3–5 Year Olds* (Sage, 2005) and *Developing the Gifted and Talented Young Learner* (Sage, 2008). She is on the editorial board of the Korean Educational Development Institute *Journal of Educational Policy*. She regularly gives keynote addresses at conferences and has led courses, workshops and seminars across the UK on gifted education. She has organised and hosted national conferences for teachers. She has been invited to work with teachers, researchers and students in Tanzania, Malawi and Korea.

Dr Georgina Wardle
Georgina Wardle teaches in the Department of Educational Studies at the University of Glasgow. Following an earlier career in schools, she has worked in teacher education in higher education institutions in England and Scotland. Her research in Developmental Psychology investigates children's motives for prosocial behaviour. She is interested in the complexity of developmental, cognitive, social and environmental factors which impact on children's ability to engage in prosocial behaviour towards peers, and the ways in which schools can foster prosocial behaviour.

Mary Wingrave
Mary Wingrave is programme leader for the BA and PG Certificate in Childhood Practice. An experienced senior school manager, Mary also develops and delivers continuing professional development relating to Nurture Groups. She teaches on the suite of leadership programmes offered in the Department of Educational Studies where she is based. She is currently undertaking her Ed D. Much of the focus of her work is on leadership, inclusion and early intervention.

ABBREVIATIONS

ASN	additional support need
ASP	Additional Support Plan
CARN	Collaborative Action Research Network
CfE	Curriculum for Excellence
CIPDE	Continuing Intercultural Professional Development in Europe
CoP	community of practice
CPD	continuing professional development
CPE	collaborative professional enquiry
DCELLS	Department for Children, Education, Lifelong Learning and Skills
DCSF	Department for Children, Schools and Families
DfES	Department for Education and Skills
DFID	Department for International Development
ECM	Every Child Matters
EU	European Union
GIRFEC	Getting It Right for Every Child
GTCE	General Teaching Council for England
GTCNI	General Teaching Council for Northern Ireland
GTCS	General Teaching Council for Scotland
GTCW	General Teaching Council for Wales
HMIe	Her Majesty's Inspectors in Education
IMF	International Monetary Fund
IQ	intelligence quotient
LECT	League of Exchange for Commonwealth Teachers
LLW	Learning for Life and Work
MDG	Millennium Development Goals
NCS	new community schools
NG	nurture group
NQT	newly qualified teacher

OECD	Organisation for Economic Co-operation and Development
OFMDFM	Office of the First Minister and Deputy First Minister
PISA	Programme for International Student Performance
PLC	professional learning community
QCA	Qualification and Curriculum Authority
QCDA	Qualifications and Curriculum Development Agency
SDQ	strengths and difficulties questionnaire
SE	Scottish Executive
SEN	Special educational needs
SLT	speech and language therapy
SIP	Social information processing
TDA	Teacher Development Agency
UN	United Nations
UNCRC	United Nations Convention on the Rights of the Child
UNESCO	United Nations Educational, Scientific, and Cultural Organization
WAG	Welsh Assembly Government
WB	World Bank

CHAPTER 1

INTRODUCTION – CONTEMPORARY ISSUES IN LEARNING AND TEACHING

Margery McMahon, Christine Forde and Margaret Martin

The focus of this book is on contemporary issues in learning and teaching, and to explore these issues we have adopted a wider perspective than just examining learning and teaching strategies. While these strategies are important, equally important is a consideration of the factors that shape the practice of teachers and the experiences of children and young people in classrooms today. To examine these factors we need to explore the landscape of education, where wider socio-political and economic trends are having a profound influence on the priorities identified for education, where research has led to an explosion in our knowledge about the nature of learning and where there have been significant changes in what is expected of teachers. To make sense of these trends and to appraise critically the impact these trends are having on learners and teachers alike, we need to first consider the purposes of education.

The purposes of education are much debated: for example, is education about self fulfilment and preparation for a purposeful life, or is education about ensuring the next generation understand and fulfil their role in society, or indeed, is education about ensuring each learner has the appropriate skills for work? To some degree all of these purposes are evident in education and often the debate is about a matter of emphasis in specific curricular programmes and outcomes. However, we can examine this question of the purposes at a much deeper level by considering why we lay such stress on education for children and young people not just in the UK but also across the world. The United Nations Charter of 1945 gave international expression to the position that education is a human right and, though universal access to primary education has yet to be achieved, we cannot lose sight of the importance we accord education. There are a range of competing purposes in education and each educator must determine and justify his or her own stance. Thus we as the authors of this book argue that education in modern societies has important functions. Leaving aside questions over the content of education there is general agreement that access to education is a personal and public good. Unfairness and inequalities can and do occur within the processes of education and through key aspects of its arrangements such as structure and conditions for access. For us the fundamental purposes of education are achieved by first, ensuring effective learning experiences for all learners and through these experiences, and second, developing the next generation of citizens who will actively contribute to the task of securing social justice and equality. This stance has significant implications for learning and teaching and for teachers which we explore in this book.

Why is this book worth reading?

This book is aimed at those student teachers making the transition from initial teacher education into the teaching profession and for those newly qualified teachers who have just begun their professional journey. The move from student teacher to fully qualified professional could be described as a developmental process where the newly qualified teacher builds on the knowledge, skills and experience gained in initial teacher education and develops a range of broader understandings about what it means to be a teacher. Understandably, new teachers are very concerned with the technicalities of teaching and the practicalities of running a classroom. However as Palmer (1998: 5) argues 'technique is what teachers use until the real teacher arrives', and although technical ability is of course important, we aim, in this book, to encourage new teachers to begin to look beyond their operational remit to deeper considerations of what it means to be a teacher in the twenty-first century.

It is, however, not always easy to persuade teachers of the need to take a wider view of their work, but we argue that this is an essential element of their development and a key area often difficult to address in the course of initial teacher preparation programmes. One of the main reasons new teachers can become so concerned with operational and practical matters is their understandable lack of confidence in their ability to deliver in the classroom. Many see this as an essentially technical matter where they need to improve planning, classroom organisation, use of resources, and so on, and we are arguing that confidence in the classroom can come from other equally important insights, derived from consideration of identity, values and purposes of education. When teachers concern themselves with these apparently more abstract issues, it focuses attention on the *why* rather than the *how* of teaching. They are asking important questions about the rationale that underpins their professional practice and subjecting their everyday professional actions to critical scrutiny. Such scrutiny allows teachers to arrive at a considered position based on critical reflection rather than 'unexamined common sense', as Brookfield (1995) argues. He advocates the use of four lenses through which to view what we do from other angles to unearth our underlying assumptions: our autobiographies as learners and teachers, the views of colleagues, student feedback and, importantly, related literature. He asks us to step outside ourselves to examine how some of our deeply held values and beliefs are informing our practice.

- Examination of autobiography provides the opportunity to explore previous experiences, with a view to understanding why specific views of the world have been internalised and become what we perceive to be 'normal'. Identifying these assumptions is seen as the first step to addressing their validity.
- The views of teaching colleagues are an important source of reflection through discussion of common contexts with others who understand the territory but may have differing viewpoints. This kind of professional dialogue around critical moments in teaching, formal or informal, can often create the conditions where ideas can be tested and explored.
- Seeking the views of students is seen as an essential element in the teacher's critical reflection where the teacher checks in with the learner about their perception of the quality of the learning in the classroom. Without this feedback, teachers are operating in purely transmission mode with little real knowledge of the experience of the learner who is on the receiving end of the teaching. There is also an opportunity here to examine the power relationships in the classroom.
- Lastly, the use of relevant theoretical literature provides an external lens through which to scrutinise ideas about practice by exploring the ideas of others who have investigated the area in question in some depth. It can allow us to name it and see generic patterns in events and processes.

Through this process, Brookfield (1995) argues, teachers give themselves the opportunity to arrive at an informed professional stance, which allows them to develop a sense of confidence about their practice, based on a wider consideration of their actions in the classroom and in the school, rather than simply their personal preferences or available resources. This reflection also addresses the myth that teachers are only interested in things practical and do not engage with theory. It can be argued that teachers have very definite theories in their heads about what constitutes effective learning and teaching, and that the kind of critical reflection suggested by Brookfield allows these theories to be surfaced, explored and subjected to scrutiny.

Many teachers find it a challenge to explain why they use the pedagogical approaches they choose to use in the classroom and tend to rely on a developing repertoire of tried and tested formulae for what seems to work. We want to encourage in teachers the facility to routinely subject their assumptions about learning and teaching to careful inspection in order to develop their professional confidence in the decisions they take. This, we argue, is a crucial dimension of being a 'real teacher', not least because of the immense responsibility carried by education professionals in carrying out their work. It is widely acknowledged that young people's life chances are influenced by their level of education. Therefore teaching can be viewed as a deeply moral and ethical endeavour and it is essential that teachers develop a sense of criticality, both about their own work and about the wider context within which they operate. If teachers can develop this facility they can claim to be truly professional and not simply technicians who go through the motions of implementing external policy and delivering centrally determined curricula using prescribed methodologies.

Making decisions about the kind of teacher you are going to be is central to the development of the identity and integrity of new professionals. This involves consideration of the purposes of education in the global arena of the twenty-first century and teachers' perceptions of their place in delivering those purposes in their everyday work in schools. These are not uncontested areas and there are controversial issues about which new teachers need to develop an informed view, for example the changing role of the teacher, the place of assessment, the nature of curricula and pedagogy. This wider context therefore is worthy of deeper exploration.

Overview of the book

In this book we examine some of the contemporary issues related to learning and teaching by considering critically the wider context in which learners learn and teachers teach. For the authors of this book one of the fundamental purposes of education is to actively contribute to greater equality and social justice. However, wider trends, particularly an increasingly competitive global economy and greater social diversity, are having a considerable impact on education and what is expected of learners and teachers. We need to explore and understand these influences in order that the focus on social justice and equality can be developed. Therefore we need to consider the wider policy contexts and the way these are shaping the processes of learning and teaching and the role of the teacher. In this book we begin by exploring the policy context, including examining the nature of policy. From this we then move on to examine specific areas where there are significant developments in learning and teaching, before considering the ways in which both the global policy trends and our increased understanding of the processes of learning are changing the role of the teacher.

As student teachers embark on their careers we cannot imagine how schools and the role of the teacher may be transformed in the future. However, we can look to some of the underpinning processes that are transforming education, and we begin this book by exploring what is often referred to as the 'very big picture' (Barber, 2001). This 'very big picture' might seem distant from the day-to-day workings of a classroom in a school somewhere in the UK. However, global trends such as economic development, environmental changes and social diversity have an increasing influence on shaping education and social policy, which in turn shape the professional practice of teachers and the processes of learning. Thus one of the key themes of this book is about policy in education.

As in many education systems globally, across the different educational systems in the UK, in Scotland, Northern Ireland, England and Wales, there are significant developments in the teaching profession, in the curriculum and in the governance of schools. However, the processes of policy development and implementation are not straightforward and, indeed, are frequently contested. We can see the way in which policy operates in education by considering the debates about specific policy initiatives designed to achieve particular outcomes as well in the actual process of creating policy. A policy in education codifies a set of values in which there will be assumptions and beliefs about the purposes of education and how best these might be achieved. If we take an example of a current area of concern in education, we can see the assumptions underpinning policy which will often be deeply contested. Thus, a current emphasis in policy in the UK is on numeracy, particularly as international benchmarking shows that education systems in the UK are falling behind other national educational systems with regard to pupil attainment in this area.

This policy drive rests on the idea that a high level of numeric skills is to be valued. In this, though, we can see different views on why numeracy should be valued. It might be argued that numeracy is a vital set of skills particularly for future work or, alternatively, numeracy must be valued because it helps form patterns of thinking that can be applied to other spheres of activity. In contrast, a case might be made for seeing numeracy as having limited relevance. Again here we can discern different standpoints. On the one hand, it might be argued that an emphasis on memorisation in the teaching of numeracy detracts from higher-level thinking skills. On the other hand, given the rise in technology, there is little need for pupils to learn arithmetical skills in the way previous generations did. These positions are based on a view of the usefulness or otherwise of numeracy, but we can go to a deeper level and ask how the focus on numeracy can serve the task of promoting social justice and equality: will the emphasis on numeracy reduce the learning experiences and opportunities for particular groups of learners, or by not ensuring achievement in this core skill will we be reducing access to many areas of the curriculum, for example the sciences or economics, which potentially would enable particular groups of learners access to higher education and employment. Policy, even in a clearly defined area of the curriculum, is underpinned by specific assumptions and values which may be contested. Teachers therefore need to understand the assumptions underpinning policy and be able to make informed decisions about their practice.

Policy is part of the landscape of education and indeed is critical in the commitment to improve the educational experiences of young people to promote social justice and equality. Educational policy has driven many positive changes evident in schools in the UK today, including ensuring inclusive education where every child and young person has access to the full set of curricular experiences that support their learning. Policy, side by side with legislation, has also helped create a concern for ensuring effective learning experiences in safe and secure settings to enable children and young people to achieve. What is important, though, is that teachers are aware of the underpinning values and ideas, are able to interrogate these and come to reasoned positions in the development of their role and practice. Thus an important aspect of this book is examining the tensions in a number of policy trends such as the relationship between education and the economy, education in a global context and education and individual rights to enable teachers to explore the values and assumptions on which these policies are based and consider their own stance.

The policy context is one arena which has had a profound effect on education, particularly since the early 1980s. At the same time, our understanding of how we learn has expanded rapidly through research in a variety of disciplines, including education, psychology, neuroscience and sociology, and some of the tensions that arise are often the balance between policy shaped by political agendas and the use of professional knowledge about the nature of learning. Thus, increasingly in the design of curricular policy and programmes we need to take into account the ever-expanding knowledge about the holistic nature of learning in which the social, emotional, physical, cognitive and spiritual areas are all of fundamental importance in the development of the next generation of citizens who will face challenges we have yet to appreciate. Therefore, teachers need to be able to look at the whole child or young person in his or her setting, and conceive of a school's curriculum as the sum of his or her experiences in order to be able to create the conditions for effective learning. A keynote of this book is that social justice has to be grounded in a vision of providing access to good learning. It is in only this way that schools and teachers can enable learners who achieve in and beyond school and who, as citizens, work for social justice in a globalised world. This position highlights the importance of the role of the teacher.

The developments in the policy context and in the learning context are having a profound influence on the professional context. The expansion of knowledge about learning has helped to develop understandings of pedagogy, and very different sets of skills, dispositions and knowledge are now demanded of teachers. They have to be able to work with their teacher colleagues as well as other professionals and, further, teachers are now expected to continue to develop their skills and knowledge throughout their careers. Thus, in this book we explore the way in which teachers grapple with these changes which are reshaping their role.

The structure of the book

This book has been designed to explore a range of different influences on learning and teaching, to highlight some of the issues facing teachers and, most importantly, to enable the reader to consider his or her position on these issues. The issues explored in this book might seem distant from the immediacy of the classroom where teachers are called upon to make rapid decisions about the learning opportunities of children and young people. However, it is because of the intensity of classroom and school life that it is essential that teachers have the opportunity to explore and understand the issues underpinning learning and teaching, and to make considered judgements about how to provide effective learning opportunities to actively work for equality and social justice.

The book is divided into three sections, each dealing with a specific context: policy, learning and practice. The section overviews map out the broad issues evident in the particular context being explored. Each chapter then examines a particular area drawing together current research and professional debates. The key ideas examined in each chapter are listed at the beginning to provide a framework for the discussion. Within each chapter there are a number of features which are intended to enable you to 'interact' with the discussion. You will find short case studies to help you reflect on how these ideas relate to your own practice as a teacher. It is also part of our aspiration that we enable you to develop, articulate and justify your own position as a professional educator, and so throughout each chapter you will find 'thinking points' as well as a list of key questions at the end of each chapter which you can use to reflect on your practice or explore with colleagues. The chapters in this book are necessarily concise, providing an introduction to specific areas. Annotated further reading lists and web resources are also included to enable you to begin to look in greater depth at specific issues.

The book moves progressively through different layers of education: the policy context, the learning context and the practice context. Section 1 explores the policy context where the intention is to foster an appreciation of the significance of educational policy, where policies come from and the debates surrounding specific policies. We look at the process of policy-making as well as some of the key current policy themes in education in the UK. As policies in the UK often relate to wider global trends and concerns, the introductory chapter on educational policy in this section is followed by an exploration of schools and schooling internationally and how all pupils can be prepared for life and work. From this we can see how policy debates around the relationship between education and the economy and education and social inclusion are shaped by wider international trends.

Section 2 examines the learning context in which research and professional experience and expertise have to come together to provide effective learning experiences for all pupils. This section begins by considering how teachers can become more skilled at looking at learning in the classroom and then explores some of the areas particularly concerned with the holistic learning experiences of children and young people, which are of critical importance in the active engagement with issues related to equality and social justice.

Section 3 focuses on the professional practice which has been profoundly altered by the developments in the policy context and the learning context. Here we consider how teachers develop as professionals progressively through their careers, particularly given that the role of the teacher has evolved radically to include aspects such as professional development, leadership and collegiality.

In the final chapter we return again to the global context of education where these changes in the role of the teacher are then set against a vision of what it means to be a teacher in an education system seeking to promote cosmopolitan justice.

We begin with an examination of the policy context.

SECTION 1

POLICY

SECTION OVERVIEW

Margery McMahon

This section looks at the practice of teaching in a wider context to enable you to explore some of the underlying issues faced by teachers today, in a dynamic policy environment, where there are evolving expectations of the role. Current policy initiatives have a direct bearing on the approaches teachers adopt to their practice in the classroom, their ways of working with other teachers and professionals, and their ongoing development as an educator.

A key focus of this section is on education in a globalised context and its relationship to political, economic and social policy. We try to show the links between this and a central theme of the book: social justice and equality. We argue that educators need to be informed and to have a critical stance. This relates not only to curriculum, pedagogy and to professional concerns, but to policy, and the political contexts in which policy is formulated. At a time when levels of public engagement with politics in the UK and the alienation of young people from political life are causes of concern, we argue for the need for greater political literacy for those involved in the education of young people.

Teachers need to know about and understand the political, socio-economic and cultural contexts in which they will teach and pupils will learn. They need to know and understand the policy drivers and decisions that shape what happens in classrooms and schools in relation to the curriculum, approaches to learning and teaching, resources, learning environments and their own role as a professional. And, as we suggest in the introduction, they need to know this in a global as well as a local context.

In this section you will engage with some key concepts and ideas that are used to describe and explain developments in policy and politics in the UK and beyond. Several key themes connect the chapters in this section. The influence of *globalisation* is a common thread in each of the four chapters and the influence of this global movement of people, ideas and commodities is seen as a key determinant for many of the changes in education in the twenty-first century. Another determinant is the influence of *neoliberalism*. The central tenets of neoliberalism are the predominance of market forces and a limited role for the state. In education this has come to be seen in the growth of the private sector (for example, in private–public partnerships); greater focus on parental choice, assessment, standards and the 'new managerialism' (Lauder et al., 2006: 7). Linked to globalisation and neoliberalism is the growth of the *knowledge economy* – where knowledge has become the driver for the economy in post-industrial Britain and beyond.

Outline of section

The growth of the knowledge economy, the force of globalisation and the dominance of neoliberalism are evident in education today, and in the chapters that follow we aim to show their influence in the contemporary world and to consider what this means for social justice and equality. In Chapter 2 Robert Doherty provides a critical perspective on the place and workings of education policy in the UK. He shows how education policy establishes the aims, values and boundaries for national systems of education and how policy authoritatively defines what it means to undertake the role of teacher, together with the imperatives laid down for the teaching workforce. Through the process of policy-making and the consequences of implementing policy in the context of practice, control is exercised over multiple spaces within the educational field. Doherty argues that a rounded education, appropriate to the needs of the active teacher, who aspires towards some degree of autonomy, would be incomplete without an informed and critical understanding of the framing influence of education policy, and in his chapter encourages readers to move beyond a technical, rationalist understanding of policy, and policy-making, to embrace a range of critical perspectives.

In Chapter 3, Margery McMahon extends this call for a more informed and critical understanding of policy by exploring the international context in which schools exist and students learn. This is looked at from two dimensions: the major policy drivers from international agencies such as United Nations Educational Scientific and Cultural Organization (UNESCO) and the Organisation for Economic Cooperation and Development (OECD) and how these are translated into national policy and curricula. In this discussion of policy development a critical concern is the idea of knowledge transfer: the movement of ideas internationally that then shape educational policy nationally in the UK. The second dimension examines the implications of these processes for schools, learners and teachers, looking at how a 'global dimension' is integrated into the curriculum, the ways in which this is developed and the role of other agencies in supporting this.

Consideration of the impact of an international perspective in shaping the global citizens of the future leads to Cathy Fagan's chapter on education and work in which she takes up the idea of the global citizen and considers the relationship between education, the economy and work. In the post-industrial economy, developing technology has changed social, political and economic parameters so that a knowledge economy is now the most influential context for living and learning. The role of education has become central to the development, acquisition and transfer of knowledge, and thereby has shifted its position in relation to the changing nature of work in contemporary society. The chapter explores the range of generic approaches being promoted in recent curricular initiatives in the UK in areas such as enterprise education, entrepreneurship education and citizenship education, dealing with broad attitudinal and dispositional issues along with more specific vocational and career skills. The chapter explores the tensions for teachers, as well as learners, of the relationship between education and work.

In the final chapter in this section George Head looks at inclusive education, another key policy imperative in the UK that resonates internationally. Here the idea of inclusion is problematised. While there have been significant achievements, the range of policies and programmes are still underpinned by a notion of 'compensation': inclusion is about compensating for deficits in the individual learner, and pedagogic practices very much reflect this viewpoint. An alternative construction is proposed in this chapter: to look to the abilities of the individual learner and to make educational provision on that basis. Thus teachers and schools would look to develop complementary pedagogies.

These ideas of a critically informed educator – both locally and globally, capable of developing new and complementary approaches to learning and teaching, that will equip learners for living and working in the twenty-first century – are explored from a range of perspectives in the chapters in the sections on Learning and Practice, and you will be able to build on your learning from this section to help you become 'the real teacher' we described in Chapter 1.

CHAPTER 2

CRITICALLY READING EDUCATION POLICY

Robert Doherty

Key ideas explored in this chapter are:

- Policy
- Policy-making
- Power, influence and policy
- Ideology and conflict
- The vocational teacher

This chapter invites a consideration of the significance of education policy for teachers and educational professionals. It sets out a definition of policy and attempts to give an insight into the nature and importance of policy. Two approaches to understanding policy-making are introduced and explored. The chapter concludes by affirming the need for the professionalism of teachers to include a critical capacity for understanding and engaging with policy. The consequence attached to policy comes from its foundational role in establishing the boundaries, horizons and imperatives of what constitutes the work of the teacher. Policy is complex and multidimensional, which in turn makes the task of defining policy problematic and characterised by definitions that differ in emphasis and priorities. A trawl through the literature on this question reveals a range of definitions that emphasise differing aspects of policy; including policy as a 'course of action' (Heclo, 1972), or the 'selection of goals' (Jenkins, 1978), 'the authoritative allocation of values' (Prunty, 1985) and 'both text and action, words and deeds' (Ball, 1994).

This chapter will take as a working definition the description offered by Olssen and his colleagues (2004: 71) of policy being: 'any course of action (or inaction) relating to the selection of goals, the definition of values or the allocation of resources'. This definition is concise and echoes many conventional definitional elements. Note that the idea of inaction, of non-decision-making or opposition to change, requires also to be understood as a course of action. Significant to education is the category of 'public policy.' This sector of policy-making is characterised by decisions taken within government about forms of action, the setting of goals and the allocation of resources concerning such areas as the economy, health care, housing and numerous sectors of activity touched by the state. It is hard to imagine a political party or politician indifferent to public policy. It is in this intensely political area that governments, elected on a range of policy promises and positions, seek to direct the institutions and functions of the state while retaining popular support.

Education at all levels and stages is an active and obvious example of public policy. The accelerating rate of policy production and the expanding areas governments have sought to code and regulate (curriculum, quality assurance, support for inclusion, health and employability) are defining features of current systems of education. An understanding of policy and how it is made and altered emerges as an area of professional learning relevant to the needs of a contemporary teaching profession committed to an ongoing concern with the meaning and goals of education. An established teaching profession needs to constantly look to strike a positive balance between control and autonomy, between subservience to political direction and activism on behalf of children, young people and their communities. Understanding policy assists teachers and other professionals to enter into the contested processes that shape education.

One of the themes unifying this book and its contributors is an active concern for social justice in education. The meaning, and indeed the legitimacy, of conceptions of social justice are an area of ongoing philosophical and political contention. What is indisputable is the implication of education policy in regulating and administering multiple issues of distribution, access and opportunity. Questions over who gets what in and from education, together with the importance attached to the consequences, are contested at every level of the policy process. The struggle for social justice in education must ultimately look to establish policies with the purpose of shaping a system that provides educational opportunity to all. This is relevant not only to the UK but beyond, as explored in Chapter 3. However, equality of opportunity is not enough for educational professionals with a commitment to social justice in education. Policy must also be advanced and actively designed to reduce the burden of disadvantage weighing on many children and young people (Miller, 1999). Many children need additional support to offset degrees of disadvantage, spanning the crucial period prior to entry into early years education and continuing right through to higher education.

Policy as an expression of power

Central to the importance attached to education policy in this section of the book is an understanding of policy as an exercise of *power*; understood as the capacity to influence or control others. From the level of the education system, down to schools and classrooms, there is a tension between the independent action required by professionals and the control and regulation in operation within a directed organisation. This fault line tends to surface between the acceptance of legitimate authority and the desire for autonomy among professions who possess specialist knowledge, skills and the requirement to exercise degrees of independent judgement. In this context policy has come to play an indispensable role in modern society, establishing what should or should not legitimately happen, in exercising control and in directing all kinds of institutions, including schools.

The making of policy

For many teachers, focused on the day-to-day demands of the classroom, policy requiring change arrives 'from above' through the mediation of school managers and leaders who are required to implement such change. The processes and interactions involved in the making of policy and in the alteration of existing policies can be complex and hard to capture. One of the ways those involved in the study of policy have developed in order to cope with a bewildering array of factors, decisions and institutional arrangements is to attempt to impose some analytical order by developing models to simplify and explain how policy gets made. Two models are discussed below as a way of illustrating both the strengths and limitations of such approaches: a basic 'stagiest model' and what could be called a 'critical model.' The most common models in policy analysis are stagiest models or cyclic models that tend to understand policy as rational, ordered and unfolding in stages. If teachers in

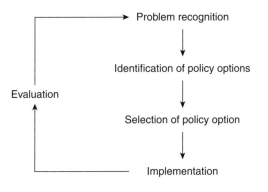

Figure 2.1   Rational decision-making, a basic stagiest model

their initial education are introduced to policy it will tend to be a stagiest approach that is encouraged; with its technical, rational assumptions.

The general stagiest approach (rational decision-making: see Figure 2.1) is easily understood, provides a logical structure to the study of policy, provides a dynamic cycle and allows a focus to be applied to any particular stage in the process. The first stage is recognition: the identification of a problem (low levels of numeracy, teacher shortages, a reduction in social mobility). This is a very significant stage in policy-making. Problems have to be defined and a decision has to be made to instigate the policy-making cycle and begin to move to the next stages. At this point the question of courses of action or inaction and the setting of goals are the main preoccupations. The power to instigate the development of public policy in response to a 'recognised' problem is located primarily in the political control of education. The subsequent phase of policy-making in general stagiest models consists of the identification of policy options, and possible responses that address the problem. This activity will generally be understood as being undertaken by policy professionals with the facility to draw upon networks of advisers and expertise. The conclusion of this phase is reached with the selection of an option or range of options formulated into a policy. The next significant stage in the cycle is implementation. Now the imperatives, goals and definition of values contained or written into policy texts have to be interpreted and translated into action within the complexity and profusion of competing activities and demands operating in the education system. It is worth noting that at any stage the process is open to being halted, overturned or alterations demanded by the political party in government who exercise control over policy and policy-making and by budgetary allocation/constraints.

Take the example of the curriculum, an essential feature of formal education, and an issue close to the heart of teachers. What comes to be identified as problematic with curricula (being outdated, failing to prepare students for employment or higher education, failing to engage a significant portion of students, not encouraging creativity, overcrowded in content or harmfully narrow) comes to the attention of government. In response, a change to curriculum policy could be instigated. The next stage in the process comprises establishing a comprehensible statement of the problem and the investigation and identification of possible responses and solutions. Such activities are normally undertaken by civil servants within government departments responsible for the administration of education. The development of policy solutions can draw upon consultation and suitable 'expertise' as required. At the selection stage politicians in government office will agree the content of the new policy. This stage is normally concluded, be it concerning curriculum or some other issue, by a statement of policy in a textual form, such as memorandums of guidance, regulations or draft bills for the legislative process. Often the final stage in the cycle is implementation; it is at this level that theoretically constructed solutions must be converted into actions, ways of working and allocations of resources. Formal evaluation of the effectiveness of implemented policy is rare; more common are forms of informal feedback to the levels of political control and policy selection.

Policy-cycle models tend to suggest a functionalist account; problems arise in education, they are recognised and expertise develops solutions. Policy-making can appear as a technical rationalist activity that happens above the heads of teachers until they must implement the solutions it provides. While acknowledging that the solution to 'problems' is undeniably a central concern of public policy and that this approach endures because it provides a structure that makes policy-making intelligible, stagiest models have important limitations. Policy-cycle models offer a weak account of how policy moves from one stage to the next, tend to assume a top-down account of policy-making and struggle to capture the multilayered and interacting cycles within each stage of the policy cycle.

Directives, conflicts and policy

The exercise of power together with the endemic existence of conflict are two significant determents of policy-making that tend to be neglected in stagiest accounts. Consequently, there are a whole range of approaches that arise from what we could call a *critical* reading of policy and the policy-making process. Critical approaches are characterised by assumptions that policy is shaped by power and takes for granted that policy is made and addresses issues within a social order in which there is conflict arising from competing interests, contradictory views of the world and struggles for scarce resources and social prestige. If policy is understood as 'the selection of goals, the definition of

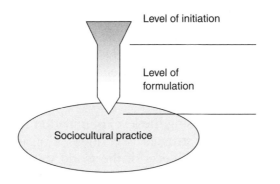

Figure 2.2   A critical model of policy-making

values or the allocation of resources', then critical perspectives have at their centre a concern with questions such as whose goals and values become encoded in policy and, within education, who gets what? Figure 2.2 attempts to represent a critical model of policy-making, moving the focus from logical stages in a policy process to the existence of differing levels of power and influence. The different activities, conflicts and actors involved at each level, and their interaction, are also important considerations in this approach. In the model, the policy process is divided into three levels; initiation, formulation and practice. Although distinct, each level is connected to form a system in which there is a permanent interaction and flow of information between levels.

The level of initiation: holding the reins of policy

The level of initiation is dominated by the possession of political authority as control over education resides with the government of the day. However, around this simple basic distinguishing aspect of the initiation level forms a complex network that transacts initiation. From a critical perspective, the interaction of this multilayered set of formal and informal relationships forms the arena in which struggles and contests over the initiation of policy take place. The idea of a 'policy problem' becomes more of a place of struggle to influence what is to be seen as problematic and how this is to be defined. One idea used to explore this arena is that of agenda-setting (Cobb and Elder, 1972). Governments put together agendas of issues for action; a feature of this process is a limit to capacity and the need for selection. Issues that manage to claim a place on this agenda can be motivated by their appeal to targeted sections of the electorate during an election, ideology, promotion by individuals, groups and coalitions, gaining importance by unanticipated events, economic trends, technological change and many other factors. In the networks around policy initiation operate special advisers, thinktanks, interest groups, and the influence of political strategists, media-led issues and moral panics. This is a hidden world of access, lobbying and influence-seeking driven by the recognition of initiation as a privileged level of decision-making and foundational to what emerges as policy.

Another approach to analysing the level of initiation that provides critical insight is attention to the struggle over ideas. Concepts and ideas are required in order to render aspects of the world thinkable, to categorise, describe and explain, to represent as valuable, desirable or contemptible. Ideas operate to make intelligible material structures, processes and relations together with the inner world of beliefs, emotions and thoughts. One conventional way to understand ideology is as a system of more or less coherent ideas. Such systems of ideas cohere, for their adherents, to provide a world view, a vision of the good society and a frame for a moral order together with a set of central values. Ideologies also tend to provide prescriptions for what courses of actions must be followed to maintain or change the social order. Such political positions are recognisable as 'isms', ideologies such as liberalism, socialism, Marxism, feminism or environmentalism. Education policy is also influenced by another significant set of ideas, what could be called ideologies of education. Educational ideologies can be thought of as comprising a relativity established set of beliefs, ideas, values and assumptions about education, its purpose, content and means of effect. Conflicts over differing conceptions of education can be seen in the struggle between traditional approaches and 'progressive' child-centred approaches to teaching, or the extent to which the purposes of education should be concerned about the interests and development of the child (liberal conceptions of education) or preparation for future employment (vocationalism).

From a critical policy perspective, policy initiation and agenda-setting take place within a climate of ideas. This is a space of competing ideas, a climate in which, for periods of time, certain ideas take hold and become dominant. In the 1980s, under successive Thatcher governments, an ideological commitment to the market as the prime mechanism for the distribution of goods and services became the orthodoxy of the policy initiation level. This belief was enthusiastically applied to public policy, including health (the internal market) and education. In education, a number of key pro-market thinktanks[1] close to government were able to exert influence at the level of policy initiation and formulation (Denham, 1996). The high water mark of the restructuring that followed is most clearly visible in the mechanisms contained in the 1988 Education Reform Act (England and Wales). This legislation contains provisions seen as essential for what has been called the 'marketisation' of state education. In other words, the organisation and operation of state education would be significantly changed in order to produce a form of market in which schools would compete for pupils and the custom of parents.

The policy climate was dominated by the idea that it would be the market, not the State, which would bring about improvement in the educational system. In order to introduce such market pressures, parents were given the right to place their children in any state school that had the capacity to accommodate them, a national curriculum was required to standardise education, and national testing was required to assess pupils according to national standards. This would open the way for schools to be measured by their performance, the introduction of league tables would allow the market to operate by providing market information. The assumed effect would force poor schools to improve while allowing successful schools to expand.

A coordinated alliance of intellectuals and politicians, ambitious to reform education, were extremely adept and successful in developing and maintaining a new educational language that reverberated with ideas such as freedom, choice, standards, excellence, tradition and parents' rights. From a perspective of social justice, this ideological commitment to the market in education has introduced retrogressive consequences. Tomlinson (1994: 8), for example, summarised the outcomes of the Conservative educational reforms as operating to 'redistribute resources towards and expand choice for middle-class students, while moving resources and choice away from working-class students and those with disadvantages and learning difficulties'. New Labour's education policy has in many respects left the introduction of marketisation untouched. As Lawton puts it, 'Labour policies on setting, selection and choice', for example, can be understood as 'representing a confused or at least weak commitment to social justice' (2005: 134). What comes to be defined as an issue or problem in education requiring a response of action or inaction is influenced by political positions, ideologies of education, public opinion and the influence of groups and organisations promoting issues and causes. From a critical perspective, the selection and definition of problems must not be seen as a neutral activity, but as an exercise of a form of control. Holders of political authority are in a position to define issues requiring a policy response and hold the reins of the policy-making process.

Thinking point 2.1

Thinking about your own experiences of education as a learner and as an educator, in what ways have you been conscious of the marketisation of education?

The level of policy formulation

Having initiated the process, policy-making activity then moves to a second level; that of formulation (see Figure 2.2). This level involves additional policy actors who are able to exert other less obvious forms of influence and inter-pretation onto a policy issue. This is a level of manufacturing solutions, of selecting arrangements, bureaucratic and administrative, and of identifying technologies and practices that can achieve the aims of policy. This stage of the process is populated by a semi-permanent stratum of policy professionals (civil servants, researchers, analysts and advisers), who undertake the design and detailing required before a policy can be implemented.

Being located within or aligned to government departments responsible for the education system, this set of policy actors have their own preferences for courses of action and conceptions of education. The administration of policy implementation and its future management, including implications for resources, will often reside within the same department. This institutional location of policy-making, aligned with responsibility for the operational man-agement of the education system, tends to dispose policy professionals and bureaucrats to favour certain formulations of policy as opposed to others. While tasked with taking forward a response to policy problems designated for action by those with political authority, policy professionals at the stage of formulation are able to exert forms of influence over the goals, details and operational arrangements of policy. From a critical perspective, the detection of this form of influence and its results can help to explain and make clear the dynamics shaping policy at this level. Policy problems come to be defined and win a place on the agenda of governments all within a particular climate of ideas. When the dominant climate of ideas shifts or changes, new problems, agendas for action and forms of policy response emerge. For teachers cultivat-ing a critical consciousness, scrutiny and insight into policy initiation and formulation provide a critical awareness of the forces steering and reshaping education.

Level of practice: performing policy

The level of policy implementation is where abstract ideas about what has come to be defined as problematic, and the solutions and responses pro-duced by the policy system, collide with the complex world of practice and the multiple demands and pressures of the classroom and the school. This is the level where teachers and school leaders must translate the demands of policy into actions, ways of working, speaking and thinking. There is no simple straight relation between the demands and mandates of policy and what happens in the material world of practice. Policy texts and guidelines require interpretation, and in this process they can be found to be vague or confusing and are open to misinterpretation. Individuated problems may motivate the policy-making process, but importantly, policy is not implemented in a vacuum. Education is a field in which at any one time a tangled grid of multiple policies will be in force. Policy is enacted in this institutional space, within which multiple polices are in operation, with the potential for contradictions, tensions and incompatibility. Policy may demand that teachers achieve high levels of academic attainment but at the same time support the inclusion in the classroom of children with complex additional support needs.

A critical perspective recognises the forms of power and influence possessed by teachers and school leaders at the level of implementation. Teachers can resist the aims and demands of particular policies, policy can be ignored, be paid lip-service or be actively subverted behind a mask of superficial compliance. All policy does not carry the same status, or level of importance or efforts to ensure conformity. Another vital aspect to the implementation of education policy is the teacher's role in the humanisation of policy; looking to negotiate a sane and ethical balance to the demands of policy with respect to the needs, emotional vulnerabilities and human dignity of children and young people. One of the recurring findings of studies of policy implementation is the disjuncture between what was conceived in the minds of policy-makers and what is to be found at the level of practice. Nevertheless, the use of policy endures and its application is intensifying precisely because of its very real capacity to shape, govern and control sectors of state activity such as education.

> Education has the characteristics it does because of the goals pursued by those who control it ... change occurs because new goals are pursued by those who have power to modify education's previous structural form, definition of instruction and relationship with society ... education is fundamentally about what people have wanted of it and have been able to do to it. (Archer, 1984: 1–3)

Teachers, critical professionalism and policy

National systems of education can seem solid, predictable and reassuringly constant with familiar roles and features such as teacher, pupil, classrooms, examination and assessments, parents' evenings and school reports. Behind, or perhaps above, the well-known symbols and arrangements of our education system sits a policy system that transacts change. The official resolutions of many ongoing conflicts over education, and the nature of demands made upon education, are to be found in the ideas, values and courses of action articulated in policy. However, such settlements have a provisional, temporary quality to them. To echo the words of Archer, those who hold the reigns of power will attempt to alter the system they inherit, to set new goals and assert the importance of different values and priorities. So it is that the direction, characteristics and structural form of education must be expected to alter. As a consequence the direction of policy and policy-making becomes a space that demands constant vigilance. It is important to note that education policy has been the means towards social progress and the demands of social justice. The extension of secondary education to all, the opening up of higher education and the allocation of supplementary resources to children with additional learning needs were all achieved through the policy process.

The national project of education is shaped by political projects together with a whole range of ideas, events and the administrative and value prefer-ences of policy professionals. Democratic forms of society depend for their vitality and health on an active and engaged kind of citizen. Society needs teachers who, as they become confident in their professional role, engage individually and collectively through professional organisations in the policy process. The importance of policy and its shifting direction requires of teachers the capacity to engage critically with official courses of action and their implications. In concluding this chapter, four dimensions to any such engagement are proposed as vital for teachers as they develop critical consciousness:

- An understanding of the power of policy to shape, alter and control the professional context in which teachers work.
- A realistic understanding of how policy is made; the politics around policy-making, the importance of ideas and the political context from which policy emerges.
- A commitment to critically interrogate policy; in particular to evaluate its impact on the education of children and young people and the ambition for a more equal and democratic society.
- Socially committed teachers should be recognised by a commitment to working for policies that are in the interests of learners and their commu-nities as part of a grander project aimed at contributing to the develop-ment of a more just and cohesive social order.

 Thinking point 2.2

As you continue to develop as a teacher, in what ways can you develop the dimensions of critical consciousness noted above?

Summary

The following three chapters explore and illustrate other aspects and dimensions of policy. This opening chapter has attempted to provide a broad introduction to policy as a deliberate course of action (or inaction), motivated by particular ambitions and purposes. In policy certain values are promoted, endorsed or assumed, and a whole range of resources including funding and time are allocated (Olssen et al., 2004). Policy is therefore a way in which power is exercised and consequently deserves scrutiny. When the policy-making process is observed from a critical perspective it is revealed as a space of conflict and influence where the direction of educational change is set. Teachers must guard against the danger of a naive acceptance of policy as the province of expertise and those who exercise political authority. Teachers require a critical professionalism; their professional learning needs to include some capacity for understanding and engaging with policy. Teachers require a critical professionalism for the reason that they share a responsibility to society for enhancing and protecting education. This means being watchful, and engaging to ensure that policy makes the opportunities and benefits of education available to all children and young people.

Key questions for reflection and discussion

- This chapter highlights the importance of education policy. To what extent do you disagree or agree with the significance given to policy?
- Can you identify a policy on an area of practice that teachers have spoken out in opposition to or in support of?
- Do teachers have a role in the 'humanisation' of policy?
- To what extent are the four dimensions of critical consciousness above realistic aims for an established teacher?
- Is a concern for social justice a justifiable aspect of the work of all teachers?

Further reading

Carr, W. and Hartnett, A. (1996) *Education and the Struggle for Democracy: Politics of Educational Ideas.* Buckingham: Open University Press. In this book Carr and Hartnett discuss many examples of the interaction between policy, politics and ideas.

Chapman, C. and Gunter, H. (2009) *Radical Reforms: Perspectives on an Era of Educational Change.* London: Routledge. This edited collection provides a critical review across New Labour's education policy around compulsory education.

Denham, A. (1996) *Think-tanks of the New Right.* Aldershot: Dartmouth. This provides an insight into policy-making, ideology and the influence of think-tanks.

Parsons, W. (1995) *Public Policy*. Cheltenham: Edward Elgar. This provides a comprehensive understanding of policy analysis.

Trowler, P. (2003) *Education Policy*. London: Routledge. This offers a readable introduction to education policy.

Web resources

For examples of current policy visit:

The Department for Education (England): www.education.gov.uk
The Scottish Government: http://www.scotland.gov.uk/Topics/Education
The Welsh Assembly: http://wales.gov.uk/topics/educationandskills/?lang=en
The Northern Irish Assembly: http://education.niassembly.gov.uk/

For an introduction to social policy: http://www2.rgu.ac.uk/publicpolicy/introduction/introf.htm

Note

1. For example, the Adam Smith Institute, the Institute for Economic Affairs and the Centre for Policy Studies.

CHAPTER 3

SCHOOLS AND SCHOOLING

Margery McMahon

> ### Key ideas explored in this chapter are:
>
> - Globalisation
> - Policy travel and translation
> - Global governance
> - Global education
> - International education

In the previous chapter we looked at policy formulation from an education perspective and argued that an understanding of *the contested processes that shape education* is important for members of the teaching profession.

We noted that many teachers experience policy as change 'from above' mediated through school managers and leaders, and suggested that teachers need to take an informed and critical perspective on policy initiation, formulation, development and implementation to be active and autonomous professionals. We showed that education policy is determined by a range of influences, including party political agendas, stakeholder interests and the organisational, administrative and value preferences of policy officers and civil servants.

In this chapter we develop this argument to suggest that education policy needs to be understood not only from a local and national perspective but also in an international context. This is looked at through two lenses: first, the major initiatives of international agencies such as UNESCO and the OECD and how these are translated into national policy and curricula. In this discussion of policy development a critical concern is the idea of knowledge transfer: the movement of ideas internationally that then shape educational policy nationally in the UK. The second dimension examines the implications of these processes for schools, learners and teachers, looking at how a 'global dimension' is integrated into the curriculum. The chapter ends by examining the impact of this international perspective in shaping the global citizen of the future.

International policy perspectives and drivers

In the twenty-first century, in most nation states, education policy is not autarkic[1] but is influenced and developed by the agendas of international bodies and agencies. This is characteristic of the move to greater international collaboration that has developed since the Second World War. While this is experienced by most citizens in political and economic ways (for example, through the application of legislation of the European Union, such as the Working Time Directive, or through access to a range of goods and products from other member states), it also impacts on developments in education at a national level.

Most nation states are members of regional, continental and international organisations. The UK, for example, is a member of the European Union (EU), the International Monetary Fund (IMF), the World Bank (WB), the Organisation for Economic Co-operation and Development (OECD) and the United Nations (UN). At the regional level, the Council of the Isles (also known as the British-Irish Council) provides for cooperation and collaboration with the British and Irish governments, the devolved institutions in Northern Ireland, Scotland and Wales, and representatives of the Isle of Man, Guernsey and Jersey (British Irish Council, 2008).

Information file

European Union (EU)

The EU emerged in the aftermath of the Second World War and since its inception has expanded from six original members to its current membership of 27. In 2002 a common currency for the region, the euro, was introduced. In 2004 eight countries of the former Eastern Bloc (the Soviet Union and East European countries) acceded to the EU. The UK joined the EU in 1973 but has not adopted the euro as its currency. The aim of the European Union is for member states to work together to bring about greater prosperity in the region. Decisions are made in the European Parliament to which representatives (Members of the European Parliament, or MEPs) are elected. (EU online)

International Monetary Fund (IMF)

The IMF was set up after the Second World War as a means of overseeing the international monetary system and to provide greater stability to international trade. Made up of 186 countries, the IMF works to 'foster global monetary cooperation, secure financial stability, facilitate international trade, promote high employment and sustainable economic growth, and reduce poverty around the world.' It does this by keeping track of the global economy and the economies of member countries; lending to countries with balance of payments difficulties and giving practical help to members. (IMF online)

Organisation for Economic Co-operation and Development (OECD)

Established in 1961, the 30 member states of the OECD work together to bring about economic development and growth; better living standards and prosperity. They do this by providing a forum for governments to 'compare policy experiences, seek answers to common problems, identify good practice and coordinate domestic and international policies'. (OECD online)

United Nations (UN)

The UN was set up in October 1945. Its initial membership consisted of 51 member states, which has grown to 192. The original aim of the UN was to maintain international peace and security and this remains its key role today. *UNESCO* is a specialised agency of the UN concerned with education, science and culture. (http://www.unesco.org/en/education/about-us/[2])

Council of the Isles

The Council of the Isles is a regional forum made up of the Irish and British Governments; the devolved institutions in Northern Ireland, Scotland and Wales, together with representatives of the Isle of Man, Guernsey and Jersey. It was set up as part of the Belfast Agreement in 1998 to further promote positive, practical relationships among the people of the islands, and to provide a forum for consultation and cooperation. (British Irish Council online)

Supranational organisations such as the EU and the UN were established and exist to promote international collaboration. The ongoing move towards greater international cooperation is also a consequence of global forces of movement and change – *globalisation*. There are many definitions and interpretations of globalisation, which is indicative of its contested nature. For our purposes, two definitions are helpful in outlining some key aspects of it.

Beck (2000) suggests that it is '*the process* through which sovereign national states are criss crossed and undermined by transnational actors with varying prospects of power, orientations, identities and networks' (italics in original) (in Jarvis, 2007: 40).

For Friedman (1999, in Jarvis, 2007: 40) 'Globalisation is not a phenomenon. It is not just some passing trend. Today it is the overarching international system shaping the domestic politics and foreign relations of virtually every country'.

While globalisation may be viewed in purely economic terms, clearly in the twenty-first century globalisation should be understood in a 'politic-socio-economic manner' (Jarvis, 2007: 40) since 'the globalisation of the economy is accompanied by the globalisation of policy making' (Moutious, 2009: 469).

Stavro Moutious observes that major international organisations have existed since the Second World War but from 1990s the size, role and scope of their policy agendas have expanded dramatically, expressing but also defining the process of globalisation (Moutious, 2009: 469). These international organisations include the United Nations, the International Monetary Fund, the World Bank and the Organisation for Economic Co-operation and Development. In this chapter we look at the role and influence of two of these: the UN and the OECD.

The influence of these international organisations on member states is experienced in a variety of ways, from commitment to common principles and universal rights for young people, to providing financial support for educational developments and programmes. The World Bank, for example, is the biggest external loan provider for education programmes, which are implemented in over 85 countries (Moutious, 2009: 470).

Moutious emphasises the pivotal role of these organisations, suggesting that 'It is essentially here, rather than in national arenas, public spheres or organisation, that the rules of the meta-power game are being negotiated, written and re-written, rules which then change national politics and societies fundamentally' (Moutious, 2009: 470). Within these organisations, he suggests, stakeholders vie for influence so that 'National education policy comes as a result of inter-state relations operating in a transnational network of research based decision making, in which the more powerful nodes can promote their own aims and make them the aims of the entire network' (Moutious, 2009: 474).

Moutious's argument is that education policy at the national level is influenced and directed by agendas and decisions at the supranational or transnational level. Given this growing influence we argue that it is imperative for teachers to apply the critical approach to policy, outlined in Chapter 2, so that they will know, understand and have a critical view on decisions that are taken remotely that impact on them locally. In the following section we look at the ways in which two such organisations (the UN and the OECD) influence education at supranational and national levels, using this to consider recent initiatives in education in the UK.

Thinking point 3.1

In what ways are you aware of the influence of international factors on what happens in your classroom?

Policy into practice

United Nations and UNESCO

The UN is a supranational and transnational organisation set up in October 1945.[3] Its initial membership consisted of 51 member states, which has grown to 192. The original aim of the UN was to maintain international peace and security, develop friendly relations among nations, and promote social progress, better living standards and human rights. It does this in a variety of ways throughout the world: through its role in peace keeping and peace building, conflict prevention and humanitarian assistance, and through its specialised agencies, funds and programmes (UN online). UNESCO is a specialised agency of the UN concerned with education, science and culture (http://www.unesco.org/en/education/about-us/[4]).

In 1945 the founding member states of the UN and the first signatories to the UN Charter made a commitment:

- to save succeeding generations from the scourge of war which twice in our lifetime has brought untold sorrow to mankind, and
- to reaffirm faith in fundamental human rights, in the dignity and worth of the human person, in the equal rights of men and women and of nations large and small, and

- to establish conditions under which justice and respect for the obligations arising from treaties and other sources of international law can be maintained, and
- to promote social progress and better standards of life in larger freedom, and for these ends
- to practise tolerance and live together in peace with one another as good neighbours, and
- to unite our strength to maintain international peace and security, and
- to ensure, by the acceptance of principles and the institution of methods, that armed force shall not be used, save in the common interest, and
- to employ international machinery for the promotion of the economic and social advancement of all peoples (UN Charter, online).

Many people are familiar with the work of the UN through its peace-keeping activities in conflict zones such Lebanon, Darfur and Kosovo. Currently troops from UN member states are involved in 16 peace-keeping operations throughout the world. However, in the twenty-first century there has been a shift in focus from peace-keeping to peace-building (UK Mission to the UN, online). Another way in which people are familiar with the work of the UN is through designated UNESCO World Heritage Sites. In the UK there 28 World Heritage sites including the Tower of London, New Lanark and Blaenavon Industrial Landscape (World Heritage, online).

Increasingly, the UN has an impact on the lives of the citizens of its member states through UNESCO, which was established as the UN agency to realise the aims of the UN Charter through education, science and culture, underpinned by the belief that 'it is not enough to build classrooms in devastated countries or to publish scientific breakthroughs. Education, Social and Natural Science, Culture and communication are the means to a far more ambitious goal: to build peace in the minds of men' (http://erc.unesco.org/websitetoolkit/en/texts/index.htm#q1[5]). Since its founding, the UN, and through it, UNESCO, has sought to uphold the Charter and, when and where necessary, to challenge abuses of its core principles.

The work of UNESCO is focused on four main areas of activity: education, natural sciences, social and human sciences and culture. Figure 3.1 outlines UNESCO's policy for education, showing its mission and how it aims to achieve this.

UNESCO works to achieve the goals outlined above in a variety of ways. In its medium-term strategy 2008–2013, five programme-driven overarching objectives were identified:

UNESCO Education Sector	
Mission to	**Strategic objectives**
– provide international leadership to create learning societies with educational opportunities for all populations.	Capacity-building: to provide a platform for intellectual and thoughtful leadership for educational innovation and reform.
– provide expertise and foster partnerships to strengthen national educational leadership and the capacity of countries to offer quality education for all.	Laboratory of ideas: to anticipate and respond to emerging trends and needs in education and develop education policy recommendations based on research evidence.
– work as an intellectual leader, an honest broker and clearing house for ideas, propelling both countries and the international community to accelerate progress towards these goals.	International catalyst: to initiate and promote dialogue and exchange of information among educational leaders and stakeholders. Clearing house: to promote the development and implementation of successful educational practices and document and disseminate successful practices.
– facilitate the development of partnerships and monitor progress, in particular by publishing an annual *Global Monitoring Report* that tracks the achievements of countries and the international community towards the *six Education for All goals.*	Standard-setting: to develop Standards, Norms and Guidelines for action in key education areas.

Figure 3.1   UNESCO's Education mission and strategic objectives (http://www.unesco.org/ en/education/about-us/mission and http://www.unesco.org/en/education/ about-us/strategy[6])

- attaining quality education for all and lifelong learning
- mobilising scientific knowledge and policy for sustainable development
- addressing emerging social and ethical challenges
- promoting cultural diversity, intercultural dialogue and a culture of peace
- building inclusive knowledge societies through information and communication (UNESCO, 2008: 16) (http://unesdoc.unesco.org/images/0014/001499/ 149999e.pdf[7])

The strategy outlined how overarching objective 1 – *attaining quality education for all and lifelong learning* – would be met by

> enabling all learners to have access to education throughout life and to ensure that they complete their studies with success, UNESCO will pursue the development of contextually effective strategies and approaches to improve the quality of education and the assessment of learning processes and outcomes. This will also include capacity development, support to national planning processes, monitoring and evaluation. (UNESCO, 2008: 1) (http://www.unesdoc.unesco.org/images/0014/001499/149999e.pdf[8])

Centre	Focus
International Bureau of Education (IBE), Geneva, Switzerland.	Enhancing curriculum development and educational content.
International Institute for Educational Planning (IIEP), Paris, France and Buenos Aires, Argentina.	Helping countries to design, plan and manage their education systems.
The UNESCO Institute for Lifelong Learning (UIL), Hamburg, Germany.	Promoting literacy, non-formal education, and adult and lifelong learning.
Institute for Information Technologies in Education (IITE), Moscow, Russian Federation.	Assisting countries to use information and communication technologies in education.
International Centre for Technical and Vocational Education and Training (UNEVOC), Bonn, Germany.	Improving education for the world of work.
UNESCO Institute for Statistics (UIS), Montreal, Canada.	Providing global and internationally comparable statistics.

Figure 3.2   UNESCO centres and institutes (http://www.unesco.org/en/education/ institutes-and-centres/[9])

To achieve these goals UNESCO, as a supranational/transnational body seeks to influence, shape and support developments locally and globally. This is done in a variety of ways, for example through UNESCO institutes and centres situated among the member states that focus on research and educational development and innovation. These UNESCO centres and institutes are shown in Figure 3.2 both to illustrate the range of UNESCO's activities and to highlight resources that can help teachers become more informed about global perspectives and issues, and that can be integrated into classroom pedagogies.

UNESCO policy initiatives and programmes are promoted locally through *national commissions*. There are currently 196 such commissions. The United Kingdom National Commission for UNESCO is the focal point in the UK for UNESCO-related policies and activities (http://www.unesco.org.uk[10]). The UK commission is an independent body that advises and works with the UK government on UNESCO's fields of activity. The focus of the commission's work is to develop UK input to UNESCO policy-making and debate, to build a more effective UNESCO and to encourage support in the UK for UNESCO's ideals and work (http://www.unesco.org.uk[11]). The UK government also has a permanent delegation in a small Department for International Development (DFID) office based in UNESCO headquarters to pursue the UK development agenda within UNESCO (DFID, online).

A current focus for UN member countries is the achievement of the Millennium Development Goals (MDGs). A commitment to universal primary education was made by world leaders in September 2000 in the *United Nations Millennium Declaration*, pledging their nations to a new global partnership to reduce extreme poverty and setting out targets to be achieved by 2015.

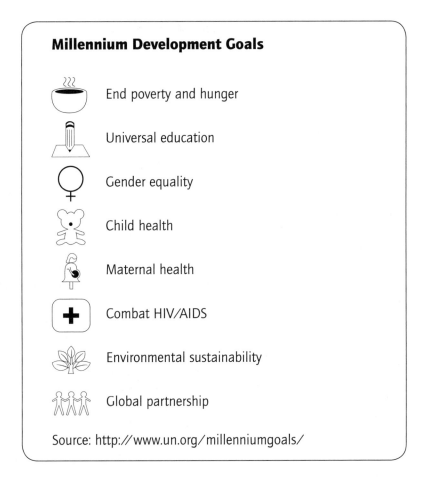

Through its programmes and initiatives UNESCO can influence and shape developments in UN member states, and member states can support the realisation of UNESCO goals though donor support. In the UK the governmental body responsible for achieving the MDGs is the Department for International Development (DFID). It does this through support for specific programmes and initiatives. For example, to achieve MDG2, universal primary education, DFID is supporting education programmes in over 30 developing countries (DFID, online).

Through initiatives linked to the MDGs, schools and pupils in the UK can become involved in the realisation of the goals through international partnerships with schools and through a curricular focus related to the MDGs. For example, a number of schools in the UK are now becoming involved in the campaign for rights through UNICEF's 'Rights Respecting School Award' (UNICEF, online).

Organisation of Economic Co-operation and Development

Established in 1961, the 30 member states of the OECD work together to:

- support sustainable economic growth
- boost employment
- raise living standards
- maintain financial stability
- assist other countries' economic development and
- contribute to growth in world trade.

The OECD does this by providing a forum for governments to 'compare policy experiences, seek answers to common problems, identify good practice and coordinate domestic and international policies' (OECD, online).

In recent years educators and classroom practitioners have become familiar with the OECD's work on education through the annual 'Education at Glance' report, through country studies and through its Programme for International Student Assessment (PISA). These serve as an international barometer or benchmark for national education systems and have been used an examples of models and practice to emulate (for example, the Finnish Model) or as a rationale for educational reform to improve performance. Through its work in these areas the OECD is able to influence and inform policy at national level with the aim of ensuring that 'education systems avoid perpetuating social and economic disadvantage and that they contribute to growth and social stability' (OECD, online).

Arguably the OECD exerts a level of influence on national policies that is disproportionate to its size (30 members) and capacity. Rizvi and Lingard note that 'It neither has the legal instruments at hand nor the financial means at its disposal to actively promote policy making at the national level; yet over the last decade its influence over member countries and others has increased markedly' (in Lauder et al., 2006: 247). Rizvi and Lingard go on to argue that:

> Over the past decade or so, the OECD agendas in education have increasingly become tilted towards social efficiency, as it has promoted a particular ideological view of educational aims linked to the requirements of a global knowledge economy and a range of ideas about educational governance divided from new theories of public management, which increasingly promote corporatized and privatized administration of education, outcome measures, and knowledge as commodity. (In Lauder et al., 2006: 248)

Moutious sees this as the prevalence of the neoliberal agenda in education policy (Moutious, 2009: 475) and international organisations have become the main promoters of this in the discourse, policies and organisational practices of educational institutions (ibid.). This agenda also includes a heavy emphasis on human capital production: education systems must produce human resources destined to upgrade developing economies and to ensure the growth of the advanced economies. All domestic education policies should be orientated towards increasing productivity and competitiveness in the global economy (ibid.).

The examples of the goals and influence of supranational organisations such as the UN/UNESCO and the OECD show that education policy at the level of the nation state is influenced by and responds to decisions and initiatives occurring beyond national boundaries. What does this mean for schools and schooling in the UK? In the following section we look at how reforms to national curricula reflect these influences, and the implications and opportunities these present for learners and their teachers. This is then developed in the following chapter in which education for work in a globalised context is explored.

A 'global' curriculum?

As world recession developed in the first decade of the twenty-first century, globalisation was blamed for the economic slump that reached most parts of the world, and the demise of globalisation as an international phenomenon was forecast. However, taken beyond economic notions of globalisation, the global movement of people, ideas, commodities and technologies is unlikely to recede, despite cyclical economic downturns. While national economies may have contracted and public spending has been curtailed, the sociocultural and political components of globalisation, or 'global interconnectedness', have proved more robust (Held, 2004: 19).

This *interconnectness* is both real and virtual, and in a world that changes rapidly learners need to be equipped with the knowledge and skills to respond quickly and flexibly to changing and dynamic political and socio-economic contexts. In the face of such changes, schools need to be able to respond, adapt, create and innovate. Schools and schooling in the UK have changed greatly since the introduction of formal schooling in the second half of the nineteenth century. In the twenty-first century the pace of change continues, evident in construction of new learning environments, revision of existing curricula or the introduction of new curricula, adoption of new pedagogies and changes in how learning is assessed and measured.

The values and principles underpinning the global ambitions of the Millennium Development Goals, and the economic rationality that shapes the agenda of the OECD, can be seen in recent educational developments throughout the UK where revised curricula have been introduced.

In England the principles underpinning the curriculum reform *Every Child Matters*[12] are that every child should:

- Be healthy
- Stay safe
- Enjoy and achieve
- Make a positive contribution
- Achieve economic well-being.

Through the curriculum young people should be able to become:

- successful learners who enjoy learning, make progress and achieve
- confident individuals who are able to lead safe, healthy and fulfilling lives, and
- responsible citizens who make a positive contribution to society (QCA, 2008: 2).

Similar values and purposes underpin the Scottish *Curriculum for Excellence* which aims to foster in young people four capacities to be:

- responsible citizens
- confident individuals
- successful learners
- effective contributors.

Figure 3.3 opposite shows how these capacities can be developed.

Curriculum reform in Wales, introduced in 2008, is designed to 'support Government policy, including: bilingualism, Curriculum Cymreig/Wales, Europe and the World, equal opportunities, food and fitness, sustainable development and global citizenship, and the world of work and entrepreneurship' (Welsh Assembly Government). In Wales this journey began with the publication of the *Learning Country* in 2001, described as a 'paving document', followed by the *Learning Country: Vision into Action* in 2006. In this document the Minister for Education and Lifelong Learning outlined Wales' ambition: 'We want to rival the best in the world. We therefore need to learn from the best by sharing experience and expertise. We are positioning Wales within the context of European and global reforms' (Welsh Assembly Government, 2006). The influence of UNESCO was noted by the Minister: 'Beyond Europe, we are working alongside UNESCO to develop important initiatives in the fields of education, culture, natural science and communications. We are helping to establish UNESCO Chairs in the University sector and teacher exchanges, especially with Sub-Saharan Africa.'

The focus on international education received a clearer articulation with the publication of *World Class Wales – Transforming Learning for Success in a Globalised World*. This document gave the political rationale for this:

successful learners

with:
- enthusiasm and motivation for learning
- determination to reach high standards of achievement
- openness to new thinking and ideas

and able to:
- use literacy, communication and numeracy skills
- use technology for learning
- think creatively and independently
- learn independently and as part of a group
- make reasoned evaluations
- link and apply different kinds of learning in new situations.

confident individuals

with:
- self-respect
- a sense of physical, mental and emotional well-being
- secure values and beliefs
- ambition

and able to:
- relate to others and manage themselves
- pursue a healthy and active lifestyle
- be self-aware
- develop and communicate their own beliefs and view of the world
- live as independently as they can
- assess risk and make informed decisions
- achieve success in different areas of activity.

To enable all young people to become:

responsible citizens

with:
- respect for others
- commitment to participate responsibly in political, economic, social and cultural life

and able to:
- develop knowledge and understanding of the world and Scotland's place in it
- understand different beliefs and cultures
- make informed choices and decisions
- evaluate environmental, scientific and technological issues
- develop informed, ethical views of complex issues.

effective contributors

with:
- an enterprising attitude
- resilience
- self-reliance

and able to:
- communicate in different ways and in different settings
- work in partnerships and in teams
- take the initiative and lead
- apply critical thinking in new contexts
- create and develop
- solve problems

Figure 3.3   How the four capacities can be developed (http://www.ltscotland.org.uk/curriculumforexcellence/curriculumoverview/aim/fourcapacities.asp)

The Government's One Wales[13] agenda makes explicit our ambitions for 'Placing Wales in the World'. These commitments include: widening Wales' membership and effectiveness in relevant European and International bodies; continuing to raise the profile of Wales to make Wales a location of choice for people to live, work, study, visit or do business; continuing to make a contribution to the United Nations' Millennium Development Goals and to support the Wales in Africa programme. (Welsh Assembly Government, 2009, 6)

The vision is further outlined through five themes:

- learning for a global world
- improving achievement, skills and well-being
- enhancing economic prosperity and social cohesion
- supporting practitioners
- driving the change.

Several strands of the curriculum serve as the vehicle for this 'international dimension', for example:

- *Wales, Europe and the World – A Framework for 14- to 19-year-old Learners in Wales*, published in 2009.
- *Education for Sustainable development and Global Citizenship* (April 2008).
- *A Common Understanding for Schools* (July 2008).
- *Making the Most of Learning* (DCELLS, 2008).

In Northern Ireland the revised curriculum, introduced in 2007, was designed to help 'empower young people to achieve their potential and to make informed and responsible decisions throughout their lives' (NICCEA, online). The curriculum focus is on helping to:

- develop the young person as an individual
- develop the young person as a contributor to society, and
- develop the young person as a contributor to the economy and environment (CCEA, 2007).

In the revised Northern Ireland curriculum the global dimension is not as explicit as in the curricula from other UK jurisdictions, although there is a clear focus on helping pupils develop the skills they need for life and work in the twenty-first century. A feature of this was the LLW component – Learning for Life and Work. This area includes the three dimensions of *Citizenship*, *Employability* and *Personal development*. At Foundation level and Key Stages 2 and 3 the global dimension runs through two strands: (1) The World around Us and (2) Personal Development and Mutual Understanding. These strands apply across school stages from Foundation to Key Stage 4 including special educational needs (SEN).

UNESCO's involvement in education in Northern Ireland is most evident in the UNESCO Centre – Education for Pluralism, Human Rights and Democracy, at the University of Ulster.

A closer look at the revised curricula in the UK reveals a number of common threads that relate closely to the *four pillars of education* outlined in 1996 by the then President of the European Union, Jacques Delors, in the report of the Task Force on Education for the 21st Century. The four pillars of education were defined as:

- learning to know
- learning to do
- learning to live together
- learning to be (Delors, 1996) (http://www.unesco.org/delors/[14]).

This refocusing on learners and preparing them to live and work in a changing world has implications for teachers. In our previous work we argued that 'teaching professionals need to be able to respond successfully to change, and when necessary, to drive change within schools. To achieve this, teachers must be secure in their understanding of their place within the profession and their teaching identity' (Forde et al., 2006: xx). Here we argue that teachers need to have a critical understanding of educational policy as part of their professional practice. How can this be gained? Central to this is the curriculum for teacher education: pre-service and in-service. In some parts of the UK this curriculum is being redesigned in a radical way such as the *Teachers for a New Era* model at the universities of Aberdeen and Glasgow. Practising teachers can continue their learning through continuing professional development (CPD). In the near future teaching is likely to become an all graduate profession with an expectation that all teachers will hold Masters degrees.

Throughout the UK, government initiatives, sometimes in collaboration with agencies such as the British Council or non-governmental organisations such as the League of Exchange for Commonwealth Teachers (LECT) support the development of teachers' professional experience at an international level through study trips and exchange programmes. Another example is the CIPDE Project (Continuing Intercultural Professional Development) funded by the EU. This was a pilot initiative for classroom practitioners to develop intercultural understanding with European partners in an online environment (CIPDE, 2009). The case studies below illustrate some of the ways teachers can become involved in professional development related to international education.

Case study 3.1 Continuing Intercultural Professional Development in Europe Project (CIPDE)

CIPDE was an EU funded project involving partner institutions in six European countries. The aim was to provide an online resource for developing teachers' intercultural understanding. Participants were classroom practitioners, recruited through teacher education institutions and professional organisations. Teachers engaged in a series of online activities and exchanges, sharing social and cultural aspects of their professional lives.

📁 **Case study 3.2   International Education CPD course**

Teachers in Scotland can participate in a postgraduate course on International Education. The course is designed to enable teachers to gain a critical understanding of International Education and to assist them in developing international initiatives in their schools.

This international perspective is also promoted through specific curricular themes such as a 'Global Dimension' or 'International Education' recognising that learning takes place through activities and in places 'beyond the school'. This can be achieved in a variety of ways, for example through the DFID-sponsored Global Partnership schemes or EU-sponsored Comenius projects. The examples in the school case studies that follow show the ways in which schools have developed a global/international dimension in a variety of ways.

📁 **Case study 3.3   Shawlands Academy, Glasgow**

Comenius Projects

Shawlands Academy is a large secondary school in Glasgow with over 1,200 pupils. Over half of these pupils have English as a second language. In an inspection report carried out in 2009, International Education in the school, together with Sustainable Development, was noted as an example of good practice. Staff and pupils in Shawlands Academy are involved a variety of international education initiatives, many of them supported by the British Council.

These include Comenius, Etwinning, Global Partnership, INDIE (Inclusion and Diversity in Education)and an exchange link with South Africa.

Innovative approaches to practice are evident in Shawlands Academy. One ICT teacher developed an initiative to deliver the ICT curriculum for Y8/S1 pupils through International Education participating in eTwinning project linking with a school in France.

International Education extends to the whole school community. In 2008 the school janitor successfully applied for a Comenius job-shadowing grant to allow him to shadow a janitor in a partner school and travelled to a partner school near Prague, to work with the janitor there for a week, learning about 'a week in the life of a janitor' in Teplice.

The school was identified as an International School by the Scottish Executive in 2000 and in 2008 was successful in gaining an International School Award from the British Council.

Source: adapted from Shawlands Academy website.

> **Case study 3.4   Warden Park Specialist School and Community Learning Centre, West Sussex**
>
> DFID Global School Partnership
>
> Warden Park Specialist School and Community Learning Centre has been in partnership with Little Flower School in Chennai in India since 2004. In 2007 the partner schools applied for a DFID Global School Partnerships grant and received a curriculum grant for three years. A central feature of the programme is teacher exchange. Ten teachers from Warden Park went to Chennai and the same number visited the UK from Little Flower School.
>
> There are currently approximately ten projects running in five or six curriculum areas. The underlying themes are global citizenship, diversity and supporting human rights.
>
> One of joint projects with Y7 pupils called 'Me, my family and friends' looks at rights and responsibilities. Pupils look at what happens in India, and what happens in the UK. Work is shared work in an online learning environment – 'a virtual classroom in the sky.'
>
> In science, pupils learn about sustainability and have undertaken projects on acid rain and pollution. The partnership coordinator says this 'helps the youngsters learn that we aren't living on a small island, but in a great big world and that we are all interdependent; that we have to support each other'.
>
> *Source*: adapted from DFID Global Partnership Case Studies, DFID online.

Thinking point 3.2

Using the case studies above, what are the benefits for pupils, teachers and schools of developing international links and partnerships? What are the potential drawbacks?

What does this mean for pupils and teachers today? The revised curricula outlined above are clearly based on a conceptual model that sees pupils as learners operating within, across and beyond a range of local, national and global contexts. They are designed to provide them with the knowledge and understanding and, perhaps more importantly, the skills and abilities, to be able to function and contribute effectively as global citizens. It requires teachers to have the pedagogical understanding, professional expertise and critical capacity to be able to mediate and facilitate this and it requires the boundaries of schools to be 'endlessly flexible' (Middlewood et al., 2005: 32).

This outward-looking perspective is a feature of the 'Learning School', outlined by Middlewood who suggests that

> Learning schools of the twenty-first century need to be less artificial as organisations, less cut off from what goes on outside them, and the learning that takes place within them needs to be felt and perceived as relevant by all those concerned. When we say 'less cut off', this in the future means not just from our immediate locality and community, but from the international world we live in. (Middlewood, 2005: 25)

Barth captures this crucial role that schools have in serving the needs of the present and the future, describing them as 'four walls surrounding the future' (MacGilchrist et al., 2004:1).

Summary

In this chapter we have argued that educational policy needs to be viewed from an international perspective and the role of supranational organisations and agencies such as the OECD and UNESCO understood in a critical way. This will equip teachers and school leaders to translate policy into practice more effectively and to provide learners with knowledge, skills and abilities to become *successful learners, confident individuals and responsible citizens who make a positive contribution to society* (QCA, 2008: 2).

This requires changes to how schools organise themselves and organise learning, how schools engage with their local communities and communities beyond, and how teachers are prepared and supported to facilitate learning.

In creating 'schools without boundaries' the guidelines for integrating the values and principles of *Every Child Matters* into the curriculum set out what is required: 'passionate and committed teaching that offers opportunities for open ended investigation, creativity, experimentation, teamwork and performance. It should also involve real experiences, activities beyond the school, parental involvement, working with others, taking responsibility for events and activities and encountering challenging and unfamiliar contexts' (QCA, 2008: 2).

In Sections 2 and 3 of this book we look at some of the ways schools are already achieving this, though collaborative approaches to learning for learners and for teachers (Chapters 6 and 11); through new understandings of learning relationships and learning transitions (Chapters 8 and 9) and through rethinking teachers' role as leaders of learning and the implications of this for teacher education (Chapters 10, 12 and 13).

In this chapter we have explored how what happens in schools and classrooms is influenced by and connected to wider international agendas and policy initiatives. Does this suggest a new form of global cosmopolitanism for the twenty-first century? This will be explored in Chapter 14 which looks at the future of education by going back to core principles of both community and the idea of individual autonomy, and argues for affirming the idea of social justice as a fundamental purpose of education.

> ### Key questions for reflection and discussion
>
> - Do supranational organisations and agencies exert disproportionate influence on education policy in their member states?
> - Is there, or should there be, a global curriculum?
> - How can you integrate a global perspective into your own learning and professional practice?
> - How can teachers help pupils develop a critical understanding of a global perspective?
> - What are the benefits locally of thinking and acting globally?

Further reading

Coulby, D. (2006) 'Intercultural education: theory and practice', *Intercultural Education*, 17(3):245–7.

Held, D. (2004) *A Globalizing World? Culture, Economic, Politics*. 2nd edn. London: Routledge. An accessible introduction to the key ideas and issues associated with globalisation.

James, K. (2005) 'International education: the concept and its relationship to intercultural education', *Journal of Research in International Education*, 4(3): 313–32.

Jarvis, P. (2007) *Globalisation, Lifelong Learning and the Learning Society*. London: Routledge. This book looks at globalisation from the perspective of lifelong learning.

Lauder, H., Brown, P. Dillahough, J. and Halsey, A. (2006) *Education, Globalization and Social Change*. Oxford: Oxford University Press. This is a comprehensive resource on globalisation.

Moutious, S. (2009) 'International organizations and transnational education policy', *Compare*, 39 (4): 469–81. This article provides a critical perspective on the growing influence of supranational bodies.

Parker, W. C. (2008), '"International Education" What's in a name? International Education signals very different ideas to different people. When it comes to your school what will you have it mean?', *Phi Delta Kappan*, 90 (3): 196–7. Some of the wider issues and questions relating to International Education are explored in this article.

Web resources

The Britsh Council: http://www.britishcouncil.org/new/

Department for International Development (DFID): http://www.dfid.gov.uk/About-DFID/Our-organisation1/DFID-Directory/International-Divisions/United-Nations-Conflict-and-Humanitarian-Division/

OECD: http://www.oecd.org/home/0,2987,en_2649_201185_1_1_1_1_1,00.html

NICCEA: Northern Ireland Council for the Curriculum, Examinations and Assessment, http://www.rewardinglearning.org.uk/

Welsh Assembly Government: http://new.Wales.gov.uk/topics/educationandskills/curriculumassessment/arevisedcurriculum forwales/? Lang=en

United Nations: http://www.un.org/en/aboutun/index.shtml

UNESCO: http://www.unesco.org/en/education/about-us/mission/

Notes

1. Autarkic – economic self sufficiency; in this context, self-contained.
2. UNESCO and Education © UNESCO 1995–2010, used by permission of UNESCO.
3. Supranational: operating above the level of the nation state; transnational: operating across nation states.
4. UNESCO and Education © UNESCO 1995–2010, used by permission of UNESCO.
5. What is UNESCO © UNESCO 1995–2010, used by permission of UNESCO.
6. UNESCO Education Mission © UNESCO 1995–2010, used by permission of UNESCO and UNESCO Education Strategy © UNESCO 1995–2010, used by permission of UNESCO.
7. UNESCO (2008) *2008–2013 Medium Term Strategy*, UNESCO, Paris © UNESCO 2008, used by permission of UNESCO.
8. UNESCO (2008) *2008–2013 Medium Term Strategy*, UNESCO, Paris © UNESCO 2008, used by permission of UNESCO.
9. UNESCO Institutes and Centres for Education © UNESCO 1995–2010, used by permission of UNESCO.
10. and 11. UK National Commission for UNESCO © UNESCO 1995–2010, used by permission of UNESCO.
12. *Every Child Matters* was developed as result of the Children's Act (2004).
13. The One Wales Agreement was the agreement reached between the Plaid Cymru and Labour groups in the Welsh National Assembly in 2007.
14. UNESCO Task Force on Education for the Twenty-first Century © UNESCO 1995–2010, used by permission of UNESCO.

CHAPTER 4

EDUCATION AND WORK

Cathy Fagan

Key ideas explored in this chapter are:

- Work-related education policy
- Education and society
- Moral citizens
- Economic sustainability
- Globalisation and knowledge economy
- Teachers' awareness of work-related requirements

This chapter looks at one particular area of policy development, that of work-related education, and considers the social, cultural and economic imperatives that have driven developments in this area. Formal education has a wide range of purposes and in school education there are two major purposes that relate particularly to education's connection with the world of work. The first purpose is the preparation of young people for their current and future social and economic roles in society and making informed choices about how they will engage with careers, career development and their prospects of making themselves economically self-sufficient in their post-school lives. Many commonly cited purposes of schooling are thus couched in terms of improving general facilities of personal enlightenment and critical thinking. Governments in rapidly changing global environments also depend on education to provide sufficient numbers of economically viable and socially adaptable workers in order to ensure sustainability and competitive advancement in world markets. Thus the second purpose is that of producing the necessary range of contributors to the social and economic prosperity of nations, internally and internationally, in relation to increasingly interconnected global economies. This approach views education in terms of its impact on the economic stability and success of nation states. Indeed we have become used to this emphasis for education and are not surprised to have economic purposes highlighted to us ahead of others. 'We are currently … so accustomed to education being discussed in terms of its economic relevance that any other reference point strikes us as curious' (Wolf, 2005: 246).

There is a social and moral importance that society attaches to paid employment that is related to the task of 'earning one's living' (Winch, 2000: 155) which obliges us, as far as possible, to provide for ourselves and thus to participate in the reproduction and continuation of society. Historically it has been the family, the church and the school, in different proportions at different times and with varying levels of awareness, that have addressed the task of preparing young people for this perceived responsibility and their progress into their adult working lives. In the more recent past the school has taken on this role to the extent that work-related aims for education are given high priority and contribute to our commonly held beliefs about the place of work in our lives as members of society.

In educational terms there has been an alienation of parents' responsibility for, and influence on, the employment destinations of their children. From early agrarian and cottage-industrial ways of life, when parents prepared their children to continue in the same occupations, lifestyle and expectations as themselves, controlling influence in modern times was transferred to the organisers of industrial society (Corson, 1993: 12). In the present day, parents may have aspirations and set challenges for their children's future careers but it is their children's engagement with education, influenced by post-industrial, knowledge-economy driven demands, that more often has the upper hand in shaping employment futures. Arguably all education that prepares for the taking up of adult roles in a society, where having a job is highly important, can be said to be addressing work-related needs. In practice, however, an academic/vocational divide can often be seen in school education that mirrors the stratified patterns of work and social status that can persist in society.

> ☁
> **Thinking point 4.1**
>
> • What are the influences on young people's career aspirations?
> • Are there other influencing factors that emerge during secondary education?
> • How can teachers make themselves aware of the range of options and new opportunities becoming available for their learners' futures?

In late eighteenth- and early nineteenth-century industrial society, the intention of providing working-class children with an education that seemed suited to their employment aspirations was realised in early forms of vocational education. There are some areas where dilemmas persistently present themselves in relation to vocational education. The first is the political imperative to encourage education and educators to produce school leavers who are well prepared to move into industry and business, with skills and attitudes developed that are of use to production, trades and commerce. There is strong emphasis in current political demands on education for relevance and preparedness for the world of work and calls for basic skills to be included among indicators of success (Pring, 1995: 6). Another dilemma is in the timing of making choices between vocational or academic routes. It makes sense to make a start on work-related training and skills development as early as possible but a premature move away from a more general education can cut off chances to alter decisions before a breadth of knowledge and appreciation of wider opportunities has been acquired. Vocational education has, despite these dilemmas and tensions, developed, albeit with varying emphases, and in 1993, Malcolm Skilbeck of the Organisation for Economic Co-operation and Development advocated a more balanced way of dealing with the divide between academic and vocational education thus:

> From the time he or she enters pre-school, to the time of graduation from college or university, the student is ... or should be ... engaged in learnings which have actual or potential value for work, employment and a vocation defined as a specific career. Conversely, vocational learnings are part of a wider set which relate to other aspects of personal and social life which have their own values that cannot be submerged in a relentless utilitarianism. (Skilbeck, 1993: 13–15)

The changing nature of work

In the post-industrial economy, developing technology has changed social, political and economic parameters so that a knowledge economy is now the most influential context for living and learning. Education has responded to post-industrial imperatives by working out policy and practice to add new areas to the curriculum to correspond with societal changes. It has taken on a central role in the development, acquisition and transfer of knowledge, and has thereby shifted its position in relation to the changing nature of work in contemporary society. This newly defined relationship between education and work can be recognised in various current and developing practices in school education in developed countries. Preparation for understanding about work and the economy in school education is part of preparation for social and cultural literacy. In the later stages of school education it can be more specifically tied to preparing for particular occupations or roles in society through vocational education or education and business links initiatives, but in the pre-vocational phases it is often referred to as enterprise, entrepreneurship or even economics education. Teachers of subjects, knowledge and skills that could be described as vocational education have traditionally been possessors of such skills themselves with a background and training in technical or industrial settings. They are usually specialists in their areas of vocational expertise, such as engineers who become technical education teachers. There are some examples of teacher education programmes that include teaching qualifications or specialisms in enterprise or entrepreneurship education in countries where these are discrete subject areas within school curricula, but often there is just an expectation that all teachers will contribute to such programmes by applying their own interests and initiative to support their efforts. This is clearly seen in countries where enterprise and entrepreneurship education, particularly in the earlier stages of education, are embedded across the curriculum or addressed in cross-curricular themes, as is the case in Scotland.

For some teachers their subject specialisms have traditionally catered for links to students' particular career choices but the more generic nature of much contemporary work-related education makes it the concern of every teacher in both primary and secondary schools. This presupposes that every teacher is able to relate their teaching to school students' needs for work-related learning and, indeed, that policy-makers can make the necessary links between theory and practice when devising and advising on initiatives. These purposes of education, however, cannot be pursued to the exclusion of others and it can be argued that learning for personal and social fulfilment and the development of individual skills and aptitudes must also be catered for in school education. Enterprise education can be understood in many different ways and much of current school policy promotes the encouragement of entrepreneurial activities and skills. Therein lies the dilemma for policy-makers, teacher educators and informed teachers who wish to promote the business and entrepreneurial features of enterprise education but struggle to accommodate the values-laden aspects of personal fulfilment and self-actualisation that arguably should underpin enterprising approaches to teaching and learning.

> ### 📁 **Case study 4.1**
>
> School A is a primary school in which the headteacher and staff raise awareness of work-related issues as part of their commitment to citizenship education. Starting in early years with a topic on 'People who help us', students examine the work that people do and the skills needed for their work. This is expanded upon later in primary school by two enterprise projects that provide opportunities to learn skills and take on roles and responsibilities that are important in work. Work-related learning is not, however, confined to topics because the teachers make use of every instance when relevant knowledge or skills emerge, for example in reading or mathematics. This is possible because the teachers agree that students should develop awareness of work-related practice and are therefore alert to teaching opportunities and are creative in making connections across the curriculum.

Apart from job-specific vocational courses and careers-related pupil support, enterprise education in its varied forms has been perhaps the most common form of work-related education to emerge in curricula in the past 30 or so years. In the UK it has taken various forms with education–industry links, business placements, mini-enterprise and young enterprise schemes being some examples of ways in which schools have made links with business and sought to emulate business practice in the classroom.

Work-related learning has been a statutory requirement in England for all Key Stage 4 school students since September 2004 when the Qualification and Curriculum Authority's *Framework for Work Related Learning* (QCA, 2004) provided guidance for encouraging students 'to recognise, develop and apply skills for enterprise and employability'. This was replaced four years later when the Qualification and Curriculum Development Agency (QCDA) unveiled the *Framework for Economic Wellbeing 11–19: Career, Work-related Learning and Enterprise* (QCDA, 2008).

In Scotland, scepticism about market-style initiatives in school education slowed the introduction of enterprise into education, and so education industry links and education for work were the terms selected in policy documents to refer to what teachers recognised as enterprise education. These were not mandatory documents for use in Scottish schools but teachers who were interested in enterprise in education were provided with resources and some support. The political landscape in Scotland altered significantly in 1999, when devolved government was established in Edinburgh. The most recent policy document relating to education and work in Scotland is entitled *Determined to Succeed: A Review of Enterprise in Education* (SEED, 2002). A group of successful Scottish entrepreneurs contributed to preparing this document and provided financial resources to support its implementation in schools.

Enterprise education has been developing in Wales, in a similar way to Scotland in that materials and resources are being made available for teachers with the intention of building work-related skills across the curriculum. Young Enterprise Wales offers opportunities for business and education skills development and Project Dynamo is a Welsh Assembly Government initiative that provides a series of entrepreneurship materials for teachers in primary, secondary and further education.

Thinking point 4.2

The first paragraph of the Scottish document *Determined to Succeed* states: 'The ultimate goal of Enterprise in Education must be the creation of successful businesses, jobs and prosperity' (SEED, 2002: 6), indicating a prime focus for economic outcomes in young people's education. This could arguably be as a result of the involvement of business entrepreneurs in the development of the policy document in much more than a consultative role.

- Do you agree with this stated goal for enterprise in education?
- Is this different from entrepreneurship education?
- Who should be in positions of power in the design of the school curriculum?

The pursuit of enterprise, particularly in education, has often been conflated with attempts to encourage more entrepreneurial aspirations in young people's consideration of their future work roles and, indeed, to boost the number of entrepreneurs supporting the nation's economy. It is not clear, however, whether it is possible for teachers and schools to 'grow' entrepreneurs in the classroom. Teachers meanwhile need up-to-date awareness of the changing needs of young people in preparing to be economically active in the current shifts in society from a welfare economy to a knowledge economy. In school education there are good reasons for building enterprise/entrepreneurship education into the curriculum. One is that political changes to the way in which society operates demand different responses from school education in preparing young people for their economic roles, and another is that we cannot afford to be left behind in the highly competitive business markets that now exist. Schools would be failing their pupils if they did not acknowledge these shifting conditions and did not try to provide support. In school education, relevance may be more achievable than realism and it is teachers' informed practice in establishing relevant learning contexts which will enthuse young people and open minds to their future economic, enterprising and entrepreneurial potential. Young people will possess these forms of capital in varying degrees. Enterprise education should then be designed to help pupils to improve their levels in those areas that *can* be altered within the school context and to allow them to utilise what they bring from outside school.

Work-related education policy must take account of the ways in which the world of work is changing. It is now essential for teachers and policy-makers to look at wider patterns influencing the nature of work, particularly the effects of globalisation on the development of a knowledge economy. Globalisation is a contested concept that relates to phenomena of interconnectedness in dealings across the globe (Held and McGraw, 2003). It relates to a rise in the interdependence of governments, corporations and people, spurred by the spread of the free market economic system. Advances in new technology have brought about large-scale changes in communication and transport that have in turn made economic systems more globally connected. The era of globalisation can be seen as a further stage in the cycle of change in human work activity. The acquisition of global knowledge capital and participation in both manufacturing and knowledge economies are heralding major shifts in the nature of work. In our post-industrial, global society and economy, the all-pervasiveness of knowledge as a prized commodity and its importance in every aspect of our economic and social lives needs to be acknowledged. If almost every occupation either produces knowledge or depends on the reproduction of knowledge, then clearly education must be prepared and at the forefront of development of the skills required to access and apply appropriate knowledge. Knowledge is now considered a central component of production, whereas in the past it was a supportive external influence. Knowledge itself is now considered the commodity, albeit a rather different and often virtual type of commodity. One of the most striking differences is that economies usually deal in surplus-scarcity environments but knowledge as a commodity does not comply with the usual conditions. It is knowledge that is the commodity in demand, that is most necessary for the growth of businesses and that has the greatest impact on economics in a global marketplace. Teachers possess subject knowledge and pedagogical knowledge, and it is now imperative for them also to have extensive awareness of the contemporary significance of knowledge and the knowledge economy.

Impact of the knowledge economy on education and teachers' practice

What can schools do to participate in these changes? Many aspects of contemporary education still have their roots in nineteenth-century practices and ideologies, but according to Valerie Bayliss (2001: 15), these will be swept aside by the requirements of the knowledge economy. There are various consequences for schools arising out of the transition to the knowledge economy which will make demands on the curriculum over and above the need for literacy and numeracy as core skills. It is becoming necessary to alter the approaches of educational systems to ensure that there will be a wide base of knowledge workers who can understand and operate within the spectrum of abilities listed above. Indeed, if nations fail to rise to the economic and educational challenges of the knowledge economy and to make adjustments in their education systems, the resulting problems of social exclusion for those not adequately prepared will present a drain on their economies. Michael Peters envisages new forms of knowledge requirement for school students as follows:

- meta-cognitive abilities and skills – thinking about how to think and learning how to learn
- the ability to integrate formal and informal learning, declarative knowledge (or *knowing that*) and procedural knowledge (*know-how*)
- the ability to access, select and evaluate knowledge in an information-soaked world
- the ability to develop and apply several forms of intelligence as suggested by Howard Gardiner and others
- the ability to work and learn effectively in teams
- the ability to create, transpose and transfer knowledge
- the ability to cope with ambiguous situations, unpredictable problems and unforeseeable circumstances, and
- the ability to cope with multiple careers – learning how to 'redesign' oneself, locate oneself in a job market, choose and fashion the relevant education and training (Peters, 2000: 3).

Whereas in industrial and post-industrial society people's occupations could be used to define their identity, post-modernism sees people constantly having to redefine themselves as the nature of work becomes increasingly disjointed. This is evident in frequent career changes, the casualisation of work, the feminisation of the workforce, people having multiple or part-time jobs and the possibility of early retirement. Many in society have become marginalised and find themselves outside the labour market altogether. Structural unemployment has increased, particularly in former industrial areas, while many unskilled or low-skilled jobs are being outsourced to Third World countries where labour is very cheap. There is no longer any security of employment or entitlement to work.

In this ever-changing environment for work, educators need to recognise that these massive shifts have indeed been occurring and that education requires some redefinition to meet the newly emerging needs of individuals, communities and societies of various sorts. David Guile (2003: 98) explored ways in which educational policy could be reformulated to develop transformative rather than informative relationships with the world. He suggests the following. First, shift the focus from the orthodox knowledge traditionally included in curricula to a social practice location for learning and to resituate forms of subject knowledge in the fields where they originated and from where they have over time become dislocated. Second, rethink and reprioritise the relationships between educational institutions and communities of practice, for example, by finding more meaningful ways of promoting work experience that enables students to gain better understanding of the links between formal education and workplace cultures and practices. Third, as well as work experience, provide opportunities to learn across activities and communities by using information and communication technology as a cultural tool in assisting students to mediate their relationships with the world. Fourth, assist learners to participate from their own knowledge bases across communities of practice so that their contributions are complementary to and not excluded from dialogues. Fifth, students need opportunities to come to terms with the traditions of social practice, but beyond that they should realise the possibilities of social practice so that they can prepare, through participation, for working and living in a knowledge society.

Case study 4.2

School B is a secondary school where a senior member of staff has the role of coordinating work-related learning. Skills for Work courses are offered, some of which are run in partnership with a local college, and the school provides careers guidance at transition points with input from the Careers Service. As well as this, all staff recognise how their own specialist areas can support the students with career choices and knowledge and skills preparation. This school, however, is concerned with more than subject expertise. Through citizenship, enterprise, personal and social and religious education, broad themes of social responsibility are introduced and all students have opportunities to engage in dialogue and action that in turn links with their subject learning. For example, the students run a long-term enterprise project that considers the impact of social entrepreneurship and promotes links with their partner school in Malawi.

Summary

School students should be able to experience at first hand the implications of their own economic and social actions and the effects of national and international trade and employment policies. All of these experiences can influence the choices that young people will make about their career paths and about how they will conduct themselves as consumers and economically active members of society. Teachers of work-related education should therefore pay attention to values and moral behaviour in issues that young people are likely to have to deal with in their working lives because the workplace is potentially an area of values conflict. Pupils need to be 'values literate' to be able to recognise and challenge such matters from a secure understanding of their own identities and ideas. Thus work-related education is inextricable from the range of aspects of education for personal, social and moral development.

The economic and financial upheavals that have come about since 2008 serve to underline a lack of moral responsibility in business and finance that highlights the need for values-driven approaches to be emphasised, from the earliest stages of work-related educational policy-making. Young people are being faced with making personal and social decisions about the global implications of their lifestyles, outlooks and career choices, and they need help and clear direction from teachers in exploring the values issues that underpin these areas. This should inform discussions about work-related curriculum matters. Work and economic activity should be presented to school students within the contexts of involvement in local, national and international possibilities. They should also be explored with student teachers and in continuing professional development activity for serving teachers to equip them with background understanding of the social, political, economic and values-based arguments for supporting education for work in schools.

Key questions for reflection and discussion

- What is the future of work and how can we change our current understandings to allow for future relevance?
- How is the expansion of new technology affecting our traditional occupations and encouraging new ones?
- What is the extent of the shift from the role of industrial workers to that of knowledge workers?
- How do teachers perceive entrepreneurs, understand entrepreneurship or relate these to teaching?
- How can we deal with knowledge management in order to promote a learning society?

Further reading

Bills, D.B. (2004) *The Sociology of Education and Work*. Oxford: Blackwell. This text provides analysis of the relationship between education and work and the interrelated social practices of both of these essential institutions.

Fagan, C. (2006) 'Three Es for teachers: economics, enterprise and entrepreneurship', *Teacher Development*, 10(3): 275–91. This article indicates that there are complex and contested ideological bases for the three Es and proposes that teachers should consider social, cultural, political and moral foundations in their work-related teaching.

Web resources

English documents: http://www.qcda.gov.uk/17872.aspx
Scottish documents: http://www.determinedtosucceed.co.uk/dts/CCC_FirstPage.jsp
Welsh documents: http: //www.projectdynamo.co.uk/application/publicAccess/default.asp?lang=eng

CHAPTER 5

INCLUSION AND PEDAGOGY

George Head

Key ideas explored in this chapter are:

- Inclusion
- Complementary pedagogy
- Human capability

In this chapter, we explore the implications of possibly the most universal and demanding policy for schools and teachers: inclusion. While there is debate about what exactly we mean by inclusion in education, there is general agreement that if it is to work, then something has to change.

Inclusion has been described as being about shared values, participation, culture and communities. It has its roots in human rights and social justice and this has created a tension between the rights of all children to be educated along with their peers and the 'needs' model that is the basis of the segregated special schools system that is challenged by advocates of inclusion. Consequently, the inclusion debate in the UK has centred on ability (including inability and disability) and place (special or mainstream) rather than what teachers and schools do. Florian (2008) argues that this is a false dichotomy and is the result of thinking on difference that sees the important differences between young people in schools as those related to disability. Instead, she argues, the appropriate differences among pupils are those based on learning and that schools and teachers are well equipped to deal with diversity in learning. This is not to suggest that we can 'do' inclusion: it is not in our gift to include anyone in anything. Rather, people must feel that they are included; that they are valued and that they belong. What we can do as teachers in our own classrooms is create the contexts in which all learners feel included. What teachers 'do' in their classrooms is, of course, pedagogy.

 Thinking point 5.1

How diverse is the range of pupils you have met in classes in terms of family background, social circumstances and subject ability, and how do these factors impact on learning?

There is general agreement among protagonists of inclusion that an inclusive pedagogy should not lead to the 'disappearance of disability' but should accept and take account of it in their teaching (Florian, 2008; Head and Pirrie, 2007; Molina et al., 2005;). There is some evidence (Head and Pirrie, 2007) that this may already be happening to some extent within special schools. One of the effects of inclusion has been to question the role of schools, both mainstream and special. Whereas in the past special schools were populated by pupils with similar learning difficulties (for example, moderate learning difficulties or social, emotional and behavioural difficulties) one of the unforeseen consequences of the move towards inclusion (complicated by an increasing demand for external qualifications for pupils in special schools) has been the introduction of a wider range of difficulties within special schools, resulting in teachers employing a range of strategies and teaching styles beyond those related to the 'specialism' of the school. Whereas, at least in Scotland, mainstream schools have coped by setting up bases and units to address the additional or special needs, teachers in special schools have responded by extending their repertoire of teaching skills. There is a danger, however, that such developments take place in isolation and therefore are fragmented, ad hoc and may lack theoretical cohesion.

A starting point for the development of a coherent approach to learning in an inclusive context might well be the changing social context that inclusion brings to schools and classrooms. Since teachers and schools are already good at dealing with diversity in learning, an inclusive pedagogy might have its foundations in diversity, in the social, moral, cognitive and affective differences that individuals bring to the class that enrich the learning experiences of everyone. An inclusive pedagogy, therefore, is rooted in the beliefs, values, skills, abilities and knowledge of the individuals and group including the teacher; in other words, practice, rather than being a matter of resources or provision only (Daniels, 2001; Molina et al., 2005). In short, inclusive pedagogy is about the importance of school as a social space and the formation of identity as well as learning (Allan, 2005).

For someone like McLaren (2009) an inclusive pedagogy is critical and operates at two levels. On the one hand, it is related to the wider world view through exploration and challenge. It questions the origins of knowledge and asks why some forms of knowledge are privileged over others. Inclusive pedagogy, therefore, draws on cultural, moral, political and social conventions, values and ideologies, and through challenge and interrogation helps learners make sense of the world. At the same time, and in order to achieve this level of critical engagement, inclusive pedagogy also operates at the level of the classroom. In inclusive classrooms, teachers seek, through engagement with curricula, to find the points where students' personal lived experiences intersect with issues within wider society (Kincheloe, 2008) for it is at this interface that deeper learning, beyond the technical knowledge required to teach and learn subject matter, becomes possible. In one sense this could be understood as the starting point of Vygotsky's zone of proximal development, and from here we would wish to argue that the appropriate form of mediation from dependency, through interdependency to independence is what, in this chapter, is called complementary pedagogy.

The most obvious testing ground and challenging context for inclusive pedagogy is that in which the learners stand to gain most from any benefits: the learning of children and young people whose difficulties in learning outstrip 'the teacher's capacity to know how to respond', that is, those with additional or special needs (Florian, 2008: 205). The remainder of this chapter offers a possible response that takes account of the arguments above to provide an interactive, collaborative and inclusive learning experience.

Compensatory pedagogy

With this focus in mind, we want to argue that there are different ways of approaching the learning of young people who are thought to require additional support. On the one hand, young people in these groups can be perceived as 'exceptional' and the teaching strategies developed for them have tended to recognise that they have special or additional needs and to compensate for them through, for example, differentiation of materials, asking for less demanding outcomes or through lowering expectations, generally. One consequence of the impact of a compensatory approach, therefore, is to construct learners as being in deficit and to adopt a pedagogical practice aimed at normalisation. By extrapolation, this argument would hold true for all learners whether they belong to one of the recognised disability groups or are, indeed, more able than their peers. The construction of lesson plans and the detailing of learning outcomes in advance of learning are based on an assumption that what is to be taught has not been previously learned and that it is the teacher's responsibility to decide what is to be learned. Furthermore, the effectiveness of teaching is evaluated by the extent to which students learn what was intended. Moreover, a compensatory pedagogy might also reinforce the identity shared by each of the discrete special needs groups; that of being somehow different in their learning from the majority of others.

Compensatory pedagogies tend to take learners' curiosity, anger and lack of knowledge and treat them as 'ignorance' that is dependent on the teacher (or other external source) for a remedy. In such circumstances, the teacher acts as instructor, provider or at best, facilitator, guiding learners towards predetermined outcomes or intentions. All learning is presumed to be at the behest of the teacher who is experienced in the normal requirements of an education system, and it is the teacher who chooses materials and decides when and how they will be used for learning. This practice assumes that learners are unable to engage successfully in learning on their own. A compensatory pedagogy, therefore, can be understood as a pedagogy of ignorance, dependency and despair.

Complementary pedagogy

By way of contrast, a complementary pedagogy begins with and maintains a perspective based on ability and the value of students' own experiences, thoughts and beliefs. Consequently, rather than compensating for a perceived deficit, it invites an approach to learning and teaching that complements the skills, abilities and knowledge that students already have and provides a context in which they can be developed in collaboration with others, including their teachers and other adults such as learning support assistants.

If such experiences are to be sustainable, however, they must be understood both in operational and theoretical terms. While the goal of compensatory pedagogies is normalisation, the goal of complementary pedagogies can be understood in more humanistic terms as autonomy within broadly communitarian principles (Smith, 2008).

A complementary pedagogy can be understood as a pedagogy of 'unknowing', interdependency and hope (Zembylas, 2007). Teachers and learners find themselves in a condition of unknowing; that is, while content and context might be familiar to all, what learners will make of it and how that will impact on the learners and teacher are unknown. Indeed, since a complementary pedagogy is posited on the learner's ability and the direction of learning is determined by the knowledge and insight generated by learners, then often the roles of teacher and learner become movable and interchangeable. Within a complementary pedagogy, the teacher does not seek to normalise learners' traits, thoughts and behaviours, but to recognise and affirm them as attributes, to enliven them and seek to give them expression. In doing so, teachers and learners seek to defamiliarise and interrogate their materials in ways that allow for a new sense of fascination and wonder, thereby generating moments of intensity, revelation and creativity in which learning takes place. Through non-conformity to the traditional roles of teacher and learner, new learner identities based on effectiveness and capability are generated. A complementary pedagogy, therefore, is affective, (meta)cognitive and creative and the role of the teacher is that of activator, mediator and instigator.

Complementary pedagogy can develop spontaneously, naturally and unselfconsciously. Learning and teaching through complementary pedagogies is a process of defamiliarisation. While learning at schools tends to present as transparent and obvious, it does so because as students and teachers we accept the conventions of education and culture that determine what is to be learned and how it is to be taught. When these conventions are undercut either by the teacher or through students' own experiences and knowledge, then curricula, subjects and topics of study are either called into question or seen in new and refreshing ways.

Learning and teaching through complementary pedagogy entails a requirement for accuracy and precision, and this is the case in both analytical and creative tasks, if, indeed, they can be separated in this way. For example, following the watching of a film, students might be encouraged, through a series of process questions such as 'How do you know that?' or 'What exactly did you see and hear?' to interrogate what they have just watched in order to tease out similarities with other films, narratives, themes or experiences they may have encountered, to pick out anything that surprised them and explain why it did so, to recognise patterns that recur and to indicate anything that puzzled them and why it did so.

Crucially, working through tasks in this fashion does not entail a search for right or wrong answers; the similarities, surprises, patterns and puzzles in the above example would be those that the young people experienced while watching the film. The purpose of the analysis, therefore, is to generate understanding of and insight into the cultural, artistic and aesthetic context of what is being learned and to generate a common sense of the topic or subject matter being studied.

Moreover, using complementary pedagogies in schools provides a context in which children and young people are required to work together in ways that are not always expected in other school contexts. In collaborative tasks children and young people come to realise that others have ideas, opinions and beliefs that are valid and valuable. Similarly, learning tasks that are creative (including in the sense that students are required to produce a piece of work) entail a range of functions from planning, justifying and challenging to ordering, structuring and making sense of what is being learned. Each of these tasks calls for a team to collaborate in the production of the particular element and the teams must, in turn, collaborate as a whole in order to ensure the successful production of a learning artefact. Importantly from a pedagogical perspective, therefore, teaching in a context of complementary pedagogy provides a milieu in which pupils may be able to differentiate for themselves and others through social support and by connecting with the material and concepts being learned at their own level (Brown et al., 1996).

Considering young people's and teachers' experiences holistically, perhaps the most important factors of a complementary pedagogy would be young people's ownership and leadership of learning projects and the creation of new opportunities it presents for their learning, and innovative ways in which teachers can work with them. Operationally, this can be understood in terms of a basically metacognitive approach within a context of creativity that might be described as a 'community' that itself consists of groups or sub-sections of communities of practice and learning (Brown et al., 1996; Wenger, 1999).

However, knowing how and why learning and teaching works operationally is itself an instance of curiosity. We have already discussed above the relationships among teaching, values and beliefs that impact on learning. Further understanding of why a pedagogical approach consistently impacts on learners and teachers in particular ways requires deeper probing into what it is that they experience.

> **Thinking point 5.2**
>
> In what ways do you adopt elements of a complementary pedagogy as part of your practice?

The importance of narrative in learning has been argued by Bruner (1996) and developed, among others, by literary theorists. Narrative, we would argue, plays a significant role as part of complementary pedagogies. Narrative allows us to make sense of past and present experiences and to dream of and predict a future based on those experiences. Narrative is both a cognitive and affective experience. We think through and construct narratives in recognisable patterns, broadly linear in Western cultures and circular in some others. Narratives, however, are built on fears, hopes, aspirations dreams and ambitions, and these help to shape our narratives of the past and present as much as future narratives.

Human capability

Human capabilities, as conceived by Amartya Sen and developed alongside others including Martha Nussbaum (Nussbaum, 2006) are based on the entitlement, in a truly just society, of human beings to lead a life based on social justice and dignity, should they choose to do so. Nussbaum identified a minimum core of 10 social entitlements that she saw as forming the foundations of human capabilities that indicate a just and dignified life. The suggestion in this chapter, then, is that the impact of complementary pedagogies on learners and teachers can be understood in terms of Nussbaum's entitlements and that this helps explain why complementary pedagogies are appropriate approaches to learning and teaching in a just and inclusive educational system.

First, complementary pedagogies provide naturally occurring contexts for Nussbaum's capability of 'senses, imagination and thought' (Nussbaum 2006: 76). Engaging in the learning processes of exploration, creation and analysis allows for the exercise of imagination and all that that entails. However, it is a context informed by the conventions of culture and society, thereby providing an 'informed and cultivated' foundation to the expression of students' ideas, feelings and thoughts. Moreover, an expansion of learning in the creation of the products of learning could be likened to an exercise in 'artistic speech' in which students' narratives are expressed. Complementary pedagogy also seeks to provide pleasurable experiences, another aspect of the entitlement to use one's senses, imagination and thought.

As a result of being directly related to pupils' own experiences of the world, complementary pedagogies can be said to operate at the level of personal narrative, as it is through narrative that we make sense of our place in the world. Consequently, complementary pedagogies should provide a context in which students are able to give expression to their emotions (Nussbaum, 2006: 76–7) including, crucially, fear, frustration and anger as well as more positive emotions such as gratitude, appreciation and enjoyment. When analysing study topics, students do so in relation to their past experiences while identifying and expressing areas of 'unknowing' (Zembylas, 2005, 2007) that are ripe for learning. The experiences used to make sense of tasks include life experiences and experiences of literature (in a broad sense) and other artefacts that are significant constituents of the learner's culture. Moreover, instances of 'unknowing' are expressed as moments of surprise or puzzlement, thereby invoking curiosity.

Since complementary pedagogies offer both cognitive and affective experiences, they also provide a context for the exercise of practical reason on those emotions listed in the previous paragraph. It is not difficult to extrapolate from the planning of and critical reflection on learning tasks to reflecting on and planning one's own life. While research indicates that the transfer of criticality from one domain to another is the most difficult aspect of any educational initiative, the literature on metacognition, for example, suggests that it is achievable (Shayer and Adey, 2002). Practical reason (Nussbaum, 2006: 77), therefore, would be one manifestation of the impact of a complementary pedagogy.

In terms of Nussbaum's entitlements, a feature of complementary pedagogy would be the emergence of a greater sense of affiliation for both learners and teachers. This would arise from the requirement of working together to create learning experiences in which the importance of each of the learners' and teacher's roles necessary for success would lead to appreciation of each others' skills and abilities. Teachers and learners alike would be in a situation of living 'with and towards others' (Nussbaum, 2006: 77) and be able and prepared to show concern for others as part of a learning team. Moreover, because study through complementary pedagogies is a search for understanding and insight and not right or wrong answers, the class becomes a place where students are able to express their opinions and thoughts without fear of humiliation and know that their contributions will be treated with dignity. Not only does this result in a sense of one belonging to others, it also produces a sense of others belonging to the one (Noddings, 2007).

🗁 Case study 5.1

A class of 10-year-olds were discussing the meaning of colour as part of a Moving Image Education lesson. The pupils made the expected observations and suggestions such as red standing for danger, yellow for sunshine and happiness and that you know who the villain is in a film because they are usually dressed in black. The example of Darth Vader in *Star Wars* was given.

At this point, one girl suggested that white signified evil. Her classmates responded by arguing that white, in fact, stood for innocence and goodness. The girl's idea, however, intrigued the film professional working with this class and teacher. He probed the suggestion through a series of process questions such as 'what if ...' and 'how might that work ...' and so on, until the girl finally explained that she had been watching a programme on television in which a group of scientists dressed in white lab coats had been plotting to blow up the world. White, therefore, signified evil.

In that instant, she had completely defamiliarised the concept of white for the class and the discussion took off on a more enthusiastic note and in a more meaningful direction. As a result of her answer being accepted and explored rather than dismissed as 'wrong', the girl had become the person who had enlivened learning. The film professional's questioning, the responses from her teacher and peers, and her reaction to them clearly indicated that this interaction provided an experience akin to Nussbaum's entitlements for all the children in this class.

Like many other forms of pedagogy, learning through complementary pedagogy can be seen as an essentially political experience. Students would have shared control over the decisions they make and be invited to contribute to the choices made regarding their own learning. In working with others they are able, if they so wish, to enter into 'meaningful relationships of mutual recognition' with their fellow students. In Nussbaum's list, this constitutes control over one's environment.

Finally, Nussbaum lists play, which she defines as 'being able to laugh, to play, to enjoy recreational activities' as one of the core capabilities. A feature of complementary pedagogy, therefore, is that learning would be fun.

> **Thinking point 5.3**
>
> What changes could you make to your practice to incorporate Nussbaum's entitlements?

At the outset of this chapter we stated that inclusion has been the most demanding of policy initiatives in education. We state this because the complexity of the concept and difficulty of implementation have led us to think about learning and teaching in the round. At one level, the inclusion debate has centred on place, that is, whether all pupils should be taught in mainstream schools (albeit perhaps within segregated bases and units) or whether it is more appropriate for some with additional or special needs to be taught elsewhere. The argument in this chapter is that place and provision constitute only part of the debate and that any serious deliberation on inclusion would have to consider teaching and learning; what we do as teachers that helps learners feel included. Nor, would we argue, is what teachers do simply a matter of the technical aspects of teaching subject matter to children and young people with a range of disabilities and none. Rather, in a context of social justice, the educational experiences available to students are dependent on the values, beliefs, morality and ethics of society in general as much as the technical skills of teachers and the learner's own ability. It is about how learners, schools and teachers engage with each of these aspects to create the experiences that are the markers of a just society, and lead to learners and teachers feeling valued and that they belong.

Summary

In this chapter, we have considered the implications for teachers and learners of the policy initiative of inclusion. We began by arguing that one of teachers' existing strengths is the ability to deal with diversity and that this should be the starting point for a consideration of pedagogy in a context of inclusion. We then argued that one way of dealing with diversity is to see it in terms of disability or inability and to compensate for the perceived deficit. In the main body of the chapter, however, we argued that a more inclusive pedagogical approach would be to start from a perspective of ability, to accept and affirm what learners bring to the learning context and to seek approaches to learning and teaching that complement them. Finally, we argued that learning and teaching through complementary pedagogy will result in learning experiences that are the markers of a dignified and just society.

Key questions for reflection and discussion

- Do you think that all children and young people can be taught in the same classroom, regardless of inability or disability?
- Is the policy of inclusion, however laudable, compatible with the other demands (for example, levels of attainment) that are made of schools and teachers?
- Considering your own and colleagues' teaching, how far would you understand it as compensatory or complementary?
- What resources are available to you in the classroom and how far do they help in supporting diversity?
- How would you plan learning and teaching so that your pupils have experiences that help them feel valued and that they belong?

Further reading

Daniels, H. (2001) *Vygotsky and Pedagogy.* London: RoutledgeFalmer. This is a comprehensive study of the implications for schools and teachers of Vygotsky's theories on learning and development. These theories form the basis of learning and teaching that can be understood in terms of complementary pedagogy.

Dweck, C.S. (2000) *Self-theories: Their Role in Motivation, Personality and Development.* Philadelphia, PA: Psychology Press. This book argues that intelligence is incremental, that is, it can develop and improve rather than be a fixed entity. The implications for learning and teaching, especially the setting of learning rather than performance goals by both learners and teachers, are explored.

Lewis, A. and Norwich, B. (eds) (2005) *Special Teaching for Special Children?* Maidenhead: Open University Press. The 16 chapters in this book explore learning and teaching needs that can be considered as special or additional. Some of these might be considered compensatory while others are more clearly complementary.

Shayer, M. and Adey, P. (eds) (2002) *Learning Intelligence.* Buckingham: Open University Press. This book offers a cognitive acceleration approach to learning and teaching across curricular areas for children aged 5–15. The theoretical foundation of the book is metacognition and contributors are drawn from psychology, the arts and science, and include practising teachers.

Trifonas, P.P. (ed.) (2003) *Pedagogies of Difference: Rethinking Education for Social Change*. London: RoutledgeFalmer. This book offers a philosophical perspective on pedagogy. Chapters 2 on difference as deficit, 5 on the emotional terrain of difference and 9 on matters of equity are of particular significance. This book should be read alongside Kincheloe (2008) and Darder et al. in the reference list.

Web resources

Centre for Studies in Inclusive Education: http://www.csie.org

Scottish Teacher Education Committee National Framework for Inclusion: http://www.frameworkforinclusion.org

LEARNING

SECTION OVERVIEW

Margaret Martin

In the previous section, the policy context was explored and it has been argued that policy can drive both positive and negative change in education. This section moves into an explicit focus on learning and the changing role of the teacher in relation to some of the trends identified earlier. These important shifts in education policy in the past 10 years make it imperative that links are made to the effects on learning, and this is particularly significant for those who are entering the profession, often with expectations of a role that in fact is no longer relevant. What it means to be a teacher in the twenty-first century is a constantly changing concept which makes it challenging for new teachers to work out where to locate themselves in the shifting landscape, and how to develop a sense of their own identity and agency.

Equally important are the developments which have taken place in what we know about the nature of learning. Recent research on the social, emotional, physical and cognitive aspects of learning have impacted on the pedagogical approaches expected in the classroom. There is often a tension between this kind of professional knowledge about learning and international policy imperatives. While the literature advocates breadth and depth of learning and understanding, rather than strategic or surface learning for the purposes of passing national examinations, international policy imperatives encourage performativity and a fast-paced improving attainment agenda. This is just one example of the dilemmas and tensions faced by teachers as they grapple with these competing demands, and there can be little doubt that a well-informed perspective on the bigger picture can assist them in working out where they stand and in developing their professional confidence to engage in the surrounding debate.

It is therefore essential that new teachers have the opportunity to learn about and reflect upon the changes which are taking place, globally and locally, in policy terms and in terms of knowledge about learning, and to begin to develop their own views on what the implications might be for them. In this section therefore we look at a range of learning contexts and the challenges which new teachers might face in ensuring access to learning and meeting the needs of all learners. We look first at the idea of collaborative enquiry into learning in the classroom which is central in persuading new teachers that they have to investigate the learning process to ensure its quality and relevance to the learner. Then we explore a range of specific examples of the ways in which conditions can be created in schools in order to ensure that effective learning takes place.

We begin in Chapter 6 with an examination of the notion of 'looking closely at learning'. Here Mike Carroll explores some of the strategies schools might use to foster a culture of professional enquiry into learning. This fits well with Brookfield's (1995) argument for looking at practice through a number of lenses: the collaborative working on the part of staff encourages the possibility of professional dialogue about learning with colleagues and the enquiry into learning offers the opportunity to get the pupils' perspectives on their experiences of learning. The chapter looks at ways in which teachers can begin to construct and implement professional enquiries which involve teachers in meaningful collaborations that lead to improvement in the school and in the classroom.

In Chapter 7 Mary Wingrave assesses what nurture groups might have to offer to children who are experiencing social and emotional difficulties which become real barriers to their learning in school. Here a rationale is put forward for a very particular environment for learning set up within a school. This safe and predictable setting can provide the opportunity for children to develop trusting relationships with adults which allow them to settle and engage with learning. The implications for a whole-school approach are also examined. There are many lessons here to be learned by teachers about the engagement of children who would otherwise be excluded from the education process.

Looking closely at learning involves many different aspects of the whole child and in Chapter 8 Georgina Wardle considers the implications of understanding children's relationships in the classroom. This is a key area of learning and often a concern for new teachers as they grapple with children's behaviour. Attention is often focused on antisocial behaviour, but this chapter puts forward an alternative perspective where the focus is on understanding prosocial behaviour and building positive peer relationships. An important aspect is not only the teacher's understanding of the reasons behind pupils' behaviour, but also some psychological factors which affect children's interpretation, or misinterpretation, of the motives of their peers.

Finally, in a different context, Niamh Stack and Margaret Sutherland examine another important aspect of inclusive education by looking at the education of gifted and talented children in schools. This is yet another area of concern for new teachers who find it challenging to develop approaches to meet the needs of this particular group in schools. The chapter explores critically a range of different approaches to wider societal and cultural understandings of intelligence and inclusion, as well as the impact of specific approaches on aspects such as identity and pupil voice. The messages in this chapter will provide important insights into learning for new teachers.

The overall focus of this chapter, then, is to exemplify how social justice, in terms of access to quality education, may be served by the possible structures and approaches to learning put in place in schools. This, however, has to be grounded in a vision of providing access to good learning and a clear vision of what good learning might look like.

CHAPTER 6

COLLABORATIVE PROFESSIONAL ENQUIRY

Mike Carroll

Key ideas explored in this chapter are:

- Individual and social aspects of professional learning
- Professional enquiry
- Structural elements of collaborative professional enquiry

The changing policy environment described in earlier chapters is significant in terms of teachers' professional learning as sooner or later policy change has an impact upon our practice in classrooms. How do we respond to this changing landscape? We could wait until we are 'told' to implement particular changes in our ways of working through top-down, centrally driven initiatives. Reacting to policy change is only one of the ways in which we come to understand and engage with the process of change. This chapter looks at a bottom-up, school-based approach driven by teachers participating in professional enquiry as a complementary response to change. Central to this is the idea that teachers naturally continue to develop their knowledge, skills and experience through-out their careers. Arguably such knowledge updating, as part of ongoing learning, is a defining characteristic of the professional as it is necessary to 'maintain and develop their professional practice throughout their career, reviewing practice, acquiring new skills and knowledge, sharing good practice and experience with colleagues and new entrants to the profession' (Forde et al., 2006: 128). Professional enquiry takes professional learning a stage further as it is focused on individual teacher's classroom practice and seeks to support teachers in understanding why good practice is effective through developing a sense of criticality, both about their own work and about the wider professional context within which they operate.

Individual and social learning

There is a strong tradition of professional learning constructed on cognitive models of learning (Wilson et al., 2006) based on an expert–novice relationship whereby the aim is to develop knowledge, skills and under-standings in the novice (that is, newly qualified teachers). What is being described here is a vertical transfer of knowledge, from the expert to the novice (that is, teacher-as-learner), with its focus on providing curricular knowledge and/or modelling 'best practice'. This is typical of formal/planned professional learning 'events' where teachers attend 'courses' and are sub-sequently expected to apply their learning in their professional context; learning is seen as being 'portable'. Essentially teachers-as-learners are seen as passive recipients of knowledge in order to facilitate more efficient and effective delivery of that knowledge in the classroom. However, this approach is not unproblematic as it does not necessarily assist individual teachers in finding solutions 'to practical problems in the lived professional lives of teachers' (Groundwater-Smith, 2007: 60) as it is difficult to predict the problems that the teacher-as-learner may encounter when back in their classrooms. Furthermore, the complexity evident in different classrooms, within and between different schools, make it highly unlikely that profes-sional learning 'events', divorced from real classrooms/schools, will provide solutions to problems, some of which have yet to arise.

In addition professional learning is a third-order activity in that it is under-taken with the intention of improving teaching which, in turn, seeks to improve pupils' learning. However, the linkage between teachers' professional learning and improved pupil outcomes is a contentious one, with an improved understanding of professional practice being taken as a future-orientated 'proxy' measure of improved outcomes for pupils. Accordingly, it is difficult to establish a link between teachers' involvement in programmes aimed at professional learning and pupil outcomes (Reeves et al., 2003). The connection is difficult to establish due to the 'time lag' between teachers engaging in professional learning and the reporting of improved pupil outcomes. This is compounded by the fact that schools are complex organisations in which there are a number of developments taking place coterminously. As such there is no simple cause-and-effect relationship between professional learning and improvements in practice.

The notion of portable learning is also disputed by theories of situated learning (Lave and Wenger, 1991) where the focus is on knowledge creation through participation in meaningful activities, focused on teachers' professional practice. Social interaction provides the context for learning to take place with teachers working and learning together with the intention of developing their practice. Consequently the learning of an individual teacher is only understandable if we set it within the context of their school; as such, individual learning and collective learning become intertwined through the discussions which take place within school communities. Furthermore, the complexity of schools within a culture of change requires all involved in education to seek knowledge from a variety of different sources entailing cooperation with different experts; consequently, learning has an impact on the individual teacher as well as being a function of the interaction within and between groups of individuals, within and beyond the school. Accordingly, Pedder et al. (2005) suggest four hypotheses regarding teachers' learning in stating that it is:

- a feature of professional practice and reflection
- extended through utilising different knowledge bases
- enhanced through collaborative activity, and
- deepened through dialogic interaction.

Dialogue between teachers is critically important in order to share and understand other teachers' professional experience on matters of teaching and learning. The intended outcome of this dialogue is to create new professional knowledge to bring about improvement in practice. The Vygotskian concept of the 'zone of proximal development' (ZPD) provides an insight as to how, through social interaction and dialogue, the cognitive capability of individual teachers is enhanced by engaging in group, problem-solving activity. Activity that is challenging at an individual level may be manageable through support (that is, scaffolding) from 'more knowledgeable others' (MKOs) within the group. Therefore a 'collegial' dimension to professional learning enables teachers to share and merge their different perspectives with the knowledge that is created being disseminated throughout their professional context.

> **Thinking point 6.1**
>
> - In your experience do schools provide opportunities for teachers to engage in discussions with each other on what they know about teaching and learning?
> - Have a look at the GTCE website where there is a short account of a group of Devon schools who used an enquiry approach to improve pupil engagement and attainment. This information is located at: http://www.gtce.org.uk/teachers/ rft/reflection0507/reflection0507cs/casestudy2/

Lave and Wenger (1991) bring these ideas together when describing engagement within a 'community of practice' (CoP); although a 'professional learning community' (PLC) is perhaps a more useful descriptor (see Chapter 11). A PLC involves professional learning brought about through collaborative interaction binding teachers together around an activity or area of knowledge. Professional enquiry takes this learning further as it involves teachers 'enquiring' into aspects of their professional practice that matter to them. This enables teachers to generate meaningful professional knowledge with a view to bringing about improvement.

Professional enquiry

School improvement is often predicated upon a top-down model whereby initiatives for improvement come from the 'outside', the 'best practice' model, with a view to implementing these on the 'inside'. The problem is that in order to nurture teachers' knowledge, skills and understanding it is necessary to articulate a connectedness between teachers' knowledge, the school improvement process, and the wider educational context within which the school and the process of improvement are located.

One way to establish such a connectedness is through the process of professional enquiry whereby teachers, using educational literature and research evidence, critically reflect upon their personal and professional values, past experiences and educational practice, and the views of colleagues and pupils with the intention of bringing about improvement in some aspect of professional practice. This is a form of professional learning which Torrance and Pryor (2001: 81) describe as involving teachers in progressively developing 'more consciously theorised practice' by 'looping back and forth' between theory and practice, with each informing the other. This is broadly similar to Brookfield's (1995) use of 'four lenses' to arrive at an informed professional stance with respect to our understanding of practice (see Chapter 1).

Thinking point 6.2

In your experience what promotes and/or hinders utilising theoretical and research perspectives to help inform practice? Have a look at the Chartered Teacher Standards of the General Teaching Council of Scotland (http://www. gtcs.org.uk/) and General Teaching Council of Wales (http://www.gtcw.org.uk/ gtcw/).

Using theory to inform practice and our practice to inform our understanding of theory is not unproblematic as Reeves et al. (2002) suggest that such practice-focused learning involves establishing linkages between new knowledge and skills, and how these are then tried out and potentially embedded in practice. There are a number of components to this that can be understood by reference to Moran's (2001) framework of four complementary categories of professional learning:

- Functionalist – this is a largely passive learning model involving pro-gramme organisers identifying the technical knowledge and skills needed along with the method of transmission. This tends to give rise to didactic presentation by an expert (for example, in-service, staff development events).
- Self-directed – individual selects professional learning targets and the learning activities that will help them achieve these goals (for example, personal learning plan as part of review of professional practice).
- Critical – process of critically analysing how to incorporate knowledge and skills into practice (for example, action research, professional portfolios).
- Collaborative – professional learning focused upon an identified 'problem' between professionals (for example, coaching). In this latter approach the commitment is not just to a single activity but rather as part of ongoing professional relationship.

Professional enquiry is a synthesis of the elements within Moran's frame-work. The first of Moran's categories is significant as Dadds (1997) noted that teachers expect to draw on others' expertise and knowledge, to come across new and stimulating ideas and practices, to learn something they did not know before and to extend their repertoire of understanding, skills and attitudes. An element of self-direction is also important as research (Cordingley et al., 2005) suggests that the more involved teachers are in selecting their learning programmes, the more likely they are to perceive these opportunities to be relevant, to feel their professional learning needs have been met and to rate the effect of their practices and professional activities more highly.

Self-direction is made possible if there is a climate of trust and openness encouraging teachers-as-learners to engage in critically challenging and evaluating their practice and the context in which they work. A number of studies (for example, Dadds, 1997) have shown that developing reflective practice in this way enables teachers to learn throughout their working lives; professional enquiry becomes a lived experience or 'way of being'. Reflection is about slowing down and taking the time to explore available theory, knowledge and experience; consequently, it is 'informed', in order to understand our practice in different ways. Reflection also involves placing a critical distance between our professional context and our learning about practice such that we are not shackled by our thinking about practice within context. Consequently, critical reflection is not necessarily about becoming more highly proficient with respect to practice but, rather, to learn in such a way that teachers are cognitively and/or affectively changed, leading to a form of transformational learning. In the final category of Moran's (2001) framework the term 'collaborative' is taken to mean sharing, enacting and changing practice with others, both within the teacher's professional context and across contexts. Furthermore the learning derived from collaborative activity has an object of attention in that the 'intention' is to bring about improved understanding of practice. Cordingley and Bell (2002) emphasise the benefits of sustained professional dialogue between teachers, focused on active 'tinkering' with and developing new approaches to practice. That teachers take time to reflect upon such activity renders it 'meaningful' as it relates to their professional lives. This describes a form of professional learning that is not about a particular form of activity but rather a range of activities that relate to the context and change purposes of teachers at different points in time. Through engagement in collaborative enquiry teachers find their 'voices' within a set of social relationships built around a set of shared visions, values and purposes. Finding their 'voice' is supported through teachers meeting on a regular basis to support each other in resolving learning problems, so creating an 'action learning set'. This relational network is significant in that it also provides emotional support; a sense of connectedness within the organisational context, while at the same time removing feelings of isolation that are often a feature of working alone to bring about change.

🗂 Case study 6.1

A secondary school sought to introduce the Assessment for Learning strategies of sharing learning intentions and success criteria along with a system of self and peer assessment.

One class teacher in the school, who had been working on a small-scale enquiry aimed at encouraging their pupils to take responsibility for their own learning, felt that this could be taken further.

They were aware of the need to tread carefully because they were not in any position of authority to offer advice or guidance to others. The teacher approached the management team with a proposal to initiate an enquiry, to run alongside the whole-school development, which would seek to develop positive attitudes to learning in classes that were causing problems for a group of newly qualified teachers (NQTs) across five departments.

Through a process of enquiry the collaborative group learned from each other and positively developed their practice, introducing:

- Classroom contracts – pupils given voice in shaping their learning environment
- Plus–minus marking – focus on personal improvement by providing indication of better (+) or poorer (−) work supported with formative comment
- Interactive seating plans – regular movement to support pupils in identifying their ideal working partner.

Collaborative professional enquiry (CPE)

Carroll (2009) describes a form of personal and professional learning which involves teachers working collaboratively with their colleagues on professional enquiries – collaborative professional enquiry – such that individual cognitive learning is complemented by social-cultural learning. These professional enquiries seek to facilitate an informed and structured reflection on professional action with the intention of improving aspects of professional practice. This approach involves teachers taking a proactive stance towards the challenges that confront them in their professional contexts. What is being described is an approach to improvement which is complementary to the dominant 'top-down', best practice notion of change as it recognises the need for 'bottom-up', locally driven policy initiatives.

> **Thinking point 6.3**
>
> In your experience to what extent do schools import 'best practice' as a means of bringing about school improvement? Do schools make adjustments to ideas imported from the outside?

Several structural elements emerge in constructing CPEs (Jackson and Street, 2005); however, it is important to stress that there is no single, definitive pathway through a professional enquiry (Woolhouse, 2005). The first phase of this process (see Figure 6.1) involves a teacher or group of teachers identifying an area of professional practice for enquiry. The focus of their enquiry is borne out of an analysis of their school context and current practice. There are a number of elements to this analysis involving teachers in identifying an area for enquiry which complements some aspect of the school's improvement plan. This is particularly important for beginning teachers as they do not occupy formal positions of power. Accordingly it is politically more sensible to locate the enquiry within the school's improvement plan rather than outside it in order to gain access to permissions, and the necessary resources, to act. The selection of an area for enquiry is also supported by 'dialogue with colleagues'; this, in turn, enables teachers with similar interests to coalesce around the enquiry. The final element of this preparatory phase consists of 'scoping the professional environment' whereby teachers start to look for literature and gather evidence that will help them to understand their professional enquiry at a much deeper level. During this phase teachers often find that they modify and fine tune the nature and scope of their enquiry as they come to understand it better. Preparing for enquiry is vital as it will be necessary during the second phase to seek 'permissions to act' from line managers. That the enquiry is located in the school's improvement plan, and that the teacher(s) have a good idea of what they would like to do and why they think this may be important is more likely to persuade others to provide time and resources to enable the enquiry to take place.

The third phase of the process involves teachers in carrying out the enquiry by developing a 'plan for action'. As part of the plan it can be worthwhile to consider establishing connections with external support networks (for example, local authority colleagues engaged in similar enquiries in other schools) where these exist. At some point it is necessary to 'implement the plan' which will involve 'collecting and analysing data' as well as re-negotiating roles, responsibilities and levels of participation as the plan progresses. The final element of this phase of the enquiry process involves teachers in 'critically reviewing the outcomes' of their action in order to determine whether

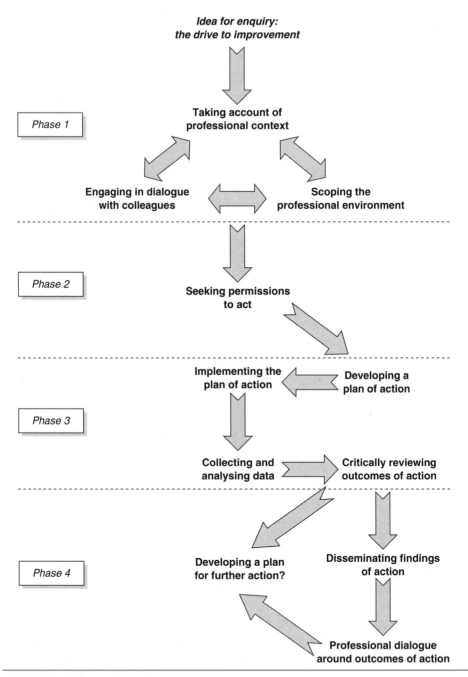

Figure 6.1 Process of enquiry

'measurable' improvement has taken place. Review often marks a transition into a fourth phase of the enquiry process. In some cases the outcomes of the process of enquiry will lead directly into further cycles of enquiry with a discernible shift in the nature and scope of the enquiry. The other possibility here is that teachers can take time to 'disseminate' their findings in order to engage in discussions with colleagues focused on the outcomes of the enquiry which, in turn, can lead to further cycles of enquiry.

This process takes time to complete and involves more sustained effort on the part of those involved. However, it is not the duration of time but rather the quality of the interactions that is significant in terms of the impact upon teaching and learning. What is being described here is a complex set of over-lapping dialogic interactions at the heart of which lies a form of three-way or 'trialogic' dialogue between those engaged in the process of enquiry, a critical examination of literature (that is, theoretical, research and policy perspectives) alongside an examination of the findings from the process of enquiry itself.

Case study 6.2

A group of primary school teachers formed their own dialogue community in order to engage in 'a dance of communication' looking at the school's drive to introduce more active learning strategies. This led them to identify a 'problem' to be tackled as, in their view, this important initiative was in danger of floundering as some children appeared to lack taken-for-granted social and communication skills.

In talking together the group probed the 'problem' which led to a plan to develop the children's social and communication skills (for example, taking turns, using encouraging language, using quiet voices, and so on) to support collaborative learning activities. The group participated in planning and implementing the 'enquiry' by gathering information about the children's behaviour and performance before and after the intervention.

The group described how the collegial dimension supported their learning and development of practice. The importance of listening and sharing reflections together were highly valued. One class teacher talked of her colleagues as being 'critical friends'.

This engagement in collaborative enquiry has led the group to identify further enquiries to undertake and they have taken some tentative steps in disseminating their findings to others within the school.

Summary

The professional identities of teachers, particularly NQTs, are often con-structed in such a way as to ensure organisational stability. This can provide a safe harbour for teachers in the turbulent sea of change; however, these identities can also act to constrain teachers' sphere of action particularly in enacting change that can potentially transform organisational practice. Such a transformation is possible through collaborative professional enquiry as it establishes a connection between professional learning and the professional contexts within which this learning is situated: in a very real sense professional practice and learning are coincident, with each reinforcing the other.

The thinking underpinning this approach is that learning occurs through teachers working collaboratively with their colleagues on professional enquiries to bring about improvement in teaching and learning. An important feature of such an approach is the belief that knowledge gained in one context cannot simply be transmitted into a different context without the active participation of the teacher-as-learner in the process of making sense of that knowledge. Consequently, learning experiences encountered on the 'outside' cannot simply be replicated 'in' the teacher's professional context without collaborative activity aimed at 'reconstruction' of the learning experience (Tuomi-Gröhm, 2003) leading to the development of 'contextualised knowledge' (that is, knowledge reframed with respect to the context teachers find themselves in). Consequently, teachers become both consumers and producers of knowledge.

Key questions for reflection and discussion

- How would you describe the process of professional enquiry?
- What do you consider to be the strengths and weaknesses of professional enquiry as a way of working?
- In your experience to what extent is the professional learning of different teachers linked together in order to bring about improvements in practice?
- What do you see as the opportunities and threats that could come from the kind of teacher collaboration being advocated in this chapter?
- How might you go about developing your knowledge and skills to undertake a professional enquiry into an aspect of teaching and learning in your school?

Further reading

Baumfield, V., Hall, E. and Wall, K. (2008) *Action Research in the Classroom*. London: Sage. The authors provide a range of highly practical insights into professional enquiry as an approach to teaching and learning. This book is a useful guide for any teacher or pre-service teacher interested in carrying out teacher enquiry in the classroom.

Burton, D. and Bartlett, S. (2005) *Practitioner Research for Teachers*. London: Paul Chapman Publishing. Burton and Bartlett's book is a good 'introductory' text for teachers wishing to embark upon classroom-based enquiry. Case studies of real-life enquiries undertaken by teachers in practice illustrate why teacher enquiry is important and how this will enable teachers to respond to the apparently ever-changing policy environment.

Street, H. and Temperley, J. (eds) (2005) *Improving Schools through Collaborative Enquiry*. London: Continuum. Street and Temperley's book provides an important insight as to the difficulties of individual teachers exploring their practice. They present a powerful argument in favour of school improvement being developed and enhanced through teachers engaging in collaborative action enquiry.

Web resources

Collaborative Action Research Network (CARN): http://www.did.stu.mmu.ac.uk/carnnew/index.php

National College for Leadership of Schools and Children's Services: Networking: http://www.nationalcollege.org.uk/index/networking.htm

CHAPTER 7

NURTURE GROUPS AND INCLUSION

Mary Wingrave

> **Key ideas explored in this chapter are:**
>
> - What a nurture group is
> - Why nurture groups are needed
> - How a nurture group works
> - Nurture groups – a whole-school approach

This chapter seeks to examine what a nurture group (NG) is, why there is a need for them and to determine whether they work. Nurture group education is a contemporary approach to inclusive education and increases the access to learning for children who are often marginalised. Initially, the development of self-esteem and attachment will be examined. Then the type of children who benefit from NGs will be looked at by discussing two case studies which highlight the type of support that is required to develop the prosocial skills that are required for learning. Finally, considerations will be given to how NG can be taken forward.

What is a nurture group?

Nurture groups were started in the late 1960s by Margery Boxall. She identified poor early parenting, poverty and lack of attachment as being responsible for the increased number of children being referred for specialist intervention in schools (Boxall, 2002). She promoted the idea that if children could develop trusting relationships it would allow them to settle and engage with learning. Her philosophy of NGs was underpinned by the theory of attachment. Bowlby's research indicated that for children to develop other relationships in life, it was necessary for them to attach to their mothers (Bowlby, 1969). It should be noted that while the results of Bowlby's research identified attachment to the mother, it cannot be ignored that his work emerged from the post-war period when the role of the working mother was being maligned by the US government, who wished women to step aside to allow the men to return to their previous roles. However, Bowlby's work is still relevant if we substitute the attachment to a mother to that of any significant adult in a child's life.

Bowlby argued that experiences in early childhood have a significant influence on development and behaviour, and can affect a child's emotional growth and even have an impact on later life. Where the initial attachment is positive the majority of children grow, develop and engage successfully. If these important early relationships, with a significant other, do not develop successfully, this can result in severe impairment to a child's ability to form other relationships. When these relationships have not formed or if they have been interrupted, children become suspicious and do not trust adults or other children. This can result in children who exhibit behaviours which can be remote, hostile or unhappy. These are very often the children who find settling into a classroom difficult and can be disruptive or withdrawn. This can result in them being unable to engage with others and the curriculum, which then increases their feeling of isolation and failure. This can lead to these children being excluded from school.

In the past decade the Labour government's policies have centred more on inclusion than any previous government's. Inclusive legislation (Special Educational Needs and Disability Act 2001, the Education (Additional Support for Learning) (Scotland) Act 2004, The Special Educational Needs and Disability Order (Northern Ireland) 2005 and the Welsh Assembly Government's *Inclusion and Pupil Support (Wales)* 2006) has resulted in schools facilitating the provision for children with a large variety of special needs. Statistics show that in England in 2006–07, 31 per cent of all permanent exclusions were for constant disruptive behaviour and the Scottish government's (2009) figures show that exclusions have been rising each year since 2002–03. Exclusion figures for Wales show a drop in exclusions, from 465 children in 2004–05 to 241 in 2007–08. The percentage of exclusions in Northern Ireland shows a fall from

1.89 per cent (2003–04) to 1.74 per cent (2008–09). However, the statistics also indicate that children who have an additional support need (ASN) in mainstream schools are more likely to be excluded than those without an ASN. Children with social, emotional and behavioural problems have the highest percentages of exclusion. Therefore, despite government inclusion policies, schools are finding the management of certain behaviours difficult.

Inclusion has to be seen as more than sustaining the presence of a child within school, it is about ensuring that the child's needs are met. Topping and Maloney (2005) assert that inclusion, like learning, is a journey not an arrival point. Nurture groups may provide a solution and they have seen a revival in the last decade (Cook et al., 2008). There is now an acceptance that children with social, emotional and behavioural problems need to be accommodated within schools as an alternative to exclusion as they too have a right to an education within a socially inclusive society.

Thinking point 7.1

Would it surprise you that boys are consistently more likely to be excluded than girls? Why/why not?

What a nurture group looks like

Nurture groups do not claim to solve social, emotional or economic difficulties that children experience in their lives. It is not a magic wand nor does it claim that the children who enter nurture will not continue to experience levels of difficulty or control. It does however help the children develop 'resilience'. Brooks and Goldstein (2002) believe that children need to have experienced levels of success in what they deem to be important, in order to develop resilience. Nurture groups help develop positive relevant, successful experiences, in order that the children are able to engage with the curriculum and develop social skills which allow them to cope with the academic rigours of education. Reid (1986) argues that while disadvantageous social and economic factors can influence children's behaviour, the impact can be diminished if the school environment provides support. Nurture groups build on the concept that social and emotional development are part of the learning process. A NG follows guidelines which give careful consideration to the children's need for structure and predictability to encourage security and trust for the children to learn (Bennathan and Boxall, 2000). The key features of a nurture group are outlined opposite.

Key features of a nurture group		
Essential within an NG	What does it look like?	Its purpose
Location	Located in a mainstream school.	The setting merges many aspects of school and the home environment. It has a comfortable sitting area, a play area, a dining table, a kitchen and a teaching area. The merging of the formal and informal learning environment allows the child to be less restricted. This helps alleviate the child's suspicions and helps support integration.
Staff	Staffed by a teacher and an assistant.	Staff model behaviour that they wish the children to adopt. Children are able to see how adults negotiate socially with each other. It is important to give a secure and predictable environment which also allows children to develop coping strategies for situations and relationships with other adults and children.
Number of children	The optimum number of children is 10–12.	Each child receives personal attention and there are opportunities for the children to work and respond within a group situation. The group is large enough to ensure that there is social interaction but is small enough to allow the children to risk interacting with each other. This number of children also ensures that there is no attachment challenge to the parent/child bond (Cooper and Tiknaz, 2007).
Breakfast	The children prepare, serve and eat.	Breakfast is an important feature, as children are nurtured through being fed. Breakfast provides opportunities which promote socialisation and learning.

(Continued)

(Continued)

Essential within an NG	What does it look like?	Its purpose
		It also provides a chance to emphasise rules, including manners. Breakfast is a predictable daily event, where the children express their thoughts and feelings freely. It also facilitates learning; matching, counting, colour recognition, and so on.
Curriculum	Learning takes place through formal and informal experiences.	The curriculum comprises core skills, language and maths with the child's plan linked to national expectations and the child's Additional Support Plan (ASP). There is a specific focus on the areas of personal, social and health education. A variety of the children's interests are planned for, with a focus on the skills which are key to the children being successfully reintegrated into their class. Not all children entering nurture have additional academic needs. Therefore, the curriculum offered should ensure that the child's academic progress is not unduly hampered. Good communication between the class and nurture teacher is essential.
Class identity	Every child starts and finishes every day with their class.	While the children are in nurture, it is important to promote and reinforce the children's identity and place within their class. If it is appropriate the child may also remain in class for certain lessons and celebrations. Many NGs encourage the children to invite classmates to breakfast. This serves many purposes: it allows the child to form relationships; it takes away the mystery of the NG for other children in the school; it promotes inclusion of all the children, not just those who require nurture, and it helps to prevent the NG being labelled as a 'sin bin' or a 'learning support unit'.

Self-esteem indictors

Children with social, emotional and behaviour problems often have low self-esteem (Cooper and Tiknaz, 2007). For positive self-esteem to develop it is necessary for children to feel that they are competent and worthy (Murk, 2006). The development of self-esteem relies on extrinsic feedback, from significant others and intrinsic feedback from oneself. Feedback allows one to control, regulate and evaluate one's own behaviour. Positive feedback helps promote the positive development of self-esteem. These are outlined below.

Positive indicators	Negative indicators
Can recognise their positive qualities	Can recognise only their negative qualities
Likes and feels good about themselves	Dislikes and makes negative comments about themselves
Optimistic and confident	Pessimistic and lacks confidence
Will try new things	Unwilling to try new things
Believes in themselves	Will not risk failure
Will recover from failure and will retry	Sees failure as inevitable and will not retry

Where self-esteem has developed negatively, children will find engaging in learning difficult as they are unwilling to reinforce the self-belief that failure is inevitable. Therefore, to deflect the focus of academic failure, certain negative behaviours may manifest themselves. Negative behaviour can be defined as behaviour which negatively affects the child or others that the child is in contact with. Nurture is not a solution for all children with difficulties in school. The children who enter an NG need to be carefully selected. There are three main assessment tools which are used to determine if the NG is appropriate to meet a child's needs.

The tools for assessment

1. The Boxall Profile (Bennathan and Boxall, 1998) is used in conjunction with the Boxall handbook which helps interpret the scores obtained. It is divided into two sections, Section I, Developmental Strands and Section II, the Diagnostic Profile; low scores in Section I and high scores in Section II are indicative of a child who may need NG intervention.

2. Strengths and difficulties questionnaire (SDQ) (Goodman, 1997) allows behaviour to be examined. It addresses four main conduct problems: inattention-hyperactivity, emotional symptoms, peer problems and helps prosocial behaviour. There is a questionnaire for teachers and one for parents. It is a complementary tool to the Boxall Profile. These questionnaires should be completed by the class teacher, as the person in school who knows the child best.
3. Observation is an effective tool for uncovering previously unidentified behaviour. This information is collected by recording a child's behaviour as it happens, without any analysis. Later this information is examined, allowing interpretations to be made without prejudice.

The following case studies will enable you to become familiar with typical children who attend NGs.

📁 Case study 7.1

Peter is a 6-year-old boy, who suffers from severe dyspraxia and behavioural difficulties. At home Peter is disruptive and defiant. Mum finds it difficult to control him. Mum and dad live together and try to manage Peter's behaviour as best they can and are generally supportive of the school. However, mum feels that Peter is unfairly blamed for incidents at school and has become disconsolate about being continuously brought in to speak to his teacher.

At school Peter can be disruptive and has a short attention span. Academically he is currently about a year and a half behind his peer group. He has been in receipt of learning support since P1 and he has a support assistant. Peter plays with materials and often puts them in his mouth. He is unable to focus and is continually restless. His dyspraxic-type difficulties result in him having problems such as clumsiness, lack of fine and gross motor skills. Peter has developed a reputation within the school and, as a consequence, his peers blame him for real and imaginary disruptive behaviour. Peter is inclined to take the blame for these incidents and, as a result, staff attitudes tend to be negative towards him.

A psychological therapist and a speech therapist have also assessed Peter, and the assessments indicate areas of weakness in language and social skills attributed partly to his dyspraxia. A contributing factor to his problems is frustration, thus leading to his disengagement and to Peter exhibiting attention-seeking behaviour. It was felt that given the severity of his restlessness, his impaired learning and poor social relationships, Peter should be put forward for assessment for nurture.

Case study 7.2

Anna is a 6-year-old girl who was born addicted to heroin. Up until the age of 3 she lived with her parents, who were both drug addicts. There were frequent raids on the house by the police and dad eventually went to prison. Once on her own mum was unable to cope and Anna went into care. Unfortunately this resulted in Anna having greater problems, as she had to cope with various forms of abuse, including emotional, physical and inappropriate social behaviour. Her parents opted to go on a methadone programme and were given supervised custody. Anna has had no secure or appropriate role models and her present home life is still unsettled. The family is experiencing problems readjusting to being together. Anna is subjecting her parents to violent and aggressive behaviour. However, at school Anna presents as a model pupil albeit that she does have emotional difficulties, which affect her learning and her peer relationships. Despite appearances to the contrary, Anna cannot read. She has covered this up extremely well. She has a remarkable ability to memorise her reading books. She is also very good at copying from the board and from other people's work. She does not socially interact with other children and on the rare occasions when she does, she can be verbally abusive and unkind. Anna came to the school in September and it was felt that due to her background she should be considered as a candidate for the Nurture Unit. The parents show a willingness to work with the school. They are struggling to cope with Anna's behaviour.

Thinking point 7.2

The children in the case studies manifest very different behaviour. What behaviours would cause you concern? And why?

Impact

For Peter and Anna, the behaviour that was depriving them from accessing the curriculum had to be addressed. For Peter there was a focus on his motor skills and for Anna there was a specific focus on her prosocial skills and the building of trust. For both children strategies were employed to build self-esteem.

In order for there to be an improvement in their behaviour, the children needed to develop self-control. They needed to become more self-aware in terms of the impact their behaviour had on others. This would have to be addressed through a combination of modelling, play and praise where the children learn to connect reactions to appropriate behaviour. Fisher (1996) views self-esteem as 'key' to the teaching and learning process and advocates the use of self-assessment to help recognise and reinforce success which can then be replicated.

Neither pupil was self-reflective nor were they aware of the impact of their actions on others. It was felt that the children should explore their behaviour and its consequences through play. Praise was an important feature; appropriate conduct was praised in order that they could start to make a connection between actions and consequences. Dewey (1933) advocated that we learn through making connections with previous learning. Consistency of approach, attitude and appropriate praise played an important role in developing this. The involvement of the children's teachers was essential to success, as any benefit experienced in the NG would be diminished on return to class if the teachers could not continue the programme.

To promote self-esteem, targets for behaviour were put in place in consultation with the children. A reward system for appropriate behaviour was also introduced in conjunction with the use of home/school diaries. Emphasis was placed on their ability to recognise their own and other people's achievements and the giving of and receiving of praise appropriately from others.

Most children who enter nurture require development of their social behaviour. Therefore interactive play is used in the form of games, sand and water play, cooperative one to one situations, breakfast, washing/drying dishes, setting/clearing table and baking. Anna and Peter were encouraged to use puppets to express their concerns and frustrations, and they were encouraged to make eye contact with those who were trying to communicate with them. The children's interaction improved and imaginative play became evident.

Parental/carer involvement

Parental/carer involvement in nurture is one of the most important elements of its success. It should be noted that unless parents/carers give permission, even if the child fits the profile for nurture, the child cannot be admitted. In the case studies above, Peter's mum had become disillusioned with his lack of progress within the system and his apparent failure. Anna's parents needed a solution to help them cope with her destructive and aggressive behaviour.

Building a partnership between the NG staff and home is of paramount importance in order that any progress is not short-lived. By inviting the parents into the NG to see their work, with support afternoons to discuss specific difficulties and by discussing strategies to minimise the impact of their child's behaviour, parents feel supported and less isolated. This can be further developed by encouraging parents/carers to come and work with their children on play activities that the children have chosen and prepared. Once relationships are established these meetings can be used for target setting to help modify behaviour which is exhibited at home. This can involve a number of targets, from the setting of bedtime routines to when homework should be completed.

Thinking point 7.3

What are some of the challenges in involving parents of this particular group of children?

The future: reintegration and other possibilities

The recommended amount of time a child spends in the NG is between three to four terms. A NG is not a long-term provision, and success in nurture is the reintegration into class of a child. A NG child needs to be aware that eventually they will be returning to their own class so that they do not feel that they have been rejected by those they have established an attachment to.

Reintegration has to be planned for and should involve the pupil and all interested adults. Emotional as well as physical preparation for returning to class is necessary. The child's readiness to return to class will be evident from observations, the Boxall Profile and the SDQ. Returning to class will involve spending increasingly more time in the class and the child will undertake more of the mainstream curriculum work. If this is successful, the time will increase until full reintegration is achieved. At all points the plan must be evaluated and, if necessary, modified in order that reintegration is successful. Once returned to class it is an option to allow the pupil to return to the NG for breakfast or specific short periods of time so that they do not experience rejection and revert to previous behaviour.

The nurturing school

An NG provides children with a safe, new start within their school. It allows children with social, emotional or behavioural difficulties an opportunity to develop skills in a predictable environment which carefully caters for their particular problems, while allowing their classmates the opportunity to learn in an environment without disruption.

It is important that nurture is not just confined to the group itself. It should be developed as a whole-school approach and staff should feel that they are involved in its development. Whole-school communication is a contributing factor to the success of NGs. Therefore it is important that channels of communication are established to allow information to be passed and for the whole staff to be actively involved in the process of nurture. Even the naming of the unit should be done at whole-school level, this is important as the NG should be an integral part of the school and its ethos. It is transformation and inclusion in schools that will provide social justice which will enable students to succeed in the mainstream of school and society.

Summary

Nurture groups are mainstream inclusive provision which enable children with social, emotional and behavioural difficulties to engage with education. Children who experience these problems are not emotionally ready to connect with learning and, consequently, their behaviour can lead to them switching off or to disrupting the learning of others. The NG seeks to build the children's belief in themselves and allow them to gradually develop social skills which facilitate them developing their educational skills. The NG is structured and promotes a predictable environment allowing the children to feel secure. It is a mixture of a home and school setting and supports learning through social interaction. It is necessary that the number of children is no more than 12 and that there are two members of staff. This helps promote and encourage trust and security. Class identification is also encouraged and every child will start and complete every day with their class. Parental involvement is paramount to the child's success in the NG, and permission from the parent must be sought before a child can be included. In order for a NG to be successful it has to be a whole-school approach.

Key questions for reflection and discussion

- Identify reasons that could contribute to the increase in the number of children who find school life difficult.
- How would you define a NG?
- Identify some interventions that you think would help support NG childrens' development.

- What measures would you put in place to ensure that the philosophies of a NG are a whole-school approach?
- What action would you take to ensure that parent/carer partnership is developed to enable nurture to be effective?

Further reading

Bennathan, M. and Boxall, M. (1998) *The Boxall Profile: Handbook for Teachers*. London: The Nurture Group Network. The Boxall Profile is a resource for helping support teachers' understanding and interpretation of the Boxhall Profile. The book contains the Profile itself with guidelines for use and support for analysis of the results.

Bishop, S. (2008) *Running a Nurture Group*. London: Sage. This book provides practical ideas for nurture group teachers. It gives advice and suggests approaches to setting up a NG in a school. It provides resources which support implementation, from planning guides to behaviour plans.

Boxall, M. (2002) *Nurture Groups in Schools: Principles and Practice*. London: Sage. This book will support those setting up a NG in schools and is a useful tool for all those who would be involved in an NG. It outlines how best to monitor and assess the children who may require support and how to deal with the practicalities of setting up a NG.

Cooper, P. and Tiknaz, Y. (2007) *Nurture Groups in School and at Home: Connecting with Children with Social, Emotional and Behavioural Difficulties*. London: Jessica Kingsley. This book supports the setting up of a NG. It discusses the roles of people who should be consulted in order to provide a holistic provision, the selection of pupils and, finally, providing key messages for those running the group.

Lucas, S., Insley, K. and Buckland, G. (2006) *Nurture Group Principles and Curriculum Guidelines: Helping Children to Achieve*. London: The Nurture Group Network. This book has great ideas and suggestions for nurture teachers to meet the curriculum demands, developmental and emotional needs of the children in NGs.

Web resources

http://www.nurturegroups.org/
http://www.digitaldesk.org/external/behaviour/sebd.html
http://www.caspari.org.uk/

CHAPTER 8

CHILDREN'S SOCIAL RELATIONSHIPS

Georgina Wardle

Key ideas explored in this chapter are:

- The definition of prosocial behaviour
- Prosocial behaviours demonstrated by children
- Theoretical explanations of prosocial behaviour
- Children's social information processing
- Prosocial behaviour in the classroom

As teachers strive to promote a culture of engagement in quality learning for all, they frequently ask how they can improve social relationships among their pupils. Part of the answer to this question lies in developing an awareness of how pupils relate to each other. This chapter will explore some aspects of children's peer social interactions, relevant to teachers because of the educational benefits of a calm and effective learning environment in schools. First, we focus on what is understood by the term 'prosocial behaviour', taking into account children's own perceptions of what constitutes normative peer prosocial behaviour. We then move on briefly to consider theories of developmental psychology which have informed our understanding of children's prosocial development, then investigate how children themselves may interpret, or misinterpret, the motives behind their peers' prosocial behaviour. Finally, we consider ways in which the development of a prosocial atmosphere in the classroom can help to empower learners and promote real social justice in the classroom.

What is prosocial behaviour?

People may engage in prosocial behaviour for different motives; for instance, to achieve some benefit for themselves (egoistic) or for others (altruistic). To complicate matters, different authors may apply slight variations in the precise types of behaviour which they define as 'prosocial'. So, for the purpose of clarity throughout this chapter, the definition of 'prosocial behaviour' adopted will be the definition used by Grusec et al.: 'any intentional action that produces a positive or beneficial outcome for the recipient regardless of whether that action is costly to the donor, neutral in its impact, or beneficial' (2002: 458).

 Thinking point 8.1

- Can you think of instances where children have demonstrated kindness to their peers?
- How did the other children – and teachers – respond?

   Prosocial behaviours are often categorised as being either 'relational' or 'practical'. Relational behaviours are those behaviours, such as caring for others, and including others in activities or games, which may be seen to foster relationships. Practical behaviours are usually described as involving sharing or helping activities. Interestingly, children place greater value on relational prosocial behaviours in peer interactions, and they consider practical prosocial behaviours to be more salient when directed towards adults (Greener and Crick, 1999; Wardle, 2007). It seems, then, that the motives behind relationship-building prosocial behaviours directed towards peers differ from the motives behind adult-directed prosocial behaviours, which tend mainly to demonstrate cooperation or obedience. When asked to identify which types of prosocial behaviour they consider to be normative, older children generally cite behaviours designed to sustain peer relationships, for example, inclusion, whereas younger children tend to cite behaviours such as sharing (for example, Greener and Crick, 1999).

📁 Case study 8.1

A typical example of children's inclusive behaviour is illustrated by the actions of Joe, aged 8. A new boy, Zach, had arrived in school from overseas and was quite shy during on his first day in school. During break, some of the boys were playing football in the playground, and Zach was standing at a distance from the others, looking lonely. Joe stopped playing, went over to Zach and asked him to come and join him in the game. Although shy, Zach joined in and felt included and more welcome in the new school.

In recent years, although there has been an increase in the number of studies examining prosocial behaviour as one of the components of social competence, the volume of research undertaken on prosocial behaviour remains less than that in the area of antisocial behaviour, perhaps not surprisingly, due to the problems posed globally for society by a perceived increase in levels of antisocial behaviour.

The philosophical background

Enquiry into prosocial behaviour has focused both on human nature itself, and on the notion of what constitutes appropriate behaviour towards others. The historical view of prosocial behaviour has considered the role of innate goodness (for example, Hume, 1957), the ability to understand the perspectives of others (for example, Smith, 1853), and the role of reason (for example, Kant, 1895). The contemporary paradigm accepts that a wide range of environmental and psychological factors influence the individual's prosocial development. The scope of this chapter, however, does not allow for consideration of all these factors, so we shall narrow the focus, by considering psychological theories of prosocial development.

Psychological theories

In evolutionary terms, behaviour intended to benefit others may be regarded as necessary for the survival of both the individual and the group. In the absence of caring behaviour by another member of the species, human infants would not survive; and customs which protect individuals may be regarded as fundamental to the functional operating of society (Radke-Yarrow et al., 1983).

Theories of developmental psychology tend to agree that instances of children's prosocial behaviour increase with age. The behaviourist approach suggests that children learn to act prosocially through a process involving modelling and reinforcement (for example, Bryan, 1971): typically, children will copy observed behaviour, and on being rewarded for their good behaviour, are inclined to repeat it, thus establishing patterns of positive behaviour. Cognitive-developmental theorists, on the other hand, often regard development as a type of progression through a series of stages (for example, Eisenberg, 1986; Kohlberg, 1969; Piaget, 1965). Stage theories of moral development argue that a capacity to reason that behaviour is 'right' or 'wrong' develops along predetermined lines in children of different cultures, and that evidence of these universal stages may be seen in the prosocial behaviour of children in culturally diverse societies. Although stage theories have much in common with each other, they differ in slight, but important, details.

Piaget (1965) regards the progression through the stages of moral awareness as the child's development from a stance of having little concept of ideas such as fairness, justice and authority, to a more mature understanding of these principles; an understanding which the child can employ in social interaction. Kohlberg (1969) claims that children progress through three levels of moral reasoning; the *preconventional (up to approximately 10 years of age)*, the *conventional,* and the *post-conventional* levels, with each level having two stages. As individuals progress through the stages, their reasoning changes from being based on considerations of rewards and punishments and the needs of others (stages 1 and 2), to the awareness of existing social arrangements, role obligations and respect for the legitimated rules of the social system (stages 3 and 4), and then to considerations as to what is 'right' and 'wrong', determined by mutual respect and contractual agreements (stage 5), and ideas of welfare, justice, and rights (stage 6) (Kohlberg, 1981).

Eisenberg (1986) claims that children progress through five levels of pro-social moral reasoning. The first level, *'Hedonistic'*, is seen in pre-school and young school-aged children, and is characterised by a self-focused outlook, illustrated by concern for self-oriented rather than moral considerations. At the second level, *'Needs of others',* also evident in pre-school and young school-aged children, children express concern for the physical, material and psychological needs of others, even though those may conflict with one's own needs. At the third level, *'Approval and interpersonal orientation and/or stereotyped orientation',* evident in pre-adolescents, the child is able to use stereotyped images of good or bad people and actions in order to justify positive or negative behaviours. The fourth level, *'Self-reflective empathic orientation',* seen in adolescents, is distinguished by judgements which show self-reflective, sympathetic responding, and guilt or positive affect resulting from one's own actions. This is followed by a *'Transitional'* level, when behaviour may be justified because of internalised norms and values, concern for society, and the rights or dignity of others. The fifth level, *'Strongly internalised'*, is seen in people of high-school age and older, and reasoning at this level is distinguished by internalised norms, values, responsibilities, individual and societal obligations, dignity, rights and equality (adapted from Eisenberg and Mussen, 1989). Eisenberg stresses the importance of the environment and the emotions in the development of children's prosocial behaviour. These stages define children's development in the capacity to reason about issues of right and wrong, yet they are highly relevant to the classroom as they help to explain developmental changes in children's capacity to reason about issues of 'right' and 'wrong', and to understand the views of others.

Are girls really more prosocial than boys?

Research findings do not seem to support the view that girls are more prosocial than boys. The meta-analysis undertaken by Fabes and Eisenberg (1996) concludes that overall, findings appear to suggest that girls are slightly more prosocial than boys. However, importantly, these modest differences seem to depend on the particular type of prosocial behaviour involved and the methodology used in the studies. In terms of the type of behaviour involved, girls were found to be more inclined to show kindness or consideration, but not to engage in sharing, comforting or helping behaviour. Regarding methodological differences, girls were more likely to be regarded as prosocial when self-reports or other-reports were involved, as opposed to observational methods. Sex differences favouring girls were also found to be more likely when the recipient of the prosocial behaviour was an adult rather than a child; a point which may be seen to support the notion of greater compliance, or a willingness to please on the part of girls rather than boys. As a result, it is important that teachers do not have lower expectations of boys' than girls' behaviour, but understand that both sexes are equally capable of prosocial behaviour; however, as adults, teachers may be the targets of more prosocial behaviours from girls than from boys.

A wide range of important factors – biological, environmental and psychological – can influence children's engagement in prosocial behaviour, and the picture of prosocial development is by no means simplistic. Hay et al. (1999) identify many complex associations, other than emotional and cognitive maturation, between prosocial behaviour and psychological adjustment. These include factors such as early peer relationships, family structure and the social dimensions of the child's background. The fact that evidence of these associations may be seen in the first three years illustrates the important and formative nature of early childhood experiences. It is crucial that teachers, striving to facilitate individualised effective learning to meet the needs of the whole child and to foster social justice, are aware of the factors beyond their control which may impact on the learning environment in their classrooms.

Teachers continually seek to establish learning environments which are physically and emotionally secure for their pupils, in which children can interact purposefully and form effective peer social relationships. An important insight into children's relationships is the way in which children interpret – or misinterpret – the social cues of their peers. If children effectively interpret peers' intentions, then they may be able to respond appropriately, in a socially acceptable manner. However, if children misinterpret the motives behind their peers' behaviour, they may choose to act in ways which are inappropriate and unexpected, thereby beginning a chain of events which may result in aggression or hostility.

🗁 Case study 8.2

Nicola is a quiet, serious 9-year-old girl, who usually works well in class, but she seems shy and lacks confidence in social situations. One day, just as she was walking to the front of the class to hand in some completed work, she tripped up on the leg of a chair, which had been inadvertently pushed back by another girl in the class, Lynn, who had been about to stand up, not noticing that Nicola was behind her. Nicola, too intent on reading over the written work she was about to hand in, had not noticed that Lynn's chair was being moved. In frustration, Nicola kicked out, hitting Lynn's leg, whereupon Lynn kicked back. The teacher then intervened and Nicola explained that she had thought Lynn deliberately caused her to trip. The teacher established that it had been an accident, and both girls apologised. This had been a classroom incident where one child had misinterpreted the social information she was receiving from another, and there had been potential for the situation to escalate.

Social Information Processing

The way in which children process social information, or cues, during interactions with others, has been shown to follow a sequence of six key stages. According to the Social Information Processing (SIP) model, children are seen to enter social situations with different biological abilities and sets of personal past experiences, which form latent mental structures, stored in long-term memory. These latent mental structures influence children's online (that is, in the moment) processing in social interactions (Crick and Dodge, 1994; Lemerise and Arsenio, 2000). Although children's online processing is believed to occur quickly, it is claimed that this happens in a sequential process. Lemerise and Arsenio (2000) describe the steps in the process as follows:

> *Steps 1 and 2: Encoding and interpretation of cues.* The relevant stimulus cues from peers' behaviour are encoded and interpreted. For example, a child may get hit by a ball while walking across the playground, and must then work out what happened (encoding), and why it happened, that is, was it an accident, or deliberate action? (interpretation).
>
> *Step 3: Clarification of goals.* The child must clarify his or her goals in the situation. For example, the child may wish to maintain a friendly relationship with peers, or may wish to show that this type of intrusion will not be tolerated.
>
> *Steps 4 and 5: Response access or construction and response decision.* The child evaluates possible responses to the situation in terms of goals and self-efficacy. For example, the child may think about retaliating, but may then decide against this because he or she does not want the situation to escalate; or, the child may be afraid that he or she is not physically able to throw the ball hard enough.
>
> *Step 6: Behaviour enactment.* The child selects the most positively evaluated response (in terms of goals, anticipated outcomes and self-efficacy), and acts accordingly (Crick and Dodge, 1994; Lemerise and Arsenio, 2000).

At each step in this model, the child's response is determined by his or her understanding, or misunderstanding, of the initial situation, in addition to past experiences stored in long-term memory. However, the child's emotion processes and cognition also both contribute to the child's responses (Lemerise and Arsenio, 2000). Anger, in particular, has been shown to be associated with hostile attributions of the behaviour of others, less friendly goals and social behaviour (de Castro et al., 2003); so, if a child is angry for some reason, he or she is more likely to think that another child's actions were deliberate rather than accidental. Importantly, it has also been shown that children who attribute hostile intent to the behaviour of others are more likely to respond aggressively (Dodge and Frame, 1982; Erdley and Asher, 1996). On the other hand, it has been shown that prosocial children are more likely to put on 'rose-coloured glasses', and to give peers the benefit of the doubt in potentially provocative situations (Nelson and Crick, 1999). Misinterpretation of another child's motives at any stage may result in a breakdown of the sequence, and may provoke potentially antisocial responses. The relationship between psychological understanding and prosocial and antisocial behaviour is therefore a complex one.

Interestingly, Arsenio and Fleiss (1996) suggest that proactive aggressive children lack, not the cognitive ability in one (or more) steps in the social information processing model, but the understanding that hurting others for personal gain is morally wrong. This claim has been supported by the findings of Menesini et al. (2003), who demonstrated that, compared with victims, bullies stressed positive personal advantages to be gained from bullying behaviour, and denied or distorted the consequences for the victim.

Thinking point 8.2

What types of motives are you able to attribute to children's prosocial or antisocial behaviour which you have witnessed? Why do you think this?

What should practitioners do to help foster prosocial behaviour?

In current curriculum guidelines in the UK, the importance of fostering healthy social relationships is clearly recognised. In the National Curriculum for England and Wales (1999), it is stressed that children should be encouraged to value themselves, their families 'and other relationships' (Woolfolk et al., 2008), while in Scotland, one of the four capacities identified in *A Curriculum for Excellence* (2008) requires that children develop into confident individuals who can 'relate to others and manage themselves'. Classroom activities, such as roleplay and group discussion, can be used to develop children's interpersonal understanding, to minimise the occurrence of misunderstandings and misinterpretations, and to develop awareness of how their actions affect the feelings of others. Similarly, it is important that children learn to appreciate the perspectives of, and to empathise with, their peers. Woolfolk et al. (2008: 486) cite evidence of the importance of collaborative and cooperative learning in developing children's empathy, friendships and self-confidence (Solomon et al., 2001). A wide range of helpful resources, designed to develop social skills and emotional literacy is now commercially available, and activities which help to increase pupil self-awareness, self-esteem, and confidence, can be used to foster a non-threatening learning environment.

Summary

Insight into children's peer relationships can help educators as they aim to improve the behaviour and learning culture in schools. However, there are some key points to keep in mind. First, each child is unique, and children vary in terms of their ease of social interaction with peers: some children may encounter difficulties in social interaction which are difficult to address at classroom level. Second, teachers do not teach in isolation, and it is important to remember that children come to school with a vast array of previous influences from life outside school, and that the effects of these may impact on children's social behaviour. Some children are fortunate in that they have supportive home backgrounds, and parents or carers who foster a positive approach to the social and learning environment in school; other children are not so fortunate, and for them, the school environment may present more of a challenge. As society strives to address inequality and social issues such as deprivation, antisocial behaviour, substance abuse, and crime, professionals who work with children on a daily basis cannot deny that evidence of these problems is seen in schools. However, schools, although not in a position to provide a panacea for all society's ills, very often do play an integral role in addressing the problems. Since the development of positive relationships and classroom culture can help foster children's self-esteem and develop confidence in their learning, it is important that professionals involved in education acknowledge the benefits to be gained from initiatives designed to help develop prosocial reasoning and behaviour in children.

Key questions for discussion and reflection

- How do young children relate to antisocial or aggressive peers?
- Why might the study of young children's prosocial behaviour help address problems of antisocial behaviour in adolescence?
- How far do you think it is reasonable – or possible – for teachers to be responsible for children's behaviour towards each other?
- What are the implications for the curriculum of initiatives designed to improve behaviour?
- Can you identify any appropriate activities which class teachers of young children could provide in order to develop reasoning skills?

Further reading

Eisenberg, N. and Fabes, R. A. (1998) 'Prosocial development', in W. Damon and N. Eisenberg (eds), *Handbook of Child Psychology*. Vol. 4. 5th edn. New York: Wiley. pp: 701–78. This chapter provides an excellent meta-analysis of studies in the field of children's prosocial development.

Greener, S.G. and Crick, N.R. (1999) 'Normative beliefs about prosocial behavior in middle childhood: what does it mean to be nice?', *Social Development*, 8: 350–63. This is an interesting paper which investigates children's own perceptions of what constitutes peer-directed pro-social behaviour.

Grusec, J. E., Davidov, M. and Lundell, L. (2002) 'Prosocial and helping behavior', in P.K. Smith and C. Hart (eds), *Blackwell Handbook of Childhood Social Development*. Oxford: Blackwell. pp: 457–90. An accessible and comprehensive chapter which is informative for the reader interested in exploring the topic of children's prosocial development.

Pollard, A. (2008) *Reflective Teaching*. London: Continuum. This very readable text contains an excellent chapter on classroom climates and interpersonal relationships, with the focus on the teacher's relationship with pupils.

Warden, D. and Christie, D. (1997) *Teaching Social Behaviour*. London: David Fulton. A text which offers a good range of practical classroom activities designed to foster children's prosocial behaviour.

CHAPTER 9

GIFTED AND TALENTED EDUCATION

Niamh Stack and Margaret Sutherland

Key ideas explored in this chapter are:

- International and national concepts of giftedness
- The importance of cultural understandings on both education and giftedness
- How each of the above impacts on the educational opportunities offered to gifted pupils
- Possible ways of ensuring curriculum challenge for all

The premise of this book was established in Chapter 1: 'social justice has to be grounded in a vision of providing access to good learning'. Given this beginning you may be surprised at the inclusion of a chapter on gifted and talented pupils as this is a cohort commonly associated with assumptions of privilege and elitism rather than discussions of social justice. A key aim of this chapter is to challenge these assumptions and to demonstrate that social justice is best achieved when pedagogies are permeated with opportunities for children to demonstrate their abilities. Learning which does not provide the required level of challenge is not 'good learning'. Within this chapter we will demonstrate that at a classroom level, teachers' deeply held beliefs about intelligence and ability are of crucial importance as they plan a curriculum that meets the needs of all. As you begin your professional journey this chapter will help you reflect on your values and beliefs about intelligence and examine what this will mean for your practice.

Gifted and talented pupils

So why is it important to discuss this particular group of pupils? On the surface they would seem to be an already advantaged group of pupils, they already do well at examinations, they achieve all the educational goals set by society, they often progress to higher education and achieve professional success. Or do they? Their gifts and talents mean that often they are not perceived as having special or additional educational needs. This can be a misconception. There are often erroneous beliefs about who these pupils are and where you will find them. And even those who would argue that these children are present in education and need appropriate provision, cannot agree as to what that provision should be and who should benefit from it. 'Like any other label, gifted and talented can be problematic for children, peers, parents and educators alike' (Sutherland, 2008: 2).

An obvious place to start a discussion about gifted and talented pupils would be with a definition, however there are over 200 definitions with little consensus and much debate. These definitions increase if you consider the different terminology used to describe this cohort of pupils. Within the UK alone England and Northern Ireland use the term 'gifted and talented pupils'; 'highly able pupils' is the terminology employed in Scotland, and Wales has chosen to use 'talented and more able pupils'. Globally, Chinese psychologists refer to these pupils as 'supernormal' and other European countries talk about 'high ability'. Each of these terms reflects a cultural understanding of who these children are, where you will find them and what educational provision they need.

Gifts and talents are often distinguished according to traditional notions of intelligence – gifts are academic, cognitive-related abilities and talents refer to abilities traditionally considered to be non academic such as music, sport and art. However these terms are considered by some as narrow, exclusive and as possibly providing a false dichotomy between gifts and talents. The REAL project, conducted by London Gifted and Talented, found that a greater number of African Caribbean pupils were nominated for the talented register than for the gifted register. However, further exploration indicated that a number of these children also had abilities that could have seen them nominated for the gifted register. These findings are in line with other studies (Ford, 1996; Sapon-Shevin, 1994) which suggest that often cultural, socio-economic and class expectations can play a role in how these definitions are understood and applied.

Theorists such as Bruner (1996), Bourdieu and Passeron (1990) and Brofenbrenner (1981) have all posited the importance of culture in our understanding of, and relationship to, the world about us. It is important to recognise the role of culture, particularly when globalisation means cultures are not static or geographically limited. As demonstrated in the case study below, globalisation also means movement between educational systems for children and their abilities.

📁 Case study 9.1

Alojzy is 14 years old. His family recently moved from Poland to the UK as migrant workers. He had just started upper secondary school in Poland embarking on a four-year course in a *technikum*. He had shown a particular propensity towards mathematics and had been nominated to participate in the Mathematical Olympiad in Poland. Alojzy speaks little English and so he was placed in lower-attaining classes for subjects until he grasped the rudiments of English.

Culture will determine understanding of who gifted and talented children are and how they should be educated. Indeed, this cultural specificity of the conceptualisation of giftedness can propagate deep-rooted inequalities within society (Borland, 2005). Underrepresented populations on gifted and talented programmes have caused concern for many years (cf. Smith, 2005). Gifted programmes are thought to have served the white middle-class community well but this only exacerbates the elitist connotations associated with such programmes. They would also seem to amplify the gap between white and minority families. Gifted programmes by their very 'existence reproduce existing economic and racial hierarchies or produce cultural capital held by an elite group of students' (Sapon-Shevin, 1994). Thus some (for example, Claxton and Meadows, 2008) suggest we concentrate less on the label and concentrate instead on appropriate and challenging learning for all. This, they argue, will narrow the gap between the 'haves' and the 'have-nots' in society.

Individual education in a universal education system

In 1948 article 26 of the United Nations Declaration of Universal Human Rights ratified the principle that 'Everyone has a right to education', demonstrating a commitment on the part of member states to employ education as a tool for social justice. In 1989 The United Nations Convention on the Rights of the Child (UNCRC) proclaimed that childhood is entitled to special care and assistance, and reiterated this right relating to children. The UNCRC provided a clear definition of a child as 'every human being below the age of eighteen years' but both treaties leave the definition of education open to the interpretation of member states. Twenty years later it is clear that although progress has been made, the Convention has not yet achieved all its aims as there are still children within the member states for whom education is not a feasible option or who are attending schools which cannot offer them an appropriate education (Seymour, 2009).

In developing countries the emphasis remains on ensuring the inherent right to basic education is met. Extreme poverty can mean even free education is expensive as it takes children out of the workplace in families where survival is dependent on the financial contribution, through domestic or paid labour, of all members of the family including children. Indeed 'free education' can be a misnomer, with pupils and families still having to pay for uniforms and books. In societies where free compulsory education is already embedded, this principle raises questions about what form education should take (Black-Hawkins et al., 2007). It extends discussions beyond the importance of a universal educational system, to asking how we best meet the needs of an individual within a universal educational system. Ideological beliefs about intelligence and measures of intelligence such as IQ have long played a role in decisions about appropriate provision. In Chapter 5 George Head examines how inclusion has been proffered as a solution in these debates. However, he problematises the idea, arguing that inclusive programmes are often about recompensing for deficits in the individual learner instead of looking at the abilities of the individual learner and focusing provision on that basis. Here we will ask what this means if you are highly able and if an inclusive approach provides challenging learning for all.

An inclusive approach to education has many merits but one of its possible shortcomings is fiscally bound. Where you have an inclusive approach to education which claims everyone's additional support needs should be met but you do not have the financial resources to match the intention, the limited resource model results in a lifeboat mentality – most deserving needs are met first. However, the decision about who are the most deserving is subjective and fraught with complexity. Within this model, gifted and talented pupils come very far down the list because the enduring and widespread perception is that their gifts and talents mean they will succeed irrespective of circumstances and that they will consequently 'be fine on their own'. At a societal level, cultural beliefs about the importance of egalitarianism and fear of elitism can also provide barriers in identifying and providing for these pupils. In practice this can mean that, for gifted and talented students, being included can mean becoming invisible. If an education system is truly committed to social justice then ability should be matched with appropriate provision irrespective of the direction of that ability.

Case study 9.2

Annie is 7 years old. Her parents report that she started walking alone at 8 months and could walk upstairs at a year and a half. She said her first word at 5 and a half months and had a vocabulary of 4–6 words by 10 and a half months. By 1 year and three months she was using simple sentences and personal pronouns. She became interested in letters and letter sounds at 2 years and by 3 years was reading simple sentences. Annie entered formal school already able to read fluently. Her first teacher was keen to ensure that she developed socially and emotionally and thought it was important for her to work as part of an established reading group, although it was below her ability. Annie continued to read at home with books that were appropriate to her ability. Annie remained in the reading group during her second year of schooling. By year three her teacher reported that it was hard to motivate Annie to participate in reading-based activities. She was showing increased disruptive behaviour during reading times and her parents reported that she was no longer 'devouring' books at home.

The above case study demonstrates that gifted and talented pupils can find learning equally as frustrating and difficult as those with other additional learning needs and that inappropriate provision can have a detrimental effect on them and lead to other difficulties such as disruptive behaviour. Not all gifted and talented children grow up to be gifted and talented adults (Freeman, 2001). If the needs of these pupils are not met through appropriate provision they will slip through the educational cracks of boredom and frustration. So does the solution lie in separate specialised gifted programmes? We would argue not. As we discussed earlier, gifted programmes are not unproblematic and are susceptible to all kinds of racial, ethic and economic inequalities. John F. Kennedy (1963) argued that 'Not every child has an equal talent or an equal ability or equal motivation; but children have the equal right to develop their talent, their ability and their motivation'. An inclusive approach to educational provision still offers the best model for meeting that right. Renzulli (1998) argues that in education 'a rising tide lifts all ships' and that by addressing provision to meet the needs of gifted and talented pupils you will improve provision for all. What is important is that care is taken within an inclusive approach to address the needs of all pupils, including gifted and talented pupils.

Regardless of your perspective on gifted education, it would seem that how frameworks are implemented, how pupils are organised for learning and how and which labels are assigned to groups of learners will be influenced greatly by what teachers believe about intelligence.

Teacher beliefs

From the moment a teacher stands up in front of a class they will be working to a set of beliefs about ability and intelligence. The very word 'intelligence' means different things to different people and grammatically the use of the word intelligence can pose obstacles. It is often used as a noun and, as such, is awarded some status – it implies that intelligence is something tangible, real and concrete. However, if we use the word as an adjective, then we might talk of intelligent behaviours or intelligent action and in this way intelligence becomes a way of acting and behaving rather than something that one has or does not have.

 Thinking point 9.1

- To what extent do you believe that people are born 'stupid/clever' and stay 'stupid/clever'?
- To what extent do you believe that education can help you to become more intelligent?
- To what extent do you believe that education can only bring out what is in you already?

Implicit theories about intelligence

Dweck (2005) argues that there are two implicit theories of intelligence that teachers can hold: entity theory and incremental theory. Implicit theories are in fact essential as they create a meaning system that provides a framework for our actions and goals (Dweck, 1995). Some implicit theories, however, are better grounded in reflection and consideration than others. It is the melding of implicit theory and theory proper that may offer a way forward when considering developments in education.

Nonetheless, implicit beliefs can often be very strong beliefs about key fundamentals in education:

- individual variation in academic performance
- the role that education can play
- what constitutes right and wrong in a classroom.

These implicit theories are then used to evaluate new ideas about learning and teaching: those that are compatible with our beliefs are recognised and accepted, while those that challenge our beliefs are discarded as theoretical, unworkable or wrong. Regardless of which route is taken, Bruner (1996) suggests that as well as teachers taking account of what implicit theories they hold, they had better take account of the implicit theories that learners already possess, because they can have significant impact on both learning and teaching.

Entity theory of intelligence

Entity theorists believe that intelligence is fixed and expect a high degree of consistency in what has been deemed to be 'intelligent behaviour'. Underlying this view of intelligence is the belief that it is a personal, inborn and genetically inherited attribute that cannot be altered. In other words, they believe that as humans we are born with a certain amount of 'brain power' and no matter what happens round about us, the amount of 'brain power' will remain constant. In addition, these views are often applied to particular socio-economic or ethnic groups – those in lower socio-economic groups or particular ethnic groups are less likely to amount to much given the gene pool from which they come and the catchment area in which they live (Sapon-Shevin, 1994). Implicit in this view is also the notion that we can measure intelligence in a meaningful way.

Incremental view of intelligence

Incremental theorists, on the other hand, see intelligence as dynamic, malleable and always varying over time and settings. Teachers adhering to this theory will be reluctant to predict future success or failure based on current performance in the belief that with a change in context intelligent action can be demonstrated or indeed prevented from being demonstrated. Incremental theorists are more likely to view learning as ongoing, believe that intelligence can be demonstrated in a wide variety of ways and that an individual can be more intelligent in one setting than another. While acknowledging that socio-economic status and genetics cannot be ignored, for incremental theorists, intelligent action becomes much more about opportunity and effort. Interestingly Choh Ssu Yee and Quay May Ling (2001) found that special school educators were more likely to have incremental theories of intelligence than those of their mainstream counterparts.

Beliefs into practice

It is therefore important to think about teachers' beliefs about intelligence as they will impact on how we view pupils, the opportunities we offer pupils and the expectations we have for pupils. A study from the 1960s demonstrates the power of raising expectations.

Rosenthal and Jacobson (1966) tested school children and told teachers that the test would identify those children who would achieve academically over the next year. Actually the children had been assigned to the experiment by means of a table of random numbers. The experimental conditions for these children consisted of nothing more than being identified to their teachers as children who would show unusual intellectual gains. Eight months later the children were retested and any changes noted. The children whose teachers had been led to expect greater intellectual gain showed a significantly greater gain in intelligence quotient (IQ) than did the children in the control group. The effects were most dramatic with younger children. The largest gain among the three first grade classrooms was 24.8 IQ points *in excess* of the 16.2 gain shown by the children in the control groups.

There is good news for schools in these findings in the sense that all pupils made gains during the eight months, whether they had been identified as ready to achieve academically or not. It is, however, worthy of note that if we raise our expectations then we are likely to create conditions whereby children perform to the level of our expectations.

 Thinking point 9.2

- To what extent would you agree that teachers hold internal and implicit theories about things such as intelligence?
- To what extent do you believe that such theories can influence teacher behaviour and/or pupil performance?

Constructing a challenging curriculum?

So how do we identify highly able pupils and create conditions which provide them with the opportunity to demonstrate their abilities? Rosenthal and

Jacobson's study demonstrated the powerful effects of labelling but what it also highlighted was the generalised acceptance of IQ tests' power to identify and measure intelligence. Children in this study were purposefully mislabelled to measure the effect of a label, but intelligence tests have long been synonymous with academic ability and consequently considered an appropriate tool to identify highly able pupils. Discussion of the validity and reliability of IQ tests is the realm of other authors. Here we would argue simply that, like all tools, IQ tests have merits and limitations. In some cases they are useful in telling you something but overdependence on them may mean you miss important cohorts of pupils.

Gifted and talented pupils, like all children, are a diverse population and it would be naive to think one testing approach would provide the solution to identification. Molzten (1996) argues identification should begin early, be continuous, incorporate a team approach, be as unobtrusive as possible and include both quantitative and qualitative measures. We would agree that identification should include all these aspects but this seems a significant amount of additional work for an already overworked teacher with a diverse range of pupils in their classroom. One possible solution seems clear, we could invert the process and instead of identifying gifted and talented pupils to enable appropriate provision, we could identify through provision (Freeman, 1998). If we create a challenging curriculum that incorporates a 'low threshold' for those with learning difficulties but also a 'high ceiling' for those with high abilities, we can provide an identification process that begins early, is continuous and is multidimensional. This would allow teachers to identify high ability as part of their daily practice.

Molzten also recommends training teachers to recognise high ability. Eyre et al. (2002) conducted a study to identify the characteristics of an effective teacher of able pupils. They found that effective teachers of able pupils: held well-developed views on teaching and learning; had an ability to focus on the needs of individuals; created a classroom climate that supports the development of high achievement; had knowledge of how to design tasks that ensure intellectual challenge and engaged in high-quality interactions with their pupils in which both played a range of roles. It occurs to us that these are the characteristics of a good teacher that would be valuable in teaching any pupils, not just highly able pupils. This being the case the training of teachers to recognise high ability and provide a challenging curriculum at all levels is best placed as an integral element of their professional qualification. To address the question of what format this training should take, a good starting point may be to return to the idea of identifying ability through provision. This approach allows teachers to expect the unexpected and access the unseen gifted and talented pupil. It provides open opportunities for pupils who are subject to other labels such as dyslexia or Asperger's syndrome to demonstrate that they may be doubly or multi exceptional. This process also allows teachers to identify when classroom provision may not be sufficient for a particular highly able pupil and additional resources, expertise or strategies may be required to support a pupil's learning.

A poisoned chalice?

As already discussed, contradictory evidence relating to the general profile of gifted and talented pupils is not unusual as it is their diversity which identifies them most. In practice this means that finding them and providing for them can be challenging, however we would recommend two additional strategies that have been empirically demonstrated as effective if often underutilised in practice: talking and listening. If learning occurs in the space between what we know and what we do not know, then it is important that conversations between the teacher and the learner also occur in this space.

Gifted and talented pupils' voices are important in developing new provision but also in reflecting on and evaluating existing provision. Leyden (1995) reports on findings from one school which interviewed their sixth form students about their past experiences and found they had to revise a number of assumptions the school had made about their provision. The pupils identified areas of the school where they felt practice could be improved and provided constructive suggestions on how to tackle underachievement in boys. When given a voice in research by Smith (2006), able pupils complained that being able means more work rather than appropriate challenge. Being good at something should not mean that you have to do twice as much work as your classroom peers; rather that work is set for you at a level appropriate to your ability.

Rogoff (1990) demonstrated that our values and our assumptions about what pupils can or cannot do at any given age or stage in development inform how we relate to and engage with children. These values and assumptions can lead to practices, often without ill intention, which exclude children from engaging in and reflecting on their own development. In developing our understanding of this cohort of pupils our best resource is the pupils themselves.

Summary

Gifted and talented pupils should be of concern to all those involved in education. While there is no consensus as to a definition of giftedness or how we cater for their needs, there are undoubtedly children in our schools who require an appropriate and challenging curriculum matched to their abilities or potential abilities.

This chapter has highlighted the contested nature of gifted education and sought to critique some of the established ways of identifying this cohort of pupils. It has also argued that some existing practices may result in marginalising or excluding some cohorts of gifted and talented students. As we progress through the twenty-first century we need to respond to emerging challenges in creative and dynamic ways. Moving away from traditional conceptions of giftedness will allow us to develop a discourse where optimal conditions for learning are paramount and where diversity is celebrated.

There are, of course, no right and wrong answers to the questions posed in this chapter. However, it is by investigating these questions that we have been able to ascertain concerns and tensions that are present in the interfaces between implicit theories, formal theories, policy and practice. It is this very investigation of the issues that allows educators to plan and provide effectively for all pupils in their care.

Key questions for reflection and discussion

- What has influenced your own personal and professional thinking on intelligence?
- In what ways can we provide an individual education in a universal education system?
- In what ways does your understanding of intelligence impact on practice?
- What does a challenging curriculum look like?
- What will gifted education look like in the year 2050?

Further reading

Balchin, T., Hymer, B. and Matthews, D.J. (2009) *The Routledge International Companion to Gifted Education.* London: Routledge. This international companion provides a comprehensive overview of contemporary issues in gifted education.

Freeman, J. (1991) *Gifted Children Growing Up.* London: Cassell. This is an interesting book which describes the experiences of 210 gifted young people from a wide variety of backgrounds over 14 years as they grow up across Britain.

Smith, C. (ed.) (2005) *Including the Gifted and Talented and More Able Learners.* London: Routledge. This edited collection provides extended reading on the issues raised within this chapter.

Sutherland, M. (2008) *Developing the Gifted and Talented Young Learner.* London: Sage. This book provides a very accessible introduction to some of the key discussions in the field and includes lots of practical ideas for using in the classroom.

Winstanley, C. (2006) *Too Clever by Half: A Fair Deal for Gifted Children*. London: Trentham Press. This is an engaging and accessible book. Using case studies of highly able children, the author illustrates the range of difficulties these children can face, and how without appropriate support they can become disaffected and underachieve.

Web resources

www.londongt.org
www.ablepupils.com
http://www.nace.co.uk/nace/cymru/nace_cymru_wales.htm

SECTION 3

PRACTICE

SECTION OVERVIEW

Christine Forde

In Section 3 we explore the professional context and consider how the role of teachers is evolving. In Chapter 1 of this book we argued that the fundamental purpose of education, for us, is to promote equality and social justice. This purpose is not easy to achieve but educators need to work actively towards this purpose by providing effective learning for all learners. However, there are many and often competing demands made on schools and teachers alike which have significant implications for what it means to be a teacher in school.

Teacher policy

One of the common features of educational policy globally has been efforts to modernise the teaching profession. Ozga (2005) argues that the drive for teacher workforce modernisation comes from the increasingly globalised competitive market from which heavy demands are placed on education to serve the economy. As in other parts of the world, across the UK there has been the institutionalisation of a range of managerial practices particularly with regard to increasing accountability of schools and teachers. First, government reforms have redefined the contractual obligations of teachers: for example, the National Agreement (DfES, 2003) and the Teachers' Agreement (Scottish Executive, 2001b) in Scotland. Secondly, professional standards for teachers have been developed. In these two areas there is a common purpose in redefining what it means to be a teacher.

Professional standards identify not only what headteachers, governors, employers and parents can demand of teachers but also wider societal expectations of the teaching profession. Professional standards powerfully define not only the prerequisite skills, knowledge and qualities expected of teachers but also articulate the values that define what it means to be a good teacher. In these standards we can see some of the ways in which the role of the teacher is changing. Thus the *Standard for Full Registration* (GTCS, 2006) in Scotland includes working with other professionals as part of the role of the teacher. Similarly the *Professional Standards for Newly Qualified Teachers* (TDA, 2007) in England and Wales highlights collaboration between teachers and the role of advanced skills teachers is to support other teachers in the development of their practice.

Being a teacher

The changing expectations of teachers alongside new opportunities for teachers to develop in their role raises some key questions which individual teachers need to consider:

- Who am I as a teacher: how do I define my role as an educator?
- What are the sources of my professionalism: what are the skills, knowledge and attributes I bring to this role?
- What do I stand for as a practitioner: what do I see as the core purposes of education?

These are critical questions as teachers grapple with how they will work in the immediate context of their classroom and wider areas such as working collaboratively with colleagues to develop effective learning and teaching, taking on leadership responsibilities to promote pupil achievement and working in interprofessional teams to ensure the well-being of children and young people. In Section 3 we explore the role of the teacher in these contexts.

Outline of Section 3

The key questions above highlight the importance of individual teachers being aware of how they see themselves in this role and how this shapes the learning experiences of pupils; in other words, being aware of their professional identity. This section begins with a discussion of the idea of 'professional identity' which is about how a teacher defines him- or herself. In Chapter 10, Fiona Patrick and Alastair McPhee argue for the importance of professional identity because how a teacher defines him- or herself is based on what they see as important in education. As expectations of the role of the teacher change, there is a need for teachers to reflect on their professional identity in order that they can respond constructively, building on and adding to their skills and understandings.

One area where there have been significant changes is in the wider contribution teachers can make to the development of the school. Greater emphasis is now placed on teachers working collegiately to achieve the aims of the school particularly in promoting effective learning. In Chapter 11 Margaret Martin explores how collegiate practice might be fostered through the establishment of a professional learning community which changes the role of school leaders and teachers alike.

Increasingly teachers are not only expected to work together but also to take on leadership roles. In Chapter 12 Christine Forde examines the idea of 'teacher leadership' which has become a keynote in recent policy and considers ways in which teachers draw on their skill and knowledge in pedagogy to foster this expertise in other practitioners in the school.

As our understanding of the learning process has increased and we appreciate the need to consider each child's or young person's holistic development, we have recognised the importance of working with other professionals to ensure children and young people in school are ready to learn. In Chapter 13 Margaret McCulloch focuses on the nature of collaborative practice across interprofessional boundaries and the impact of this on the role of teachers.

In Chapter 14, the final chapter, Penny Enslin draws the themes of this book together in order to explore the future of education in a globalised context.

CHAPTER 10

PROFESSIONAL IDENTITY

Fiona Patrick and Alastair McPhee

Key ideas explored in this chapter are:

- Professional identity
- Identity and career stages
- Professional culture
- Reflection

All professionals develop a sense of themselves in relation to the work they do. Some will form a clearer sense of professional identity than others, and will consciously reflect on the values, attitudes, beliefs and behaviours which underpin their practice. Overall, this book argues the importance of each teacher articulating and justifying their own stance as an educator. Part of this process involves teachers considering who they are as professionals, in other words, in shaping their professional identity. Conscious reflection on professional identity and how it informs practice can help teachers to understand how they respond to various professional situations, and to decide whether or not these responses are the most effective ones they could make. This chapter focuses on what professional identity is and how it is formed.

Exploring professional identity

Professional identity has been described as the 'enduring constellation of attributes, beliefs, values, motives, and experiences in terms of which people define themselves in a professional role' (Ibarra, in Dobrow and Higgins, 2005: 569). Current interpretations of professional identity do not see it as an entirely stable entity. Particular aspects of identity such as confidence in professional knowledge and skills can fluctuate depending on circumstances – what Colley et al. (2007) call a 'shuttling' between confidence and self-doubt. In addition, Watson points out that the 'relationship between professional identity and practice is not a simple unidirectional one in which some essential core of self … determines how we act in a given situation' (Watson, 2006: 525). The situation is more complicated than this, but exploration and awareness of how professional identity shapes our practice can help teachers to respond more effectively and purposefully within what can be a challenging career.

Professional identity rests on personal identity. It is therefore based on individual values, beliefs and feelings, as well as on professional knowledge and understanding. Broader social and cultural aspects such as ethnicity, culture and religion also play a part in how we define ourselves personally and professionally (Kostogriz and Peeler, 2007). In addition, research highlights the role emotions play in constructing and changing identity (O'Connor, 2008). All these aspects influence how we respond in professional situations but, while some of them are givens, they are not immutable. We can develop aspects of ourselves to enable us to respond more effectively in professional situations. In order to develop these aspects we have to reflect on them and how they affect our professional practice.

Professional identity usually develops throughout a career (Flores and Day, 2005). Early career teachers may well have a different perception of themselves from those nearing retirement, and more experienced teachers may have an identity which is more stable than that of a beginning teacher. Of course, this need not necessarily be the case and we should guard against stereotyping. Beginning teachers can be resistant to reflective practice and developmental change, while more experienced teachers can consistently review their practice, attitudes and beliefs.

In terms of career phase, shifts in identity are commonly seen as teachers move into posts of responsibility and begin to respond to changing expectations of how they are perceived in their new role (Reeves et al., 2005). There is potential here for mismatch between how others expect an individual to behave in a given role and how the individual might choose to behave based on their own professional beliefs. In thinking about professional identity it is important to consider the expectations of others and how those expectations affect individual practice.

The importance of professional identity

Professional identity is important because it shapes how teachers interact with pupils and parents, with the wider community and with other professionals. It can also influence teachers' responses to implementing education policy and school policy as well as shaping how teachers react to broader educational issues (such as inclusion or challenging behaviour). Exploring professional identity helps teachers to consider whether their responses are evidence based, helpful to their pupils in terms of promoting learning, helpful in terms of collegiate working and helpful to themselves in terms of developing their skills.

Some professionals have a strong sense of their professional identity and have thought specifically about what their professional role means to them. Others have an unclear sense of identity which can lead to anxiety in fulfilling a professional role, or to a less certain sense of career direction. There are internal and external factors to identity development, and these factors will be explored next.

Constructing professional identity: internal factors

At the internal level, we construct identity partly through the stories we tell ourselves and others about our work (Søreide, 2006: 529). At this stage it is worth exploring how we construct identity in more detail through active reflection.

Thinking point 10.1

Using the idea of stories or descriptions, how would you describe yourself as a teacher? You might like to think about this from different perspectives:

- How do you think of yourself as a teacher in your own mind?
- How do your describe yourself as a teacher to others?
- What aspects of your personal identity affect your teacher identity?
- What do your responses to these questions reveal about what you believe your professional identity to be?

Narrative construction of identity

By describing ourselves in certain ways, we align with professional norms and expectations. Within the profession, we might describe ourselves as taking a 'child-centred' approach to teaching. This description would stand less as a fully defined pedagogic position and more as a shorthand for focusing on children's learning (rather than being 'subject centred' which risks being seen as functionalist and less caring about the human dimensions of teaching). How we describe ourselves may therefore partly be a response to expectations of the teacher role, whether these are public or professional.

Often we do not reflect explicitly on these stories and what they can tell us about our professional beliefs. But we can think of these narratives as revealing a core level of professional identity, and if we openly reflect on why we refer to our work in certain ways, this can help us to uncover our most basic assumptions about our practice and enable us to revisit what we see as our core professional values and purposes.

Reappraising identity

At times we may choose to, or be forced to, reconstruct or adapt our professional identity and this can prompt explicit reflection. In such situations we might have to apply effort to reshape our identities and this can feel uncomfortable as we reassess who we are as professionals. However, reflection need not imply extensive effort to radically alter our professional identity. It can mean an ongoing (but periodic) process where we develop as professionals by reconsidering our professional motivations, beliefs, assumptions and practices in order to think about what we need to do to respond to changing circumstances. If we see identity development as ongoing, and if we can make reflection habitual, then major change should feel less discomforting in terms of making us question our professional role.

Constructing professional identity: external factors

If the internal construction of identity can be thought of as providing a core, then external factors can be seen as adding further layers to identity development. Professionals respond to external demands in various ways, and the responses arise from how they view their role and how they believe they should react to these demands. They can resist or accept social, cultural and political expectations, but may do so without reflecting on why they choose certain courses of action. Thinking about the range of expectations placed on teachers gives an indication of how complex teaching is, and can also indicate the various aspects of identity which are shaped by these expectations.

The teacher as subject expert

Teachers are expected to show subject expertise. Demands relating to curriculum delivery and assessment are becoming more complex and rate of change can be rapid in response to changing policy influences. Frequent changes of policy direction can lead to a sense of uncertainty with respect to our professional identities in terms of what is being expected of us regarding curriculum expertise. This can be the case particularly where education policy attempts to shape practice openly (for example, *Curriculum for Excellence* in Scotland, or the 14–19 reforms in England).

The teacher as expert on learning

All teachers are expected to have pedagogic expertise. Earlier in this book we explored different facets of learning because teachers' understanding of how children learn effectively should rest on evidence gained from research and observation rather than on common sense ideas of 'what works' (see Chapter 6). This reorientation from models of transmission to emphasis on understanding how children learn has implications for teacher identity. Contemporary teachers have to think of their professional role as a broad entity, consisting of a range of knowledge, understanding and skills.

The teacher as continuing learner

Professional development is now expected to continue throughout a career but there is a need for greater understanding of the potential impact that this can have on professional identity. Continuing Professional Development (CPD) is increasingly seen as an indicator of a professional approach to work and is often a contractual obligation. There is a risk within this culture that professionalism is always under review and that professional practice is never regarded as being good enough. However, this view has to be balanced with the need for CPD as necessary to support and develop practice to enhance pupil learning. Identity becomes modified through professional learning and teachers can develop a greater sense of expertise by actively seeking to improve their professional abilities. An important source of continued learning can be found where schools act as learning communities for staff, giving the opportunity to share professional learning (see Chapter 11).

The teacher as publicly accountable

The teaching profession exists because society has a need for it. There is a broad consensus among the main political parties in the UK about the purposes schools should have, and the role teachers should have in them. Teachers are held accountable for pupil learning at a political level within the devolved governments of the UK. In England, this agenda has led to teacher professionalism being defined much more in line with government policy and the outcome has been a move to a 'more managed teaching profession' (Furlong, 2008: 731). This can leave teachers in any sector feeling deskilled where policy implies that their role is as deliverers of the curriculum rather than creators of it (see Jones, 2008).

The teacher as accountable to management

Teachers must respond to the expectations of management in their schools, but they also have to respond to the overall management of the education system by local education authorities and through government policy. In responding to sources of accountability, professional identity is influenced by the extent to which each teacher feels they should have autonomy within their work. The more autonomy a professional feels they should have, the less they will respond positively to managerialism which tends to construct professionalism in terms of compliance and conformity and so tends to deny individual agency (Forde et al., 2006: 5). However, in some schools work is more collegiate than in others, fostering teacher leadership rather than a top-down approach (see Chapter 12).

The teacher as accountable to clients

Teachers are increasingly seen as accountable to pupils and parents for the educational service they give. This can lead to tension as teachers struggle to give the quality of service they want to because of various challenges (such as lack of resources, lack of time, or curriculum prescription). This tension may be compounded because teaching is often regarded as being 'of low status in the hierarchy of professions' (Colley et al., 2007: 186). Accountability tends to be framed in simplistic terms socially and politically because many do not understand the complexities inherent in teachers' work.

Thinking point 10.2

We have explored a range of expectations that can impact on teacher professional identity.

(Continued)

(Continued)

- To what extent do you recognise these expectations as affecting your sense of professionalism and how you approach your work?
- If these expectations seem less relevant to you, what are some of the expectations that can affect how you are perceived as a professional? Where do these expectations come from?

What does this mean in practice?

Teacher identity has an important impact on a range of professional activities as well as on our sense of self-efficacy (the extent to which we feel we can perform tasks successfully). How we view our professional role will have an impact on how we:

- plan and develop the curriculum
- relate to pupils, parents and wider communities
- interact with managers and colleagues
- interact with other professional groups
- respond to systemic change
- form communities of learning where approaches to practice are shared.

Through reflection on professional identity teachers mediate how effective their practice will be. The following sections of this chapter look at case studies which illustrate how identity potentially affects teaching practice. These case studies are fictional but have been developed to show specific challenges to identity, which many teachers will recognise. After you have read each scenario, you might like to note down what you think are the main issues for each of the teachers with regard to their professional identity before you move on to read our thoughts on these issues.

Case study 10.1 Kate

Kate is a newly qualified teacher. She is being mentored by a more experienced teacher with whom she has weekly meetings and who also periodically observes her teaching. Initially Kate was apprehensive about being under scrutiny (as she saw it) but she has gradually appreciated how peer review can help her develop as a teacher. Kate regularly interacts with colleagues who have a range of experience, and gains support from them. She has been involved in developing approaches to learning in her own classroom, which she has been invited to share with her colleagues at a staff development day. She has brought back ideas from her CPD courses for newly qualified teachers which more experienced colleagues have expressed interest in learning about. She has also been involved in policy-making in the school by being a member of a working group.

Kate's situation highlights some important aspects of how early career teachers develop their professional identity after leaving initial teacher education:

- Through mentoring during their induction into teaching.
- Through interaction with colleagues (with a range of experience).
- Through continuing professional development.

We will discuss these as they relate to Kate's developing teacher identity.

Mentoring for beginning teachers

Mentoring is increasingly seen as vital to teachers' early career development, and '[o]ne of the most important functions of mentoring is the cultivation of professional identity' (Dobrow and Higgins, 2005: 567). Reflection on practice is expected from the probationer within the mentoring process. At this early career stage we might expect professional identity to be fairly fluid and subject to shaping by outside influences (such as peer review and mentoring). Although peer observation and review have the potential to feel like scrutiny, mentoring should be supportive while inviting reflection on practice. While Kate shows signs that she has already developed a strong sense of herself as a professional, the support she is receiving through mentoring is helping her to shape this identity further.

Interacting with colleagues

Identity development does not take place in isolation. It depends in part on being socialised into a profession, and this is a complex process 'by which a person acquires the knowledge, skills, and a sense of occupational identity that are characteristic of a member of that profession' (Adams et al., 2006: 57). Part of this early identity formation can be influenced by role models such as mentors or more experienced staff. Kate seems to have been encouraged to take part in collegiate activities in her school and has been viewed by experienced colleagues as a source of support for their own professional development. This in turn has impacted positively on Kate's sense of professional identity.

Teacher as learner: the role of continuing professional development

It is important for newly qualified and early career teachers to feel that they benefit professionally by undertaking CPD. Part of developing our professional identity consists of the extent to which we are open to new learning and to sharing practice. As teaching moves towards more collegiate forms of working, this aspect of professional identity and practice is becoming more important. There is also growing awareness of the CPD needs of early career teachers like Kate. This can be seen in responses to professional development needs such as local education authorities' programmes for NQTs and by the framing of early professional development as a distinctive career phase by the Teacher Development Agency (TDA) in England and by the general teaching councils in the UK. At this early stage in her career, it appears that Kate has an identity made up of different facets: learning professional, reflective practitioner and teamworker. Overall she is able to see herself as someone whose knowledge and skills are valuable to the school community.

> ### 📁 Case study 10.2 Eddie
>
> Eddie is an experienced classroom teacher of a subject, working in a secondary school. His school has been through recent changes which have forced him to reappraise his teacher identity. As a subject teacher he saw his main tasks as being teaching, assessment and curriculum development for his classes. However, the school has moved from departments to a faculty-based structure where several subjects have come together. Eddie found this difficult because as an experienced teacher he had been highly autonomous. He also felt the subject department staff got on well together and made a good team. At the same time, the school developed interdisciplinary programmes of study and so teachers began working in cross-curricular groups. Again Eddie struggled with this new context but gradually saw how these new programmes reaffirmed his beliefs about the importance of learning opportunities for pupils. Eddie is now hoping to follow the portfolio route to demonstrate that he meets the standards required of a Chartered Teacher as set out by the General Teaching Council for Wales (GTCW).

Eddie's situation highlights the following aspects in identity development:

- Perceptions of self as a teacher: collegiate or individual?
- Identity and structural change.

Perceptions of self: collegiate or individual?

Eddie frames his role predominantly in individual terms, emphasising professional aspects for which he has particular responsibility. The core of Eddie's professional identity is that of classroom teacher, and this is a complex and dynamic role. His perception of himself as a teacher seems most strongly linked to an individual construct of professional identity, although his sense of unease at the loss of the subject department suggests that part of his identity is allied to a sense of his working relationships with colleagues. Professional identity does have collective aspects to it and can be affected by the culture and ethos of the departments or schools in which teachers work.

Identity and structural change

The move to a faculty structure impacts upon Eddie's professional identity in terms of his ability to feel autonomous as a subject teacher and his sense of belonging to a clearly defined professional group. Part of Eddie's task was to 'rethink' his role in the new faculty context. Losing a specific identity is one of the situations which could lead to Colley et al.'s 'shuttling' (2007: 184): self-doubt can arise when the rationale for your identity is removed. Imposing change can lead teachers to feel that they have been disempowered and this can have a negative effect on professional identity. Without a sense of being valued, professionals can begin to doubt themselves and their place within the school system and this may lead to a situation where professional identity becomes less robust. New roles can lead to uncertainty, particularly where role change is forced. However, as Eddie's case study shows, we can adjust to those new roles and reflect on how our professional skills have developed, or can develop, within them. Despite narrowly defining his identity as a classroom teacher to begin with, Eddie's confidence in his skills is now such that he can consider how his skills match with those outlined in the *Chartered Teacher Standards* (GTCW, 2009).

Summary

Professional identity is multifaceted and builds on our personal characteristics, beliefs and values, as well as on our professional learning, our interactions with others, and the nature of our professional role within the education system. Thinking consciously about who you are as a teacher can promote resilience in a stressful profession (see Forde et al., 2006: 40). Reflecting on your professional identity can help you to understand what you do well, and what you need to do to be more effective in specific areas of your work. Reflecting on professional identity can also help you to clarify your professional goals and how you can achieve these and can therefore have an impact on how you shape your career path.

Overall, reflection can help build self-efficacy: that is, the extent to which we believe we can achieve certain outcomes we think are desirable, and the extent to which we have confidence in our abilities based on evidence rather than on supposition (Forde et al., 2006: 16). Exploring professional identity is important in terms of maintaining individual confidence and motivation within a professional world often characterised by rapid change, bureaucracy, complexity and uncertainty.

Key questions for reflection and discussion

- In what ways could professional reflection support you to develop teaching and learning approaches for your pupils?
- How would your pupils and colleagues describe you as a teacher? Would you feel confident enough to ask them so that you can develop knowledge of whether or not the role you *think* you have aligns with the perceptions other people have of you?
- How would you describe the professional culture in the school you work in (or have your placement in)? To what extent does this culture enhance or limit your professional identity?

Further reading

Bolton, G.E.J. (2010) *Reflective Practice: Writing and Professional Development*. 3rd edn. London: Sage. This text provides an introduction to practical aspects of reflection. It includes an introduction to reflective practice which leads into discussion of various possibilities for exploring professionalism through writing.

Dillon, J. and Maguire, M. (eds.) (2007) *Becoming a Teacher: Issues in Secondary Teaching*. 3rd edn. Berkshire: Open University Press. Chapters 1, 7, and 8. Although aimed at teachers in secondary schools, the chosen chapters have wider appeal. Chapter 1 might be of interest to beginning teachers in its exploration of how student teachers develop their professional role.

Forde, C., McMahon, M., McPhee, A. and Patrick, F. (2006) *Professional Development, Reflection and Enquiry*. London: Paul Chapman Publishing. Chapters 1–3. These chapters discuss key elements of professional identity for beginning and experienced teachers. They explore what it means to be a professional and what challenges and tensions arise in modern teaching.

Pollard, A. (2005) *Reflective Teaching*. London: Continuum. Chapter 5 of Pollard's text (Values and identity: who are we?) has useful reflective activities to help with exploration of the teacher's professional role.

Sachs, J. (2003) *The Activist Teaching Profession*. Buckingham: Open University Press. Chapters 2 and 3. In these chapters, Sachs looks at how teacher professionalism has changed in recent years and what some of the political dynamics around the professional role might be.

Web resources

GTC Scotland Teacher Researcher Reports: http://www.gtcs.org.uk/Research_/TeacherResearcher Programme/TeacherResearcherReports/teacher_researcher_reports_2.aspx?

Smith, C. (2008) *The Use of Learning Journals as a Self Reflection Tool to Support and Develop Probationer Teachers' Skills in Critical Evaluation and Reflection*. Edinburgh: GTCS. http:// www.gtcs.org.uk/Research_/TeacherResearcherProgramme/TeacherResearcherReports/use-of-learning-journals-critical-evaluation-reflection.aspx

Teacher Development Agency (no date) *CPD in Practice*: http://www.tda.gov.uk/teachers/ continuingprofessionaldevelopment/cpd_in_practice/cpd/park_school.aspx?keywords=reflecti ve+practice

CHAPTER 11

PROFESSIONAL LEARNING COMMUNITIES

Margaret Martin

Key ideas explored in this chapter are:

- Defining a 'professional learning community'
- A rationale for adopting this approach in a school
- The challenges for teachers and school leaders

Teachers are now expected to contribute to the development and improvement process in schools. The leadership role they are asked to assume is a significant shift in the way schools are organised and makes very different demands on teachers. This chapter explores how that changing role can contribute to the development of more egalitarian and equitable environments for learning for teachers and pupils, through the development of a professional learning community.

Defining a professional learning community

The term 'professional learning community' (PLC) is now widely used in education but is often interpreted in many different ways. For the sake of clarity it is therefore important to define the term as it is being used here and the approach to improving learning being advocated. Essentially a PLC is a way of working in a school – a set of relationships and structures designed to encourage real collaboration by staff to ensure improvement in pupil learning. There are a number of key features of a PLC, which need to work together if the quality of learning is to be improved for teachers, and through them, for pupils (DuFour et al., 2006; Hord, 2004; Huffman and Hipp, 2003). I would like to simplify the many definitions in the literature to the following three crucial elements:

- shared and supportive leadership
- a clear focus on enquiry into the pupil learning experience
- collaborative approaches to learning for teachers and pupils.

Shared and supportive leadership

For a PLC to thrive, the conditions have to be created in the school where there is mutual trust and respect to support it. Shared leadership, shared power and genuine collaboration with stakeholders could be seen as the building blocks upon which such trust and mutual respect can be built. Teachers' attitudes to taking risks and working collectively will be strongly influenced by the culture of the school and quality of the relationships which exist there.

A sense of ownership of the school's purposes and practices can only be achieved if the stakeholders in the school are involved, in a meaningful way, in the creation of the school's aims for its pupils, their families and its community. In many schools, although statements of values are often available, because of limited discussion with stakeholders, there is sometimes a lack of any real clarity about why they are important and what they actually mean in practice.

The idea of distributed leadership has become increasingly popular in recent years and is now advocated as a desired leadership style in UK schools. (Gronn, 2003; Harris, 2008; Spillane, 2006) While many school leaders may profess to 'distribute leadership', the reality is that often they are simply delegating management tasks to those who are willing to accept them. A clear distinction needs to be made between the two – distributing leadership and distributing tasks.

Where tasks are delegated, this often involves organising people to operationalise decisions made by others, to which they may have no commitment and with which they may even disagree. When leadership is genuinely distributed, there is a sense in which stakeholders are involved at a much earlier stage in the process. They are involved, because their opinion is valued, in deciding what initiatives need to be taken forward to meet the agreed purposes of the school, and then involved in the process of deciding how these changes might be taken forward. The underlying premise here is that staff have a pivotal role to play in improving the quality of learning in classrooms and that they need to be centrally involved in identifying barriers to learning and in devising strategies to overcome those barriers. School leaders cannot do this on their own and the role of the class teacher is therefore important.

📁 Case study 11.1

In one large secondary school the head teacher consults regularly with the heads of department and openly values their contributions to the school's improvement agenda. She recognises their expertise and pivotal role in influencing the quality of learning and teaching.

They have been centrally involved in the decision-making discussions about what needs to be changed in the school to improve learning and have not only identified areas for development, but have suggested the possible strategies to address them. Their subsequent involvement in design teams to take forward the work is based on commitment to a change agenda which they themselves created.

The staff in this school feel increasingly valued as they are routinely consulted about the direction of the school improvement plan in a meaningful way and then see the results of their input translated into practice.

The culture of the school is therefore significant in determining the readiness of its constituents to consider the idea of building a professional learning community (Stoll, 2003). The extent to which trust has been built will be important. This involves attention to the quality of relationships, and the recognition of the human and emotional dimensions of working together in a school. These essential foundations need to be laid over time to create a solid basis for the building of a PLC. So it is necessary to build what Huffman and Hipp (2003) refer to as people capacities, as well as looking at the structural conditions required to support the creation of a PLC. The structural support is also vital if ideas are to be translated into practice.

The time and space for teachers to engage in professional dialogue about learning is a necessity in this approach to school improvement, and the challenge is for schools to find ways to carve out the time to allow cross-fertilisation of ideas. The important issue is that teachers need to be given time to make meaning and make sense of new developments, to experiment in an atmosphere of safety, and engage in structured conversations about their own and pupils' learning. In short, school leaders need to remove as many logistical barriers as possible to allow this approach to be translated into practice.

Thinking point 11.1

- What, in your opinion, do class teachers have to bring to this approach to improving learning?

A clear focus on enquiry into the pupil learning experience

In a PLC, it is important that a shared commitment to a particular set of purposes for the school is very clearly focused on the quality of learning. The link between teachers' learning and pupils' learning is crucial. Detailed attention to the learning experiences of the pupils is at the heart of a PLC, where the adults in the school take collective responsibility for the learning of all the pupils and understand the importance of early identification of barriers to learning and appropriate intervention where required.

This idea is explored in some detail in Chapter 6 by Mike Carroll and essentially means that as a matter of routine practice, staff are gathering evidence about the impact of their teaching on pupil learning and using it to improve the learning experience.

It would therefore be important for teachers to become comfortable with the collection and sharing of data about pupil learning which is relevant and useful in making decisions about teaching. Rather than a narrow focus on examination results, this would be widened to focus on the effects of particular instructional strategies, the nature of the pupil learning experience and a much deeper exploration aimed at uncovering barriers to learning. Schools have been described as 'data rich and information poor' (Earl et al., 2006) in that they are surrounded by all kinds of data, but need to become more skilled at identifying its uses and its relevance and at generating appropriate data of their own related to their values.

In a PLC, this interrogation of the learning is taken to a deeper, more rigorous level where teachers begin to systematically gather evidence about the impact of their teaching and establish criteria for judging the quality of the learning they organise. (Baumfield et al., 2008) This is not the same as the testing regime often used to gather performance data with which to compare schools, rather it is practitioner enquiry, where teachers take a professional interest in finding ways of evaluating the learning and use the evidence to inform their teaching. 'Results' in this sense are still important for teachers but, in this case, they are experimenting with new ideas and approaches, and evaluating their effectiveness.

It is easy for teachers to become consumed with their 'delivery' and spend less time focusing on the experience of the learners on the receiving end of that 'delivery'. The notion of seeking and acting on feedback from pupils about the impact of teaching and their experiences of learning is worth exploring.

📁 Case study 11.2

In one primary school, the teachers interviewed the children to gather their views on what made for a good learning environment. The children's responses were recorded on video and played back to their teachers as the basis of a staff discussion.

The children were adamant that they were not sufficiently praised by teachers and felt that they could be encouraged more in the classroom. The teachers were very surprised to hear this and maintained that they did in fact praise the children and gave many examples of how they did this.

This led to a very interesting discussion about what praise actually looked like – to the teachers and to the pupils. It became clear that the differing perceptions of what constituted praise were at the heart of this problem and that this needed to be explicitly discussed to clear up the confusion.

Teachers were heard to remark that there might be sometimes a similar mismatch of perceptions when teachers were under the impression that they were employing helpful strategies to assist children in their learning. It was then agreed that this would be fruitful territory for future exploration with the children.

💭 Thinking point 11.2

- What would you see as the advantages and disadvantages of seeking feedback from pupils?

Collaborative approaches to learning for teachers and pupils

Teacher learning is at the heart of a PLC. It is through the developing skills, knowledge and understanding of teachers that improvements in the effectiveness of pupil learning can be made. Teaching has traditionally been a fairly isolated activity and teachers in the UK are only recently beginning to venture into one another's classrooms to observe teaching and, more importantly, to discuss what they have seen. Louis and Kruse (1995) describe this as the deprivatisation of practice which involves peers helping peers and routinely working together in classrooms with colleagues with the express purpose of sharing expertise and stimulating debate and discussion about approaches to teaching and learning. This mutual examination of practice provides the opportunity for structured conversations about learning which help teachers to make sense of the new ideas they are experimenting with by sharing their successes and failures.

Traditionally, much of teachers' professional development involves out of school attendance at courses, often short, and with little or no follow-up or support. Individuals attending such courses are often then expected to negotiate the link between these isolated experiences and their own practice in school. There is evidence that in the space between the professional development experience and the routine day-to-day practice in school, much of the momentum to change practice is lost (Joyce and Showers, 1995). Teachers will often default to their original teaching repertoire, as they experience the inevitable discomfort that accompanies a change of practice (Palmer, 1998). In a learning community, a different approach is taken where the need for particular areas to be developed the need is identified through enquiry and evaluation. Relevant strengths and skills of staff within the establishment can then be harnessed to meet those needs in a relevant and meaningful context.

To be effective in a PLC, enquiry into pupil learning is not done in isolation, but as part of a collaborative endeavour. The development of a culture of mutual trust and safe risk-taking is vital to the success of the introduction of peer observation and relates closely to the style of leadership outlined above. If the ultimate shared aim of the school is to provide the highest quality learning, then the advantages of teachers learning from one another are clear.

Thinking point 11.3

- How do you feel about peer observation?
- What support do you think a teacher might need to be able to engage in the process?

Why should schools consider this way of working?

Values

The notion of a PLC is not just an alternative way of organising things in a school. It is a fundamental paradigm shift in the relationships in the organisation. There is a very basic realignment of the power relationships which is at the heart of the approach and which means that to be convinced of its value, those involved would need to be comfortable with that change. Professional learning communities are predicated on the idea of equity and genuine participation in decision making, especially in relation to the core business of schools–learning and teaching. The central issue here is one of values. School leaders have to believe that other stake-holders are trustworthy, that pupils have the right to be consulted about their learning, that parents are important partners and that school leadership is a joint endeavour and not a solo activity. And stakeholders have to decide whether they are willing to 'buy in' to a different way of working and how this kind of approach fits in with their own beliefs about how a school should operate.

Community

The idea of community is also important here and given the prevailing con-cern in the UK about the number of young people who are disaffected and disconnected from school, and often family, there is a powerful argument for building community in schools. Sergiovanni (1994) argues that we cannot replace the community missing in the lives of many young people, but we can offer a substitute which may prevent young people seeking an alternative subculture to find a 'sense of belonging'. It is possible to create schools where young people feel that they belong and where they feel that their contribution is valued, and, within a PLC, that would apply equally to staff and parents.

Quality of learning

The purpose of schooling here is not an uncontested area. There are many who would argue it is not the job of schools to build community, but to con-centrate on improving attainment. It is easy to understand why some teachers and school leaders come to hold this view. The clear accountability and improvement agenda in UK schools, outlined in Chapter 1, means that the school's performance, in terms of examination results, is a key driver in determining the activities and outcomes, which are easily measured and highly valued in the organisation. It is therefore a challenge for schools to see beyond this very public accountability, reflected in published league tables, and to consider the quality of learning, rather than the security that comes from being able to prove curriculum coverage. There is then an inevitable focus on the preparation of pupils for testing and less concern with depth of understanding.

It takes considerable courage and a very strong sense of vision and values to stand firm in the face of this agenda, and for teachers to remain focused on the quality of learning – both their own and their pupils'. The arguments about the time required to take an approach other than relentlessly delivering course content, are very real to teachers and they have to be convinced of the benefits of alternative, more learner-centred approaches. This means they need to be ready to enquire into and investigate the learning experiences of their pupils, and be prepared to use the results of their investigations to inform their practice in the classroom and as evidence to others of high-quality learning.

This shift is one that can be accomplished within a PLC, but only if staff and school leaders are willing to go on that journey. There are clearly risks involved in experimenting with new approaches, sharing findings with colleagues and worrying about coverage, and so the levels of trust in the school are critical. Most teachers are keenly aware that what they are required to do to help children pass tests is not necessarily what produces the highest quality learning, but feel there is no alternative. With the right conditions, it may be that teachers could gain the confidence to do things differently in the best interests of the children they teach. One crucial factor in their agency and commitment here will be the values and beliefs they have developed about learning and teaching, based upon their experience. The kind of critical reflection advocated in Chapter 1 is important in developing a professional who is able to make informed choices about these dilemmas outlined above.

Thinking point 11.4

How do these arguments fit with your own developing beliefs about how a school could or should be organised?

What are the challenges in adopting this approach?

There are significant tensions for teachers and school leaders in adopting this more egalitarian and collaborative approach. Schools are historically intensely hierarchical organisations and there are deeply ingrained attitudes towards 'management,' which make it challenging to begin to work in less hierarchical ways. Where distributed leadership is presented as distributed workload, little progress will be made, and understandably so. However when it is construed as distributed power, then it may be possible to convince stakeholders of the importance of their contribution at different levels and the centrality of their collective role in affecting sustainable change.

Another tension relates to the high levels of public accountability associated with academic attainment. This external pressure results in schools being very focused on teaching to ensure continually improving examination results, and works against the creation of conditions where staff feel able to experiment and take risks, so that even if they are persuaded to become actively involved in driving the learning agenda forward, they feel constricted by the need to 'cover the curriculum'. These external influences are not conducive to shared leadership in that they encourage schools to stick to the status quo, even in the face of the need for change.

And for the leaders themselves there are significant tensions. It takes considerable courage to step back from being the 'hero leader' to see leadership in terms of creating opportunities for others to lead. The external agenda mentioned above is a driver for school leaders, as much as it is for teachers, and limits what seems possible in terms of taking risks. The ultimate accountability for what happens in school remains firmly with the head teacher, no matter what the leadership approach taken to decision-making.

So within the current context of schooling, the creation of the necessary conditions for a PLC is essentially still in the gift of the head teacher. Head teachers in the UK are being encouraged to work in ways which promote leadership in others, but just as the historical hierarchies of schools have led to ingrained attitudes towards management, they have also led to some deep-seated views on the part of school leaders. The current climate of increasing and public accountability may explain their concerns about sharing leadership in this way. Many feel that since they are ultimately solely responsible for what happens in a school, there is almost a leap of faith required in terms of willingness to trust that the sum of the expertise and creativity of staff and other stakeholders is greater than the wisdom of one individual. This dilemma is a perennial one for leaders who, in a very hierarchical education system, have to negotiate the difficult terrain between the seductive nature of hero leadership and the push towards collegiality and shared leadership.

Often the challenge is in persuading teachers of the approach. Some may feel they are not being paid enough to make such a contribution to school development, but motivation comes in many forms (McLean, 2003). The drivers for many teachers are not necessarily related to financial rewards, but to children's learning and the job satisfaction of making a difference to children's life chances. Tapping into this very positive force in schools is possible through the building of a PLC, where those skills and attributes are highly valued and utilised to improve the learning experiences of the children who attend those schools.

There is no doubt that the external political agenda, the structure of school career hierarchies and the associated differentials in remuneration are barriers to collective endeavour, but it may be possible to overcome these obstacles by building relationships where people feel their work and their opinions are highly valued and that they make an important contribution to the school.

Summary

This chapter has aimed to define a professional learning community. The key components have been described:

- supportive and shared leadership
- a clear focus on enquiry into the pupil learning experience
- collaborative approaches to learning for teachers and pupils.

A range of arguments have been put forward for this way of working, including the central importance of the place of values in determining the approach to working together in this way, the benefits in terms of building community and, not least, the possible impact on the quality of learning for both teachers and pupils. All of these are seen as essential planks in delivering a more egalitarian and equitable environment for learning which empowers learners and teachers alike to have a say in the decision-making process. The shift in power relations and the emphasis on genuine participation are seen as crucial elements in the model.

Finally, the challenges of dealing with the external political agenda, the unhelpful structure of traditional school career hierarchies and the associated salary differentials are identified. A plea is, however, made for ways of creating the kind of learning environment where pupils and staff are both highly motivated to come to school and learn.

Key questions for reflection and discussion

- How would you describe a professional learning community in your own words?
- What do you consider to be the advantages and disadvantages of this way of working?
- How willing/prepared do you feel to become involved in making decisions in your school?
- What do you see as the challenges/benefits for teachers in seeking honest feedback from pupils? How would you tackle them?
- What benefits/challenges could come from the kind of teacher collaboration being advocated in this chapter?

Further reading

Brookfield, S.D. (1995) *Becoming a Critically Reflective Teacher*. San Francisco, CA: Jossey-Bass. This gives a very clear picture of the ways in which teachers can become more critical in reflecting upon their teaching. Brookfield encourages teachers to look at their practice through a range of lenses to come to an informed professional view. He gives many useful examples of ways in which learners can be involved in giving feedback and teachers can be encouraged to share their learning and practice.

Dufour, R., DuFour, F.R., Eaker, R. and Many, T. (2006) *Learning by Doing: A Handbook for Professional Learning Communities at Work*. Bloomington, IN: Solution Tree. This is a practical guide to action in relation to developing a professional learning community. It answers many of the questions around the what, why and how of the process. It gives guidance, based on evidence and case studies, on putting principles into practice.

Harris, A. and Muijs, D. (2005) *Improving Schools through Teacher Leadership*. Maidenhead: Open University Press. The notion of distributed leadership is outlined and the authors argue for a shift of focus from the head teacher as the main agent of school improvement to the class teacher as a central player. There is a strong emphasis on the place of meaningful professional development for staff and a focus on the creation of the conditions for shared leadership.

Huffman, J.B. and Hipp, K.K. (2003) *Reculturing Schools as Professional Learning Communities*. Lanham, MD: Scarecrow Education. This book addresses the concept of a professional learning community through research and a range of case studies. There is a helpful review of the related literature and schools are provided with a useful tool for self-evaluation in relation to the principles and practice of professional learning communities.

Web resources

National College for School Leadership: http://www.ncsl.org.uk/networked/networked-o-z.cfm

Southwest Educational Development Laboratory: http://www.sedl.org/change/issues/issues61.html

The Effective Professional Communities Project: http://www.eplc.info/

CHAPTER 12

BEING A TEACHER LEADER

Christine Forde

Key ideas explored in this chapter are:

- Leaders and teachers
- Distributed leadership
- Teacher leadership
- Being a teacher leader
- Developing as a teacher leader

This chapter explores a key dimension in the evolving role of the teacher, that of teacher leadership. There is an increased emphasis on the active participation of teachers and other professionals in the ongoing development of a school as a professional learning community to enhance the conditions for effective learning. As part of this development the idea of 'teacher leadership' has come to the fore with an emphasis on the role teachers play in contributing to effective learning in and beyond their classrooms. However, the role that teacher leaders play in school is not without some controversy. In this chapter we will, first, look critically at the contested nature of the term 'teacher leadership' by drawing on some of the theoretical discussions of distributed and teacher leadership. Then we will consider some case studies of teacher leadership to consider what it means to be a teacher leader in the classroom and in the wider school and the skills, understandings and practices that are necessary to enable teachers to take forward leadership roles.

Leaders and teachers

'Leadership' is a slippery term, evidenced by the range of descriptions to be found in the theoretical literature as well as in policy documents describing leadership in schools. Thus we have terms such as 'strategic leadership' (Davies, 2006), 'instructional leadership' (Blasé and Blasé, 1998) even 'servant leadership' (Greenleaf, 1998), with each highlighting a particular dimension within the broad idea of leadership in schools. Davies emphasises the importance of strategic leadership in the setting of overarching aims of a school and the long-term development of the school, and is a form of leadership associated with, though not necessarily exclusive to, headship. Blasé and Blasé's characterisation of 'instructional leadership' underlines the relationship between leadership and learning that is distinctive in education. The idea of 'servant leadership' might seem a contradiction but Greenleaf is deliberately seeking to challenge the idea of leadership as a role played by a single exceptional individual. If we use this idea in school, leaders are there to 'serve' the community of the school by engaging with all concerned and working to meet their needs. There are many other descriptions of leadership in school and the common idea in all of these is that of influencing others to act in certain ways (Gronn, 2002). Leadership is fundamental to learning in schools having been consistently identified as a key factor in ensuring the ongoing effectiveness of a school to provide appropriate learning opportunities for all pupils (Leithwood et al., 2008). Therefore, leadership is about influencing the actions of teachers, support staff and pupils to achieve the common goal of effective learning. This raises the question about who are the leaders in school.

Historically there has been a separation of leadership and teaching. In this context, leadership is seen as a 'top down' function, with those in middle or senior management roles exercising influence over those they managed, that is, non-promoted teachers and support staff. This close scrutiny of the teaching has positioned the teacher as deliverer of a government-sanctioned curriculum, as a technician. In neither of these positions do teachers have a role in contributing to the development of the school. However, studies of school effectiveness and improvement (Leithwood et al., 2008) have highlighted the importance of teachers being involved directly in decisions about teaching and learning, and has opened up possibilities of the role of the teacher within and beyond the classroom. It is from the need to develop greater participation by teachers and other staff in shaping teaching and learning that the idea of 'teacher leadership' has gained support.

Thinking point 12.1

What case would you make for the importance of leadership in schools?

The importance of leadership being exercised across a school, and indeed the opportunities this might afford teachers, is clearly recognised in education. However, we have to be cautious here because while teacher leadership seems an attractive idea and teachers and headteachers alike are urged to develop leadership across a school, we have to recognise that there are a number of issues we need to grapple with. One of the areas of contention is found in defining teacher leadership, and to explore this further we will draw on recent discussions of distributive forms of leadership of which teacher leadership is one form.

Distributed leadership

In 2003 Harris noted that the idea of teacher leadership has emerged as a 'new idea' in education in the UK but has a longer currency especially in North America. Since then policy and thinking in the UK have moved on substantially to endorse this idea of teacher leadership and we have seen a move away from an understanding of leadership as something exercised by individual people with substantial authority to something that can be constructively invested in a range of people in school – teachers, support staff and pupils – to enrich teaching and learning. Teacher leadership has emerged out of a greater appreciation of the importance of distributed leadership in creating a school culture that fosters this involvement: 'leadership is about learning together and constructing meaning and knowledge collectively and collaboratively' (Gronn, 2000: 314).

Gronn's work on leadership provides a searching conceptual analysis of distributed forms of leadership and has been highly influential in both theoretical discussions of leadership as well as educational policy. An unspoken assumption in leadership in a hierarchy is that for there to be leadership there must be followership, in other words if someone leads, someone else must follow. Gronn dismisses this idea of leadership and followership and instead sees leadership as something exercised 'co-jointly' in an organisation in which a number of people act collectively to bring about the desired transformation. As Gronn acknowledges, there are 'typical kinds of collaborative decision-making forums common to most educational settings, such as teams or committees' (2000: 332) but there are other processes we need to recognise and foster. Distributed forms of leadership can be exercised formally and informally through the interactions of staff, one-to-one and in groups, and so the flow of influence moves in different directions: down, up and across the school through which functions, staff and pupils become connected, develop shared understandings and undertake collective actions co-jointly to work towards common goals and thereby enhance the processes of teaching and learning. Gronn's analysis here provides an explanation of distributed leadership but there is still considerable work in developing these forms in practice.

There are a number of issues relating to the establishment of distributive forms of leadership including teacher leadership in schools. Some of these issues are concerned with the organisational structures of schools and some are concerned with attitudes and expectations, particularly how staff perceive the nature of teacher leadership and the roles they might play in school. Schools remain hierarchically organised with greater power and authority resting with those in posts higher in this structure. In these structures distinctions are drawn between 'teachers' and 'leaders', with teachers largely having classroom-focused responsibilities to deliver the curriculum or provide pastoral care and leaders having out-of-class management responsibilities ranging from the coordination of activities to strategic planning and decision-making. The current organisational structures in schools pose a considerable issue in the development of teacher leadership. There are significant pay differentials between teaching and management posts. Even where schools adopt flatter structures and remove layers of management so there are fewer staff in promoted management posts, the perception might be that teachers are forced to take on management responsibilities without the financial rewards and status previously attributed to these tasks. However, this perception arises from the conflation of leadership and management in schools and leadership being constructed as the preview of a few staff rather than being a role for all teachers. There are roles such as chartered teacher or advanced skills teacher which may carry additional payment where leadership activities very much centre around teaching and learning, such as working with and supporting other teachers to develop teaching. However, there need to be opportunities for all teachers as professionals to be able to participate in decision-making and development work to further the school's aims.

Macbeath (2005), using a series of case studies to explore different forms of distributed leadership, found a number of tensions which need to be resolved if distributed leadership is to flourish and these can apply equally to teacher leadership. One of the central issues is the balancing of trust and accountability. Schools are visibly accountable for their activities, particularly the achievement and care of pupils, and there may be significant risks in 'experimenting' with teacher leadership. Though establishing teacher leadership may bring long-term benefits, there may not be the immediate improvements demanded of schools. Schools organised hierarchically have clear lines of accountability internally and externally to ensure external priorities are focused on. As Margaret Martin argues in Chapter 11, for teacher leadership to flourish there has to be a high degree of trust on the part of head teachers, who have to enable teachers to contribute to the development of the school and of teaching and learning while at the same time ensure teachers exercise this leadership towards the agreed goals through which the expectations of parents, governors, local and central government are met.

Harris (2003) and others have found that both attitudinal and structural barriers can be overcome, particularly where there is a concerted effort and a shared view that teacher leadership provides opportunities not available in a top-down management system. In a top-down structure, where all roles are clearly defined by their place in a hierarchy, opportunities for teachers to take on tasks beyond their classroom are severely limited. However, with more flexible structures such as those in professional learning communities, there are opportunities for teachers both individually and collectively to take on a range of roles, such as mentor, project leader, liaison teacher, where they have a leadership function. The critical aspect in all these roles is the focus on pupil learning.

For Frost et al. (2000) we need to consider how teachers can 'make a difference' in their schools. In their study they firmly place teachers at the centre of the school improvement. Although Frost and his colleagues do not specifically examine the notion of teacher leadership, it is very much a model of improvement with teachers working collaboratively beyond the boundaries of their individual classroom:

> They [teachers] act strategically to improve their own practice and tackle issues from classroom to whole school level, leading to more effective student learning. Through strategic action for change informed and energised through inquiry and critical discourse, they recapture a sense of professional excitement and are able individually and collectively, to make a substantial contribution to the school development process. Teachers become 'skilled in change', the prime movers in reshaping their schools for the future. (Frost et al., 2000: 4)

They propose that every teacher should be a change agent and have developed a process called 'reflective action planning' (RAP) though links can be made between whole school and classroom practice.

Thinking point 12.2

What facilitates the development of teacher leadership and what hinders the development of teacher leadership in school?

Teacher leadership in the school

Crowther et al. similarly argue that we need to move the idea of teacher leadership beyond that of the development and sharing of expertise in teaching and learning in the classroom to a construction of teacher leadership as part of institutional-wide development: 'Ultimately teacher leadership, as we intend it, is about action that enhances teaching and learning in a school, that ties school and community together, and that it advances quality of life for a community' (2009: xvii). They also see teacher leadership as a practice reflecting mature forms of democracy which schools must nurture. If we are seeking to develop the citizens of the future, schools should model democratic processes by enabling all in the school community to contribute to decisions that shape their experiences and opportunities. The central purpose of promoting equality and social justice remains at the heart of teacher leadership.

Given the ever increasing demands made by legislation, the explosion of knowledge, parental and wider community expectations, Crowther et al. regard our current understandings of the role of the teacher as misguided. Earlier we looked at the limitations of seeing the role of the teacher situated solely in the classroom. Crowther et al. also question this model and argue that what is needed is a new conception of the teacher which is situated in the school rather than limited to the classroom. Teacher leadership is founded not just on pedagogical expertise but is about using this expertise to contribute to the development of a school and so we need to consider teacher leadership in the light of the purposes of education. Teacher leadership has to be seen as a means of achieving the core moral purpose of education, that is in the betterment of lives individually and collectively. Thus Crowther et al. (2009:10) propose that:

teacher leadership is essentially an ethical stance that is based on views of both a better world and the power of teachers to shape meaning systems. It manifests in new forms of understanding and practice that contribute to school success and to the quality of life of the community in the long term.

Teacher leaders have a crucial role in the development of a school, particularly in efforts to improve the learning experiences of all pupils. There is then the question of what teacher leaders do in school.

Teacher leaders in school

Crowther et al. (2009) identify six elements in a framework which makes the connection between the practice of teacher leaders and the wider school development. Teacher leaders:

- convey convictions about a better world
- facilitate communities of learning
- strive for pedagogical excellence
- confront barriers in the school's culture and structures
- translate ideas into sustainable systems of action
- nurture a culture of success.

One central aspect in Crowther et al.'s discussion of teacher leadership is the development of teaching and learning. For them this has an institutional as well as an individual perspective. Thus there are two aspects to the role of teacher leaders: first, developing their own pedagogic practice and, second, influencing and developing teaching, learning and assessment at a whole-school level. In addition, Crowther et al. include an activist element where, by working with other teachers in community-building, teacher leaders can challenge inequalities and promote access to learning. We discussed earlier the way in which the role of the teacher had become restricted to delivering externally devised programmes. In this idea of teacher leadership, teacher leaders not only lead others for change but create the setting in which fellow teachers become the constructors of change. Thus, teachers set the agenda for change. Now it would be useful to consider how teacher leadership might be exercised in school.

Day and Harris (2002) identify four dimensions where a teacher may take on a leadership role. We will explore each one of these dimensions by considering a short case study of a teacher leader in school.

Dimension 1: in the classroom where a teacher takes forward strategies which contribute to the school's ongoing improvement.

📁 Case study 12.1

Simone has been teaching for four years in a primary school. As part of the school's development plan, a group of teachers have been working on literacy. Simone is piloting the use of 'literature circles' with her class of 10-year-olds. Simone's task is to build up some resources and guidance notes for teachers and to report back to the project team. These resources will form part of the forthcoming staff development day. Simone was initially daunted by the prospect of taking on this role but she feels both her teaching and her confidence in working with other staff have been developed. For her, however, the most important aspect was the effect the literature circle had on the pupils particularly those who had previously been reluctant to read novels.

Dimension 2: with colleagues where teacher leaders work with and support other teachers in taking forward areas for development.

📁 Case study 12.2

A cross-department group has been working on the development priority on cooperative learning which Andrew has been leading. Andrew has provided the group members with some initial material and then set up a number of pupil tasks which would be undertaken in the classroom. Here Andrew arranged for the teachers to be able to observe in each other's classrooms following which the group came together to share their observations and plan further activities. This was a new role for Andrew but taking this on he feels has helped him develop project management skills and to communicate better with his colleagues.

Dimension 3: developing and sharing expertise: where teacher leaders develop expertise often in specific areas and then become a resource for other teachers by sharing this expertise.

> 📁 **Case study 12.3**
>
> Liz has recently completed a course on Moving Image education as part of her Master's degree, which is a new area for the school. Having seen the pupils' work, three other teachers are interested in developing this area. Liz ran an initial workshop for these teachers to introduce them to Moving Image education from which the staff decided to try out a mini-project. Some time out of class was agreed for Liz who was then able to plan and co-teach with the other three teachers. The response from the teachers and the pupils was very positive and this area will now be extended over the school. For Liz this has been a very positive experience, she has enjoyed sharing a new area in which she is really interested.

Dimension 4: building relationships to enhance their own and other teachers' learning and the development of their practice as teachers.

> 📁 **Case study 12.4**
>
> Tim is a highly experienced teacher but has always enjoyed working in the classroom with the pupils. However, recently he has been looking for a new challenge and his head teacher suggested he mentor two newly qualified teachers. He had a number of planned meetings with the teachers as well as lots of informal discussion and observed them in their classrooms and so was able to give them valuable feedback. The two newly qualified teachers have grown as professionals under his guidance. He has been working with them over the year and built good relationships where they exchange ideas and work together on different areas of the curriculum. Tim feels that mentoring the newly qualified teachers has also energised him as a teacher.

These case studies on teacher leaders illustrate some of the different contexts in which teacher leaders work and some of the different activities they undertake. An important consideration is how teachers develop their leadership skills.

> ☁️ **Thinking point 12.3**
>
> What are the qualities and skills of teacher leaders evident in each of these case studies?

Developing as a teacher leader

Frost et al. (2000) in their discussion of teachers taking forward change projects see all teachers making this type of contribution. However, Crowther et al. (2009) do not see teacher leadership as something engaged in by all teachers and it may be something that teachers are involved in for periods of their career. This process of teacher leadership is more transient, with different teachers taking on the role at different points in their career and that may be a source of its strength allowing new ideas, new energies and different groupings of staff to make the important connections to support pupil learning. It seems then that teacher leadership can operate in different ways, in which some teachers adopt a more extensive role in leadership while others collaborate with their colleagues at a more informal level. Macbeath (2005) highlights the importance of head teachers or principals creating the conditions for teacher leadership to flourish. However, it is also important that teachers recognise and take these opportunities. 'Stepping out' of the classroom is now an expectation of teachers, as teachers working collaboratively with other teachers and making a contribution to the school's development is crucial to providing effective learning experiences for pupils.

Summary

In this chapter we have examined the question of teacher leadership and the distinctive characteristics of this role and its contribution to a school. Teachers in classrooms play a fundamental role in motivating children and young people to achieve and they do this using a range of leadership skills to influence the attitudes and actions of learners. Further, teachers in classrooms also develop their expertise in pedagogy and their knowledge of the curriculum area. These two aspects – influencing others and expertise in teaching and learning – are the foundations of being a teacher leader. A critical aspect of being a teacher leader is a willingness and skill in sharing ideas, experiences and practice with fellow teachers. Here trust by other teachers is vital and so, for a teacher to exercise effectively this influence, he or she must be seen as credible and accepted as a leader by other staff. This is partly built on the expertise demonstrated in the classroom and partly by being regarded as someone who is willing to seek opportunities to work with other staff constructively and to support their work. Key areas for development for aspiring teacher leaders are building their confidence, their ability to build positive relationships and to communicate effectively with their colleagues.

Key questions for reflection and discussion

- What do you see as the similarities and differences between being a teacher, a teacher leader and a head teacher?
- Crowther et al. (2009) highlight the importance of values and a clear sense of purpose as core to the role of teacher leader. Do you see this as unique to teacher leaders or should it be a core consideration for all teachers?
- In what ways do the teacher leaders in the case studies achieve the six aspects identified by Crowther et al.?
- What examples of teacher leadership have you observed in school? How have these teacher leaders contributed to the school and to pupil learning?
- How might you go about developing your skills and qualities to take on a teacher leadership role in school?

Further reading

Crowther, F., Ferguson, M. and Hann, L. (2009) *Developing Teacher Leaders: How Teacher Leadership Enhances School Success*. 2nd edn. Thousand Oaks, CA: Corwin Press. Crowther et al. explore the role of teacher leadership in some depth and provide a number of self-evaluation and planning tools to enable teacher leaders to reflect on and plan their development.

Day, C. and Harris, A. (2002) 'Teacher leadership, reflective practice and school improvement', in K. Leithwood and P. Halliger, (eds), *Second International Handbook of Educational Leadership and Administration, Part Two*. Dordrecht: Kluwer Academic. pp. 957–77. In this chapter the authors examine closely how reflection can sustain the development of teacher leaders.

Harris, A. and Muijs, D. (2005) *Improving Schools through Teacher Leadership*. Maidenhead: Open University Press. In this book the authors consider ways in which teacher leadership can be actively fostered in school and what teacher leadership will contribute. A key element is the importance of meaningful development opportunities for teachers.

Murphy, J. (2005) *Connecting Teacher Leadership and School Improvement*. Thousand Oaks, CA: Corwin Press. The author presents a comprehensive review of the literature on teacher leadership and considers the relationship between teacher leadership and the improvement of learning.

Reeves, J. and Fox, A. (eds) (2008) *Practice-based Learning: Developing Excellence in Teaching*. Edinburgh: Dunedin Academic Press. This book looks at the way in which chartered teachers take forward collaborative projects to enhance teaching and learning. The book includes a number of case studies written by chartered teachers.

Web resources

Harrison, C. and Killion, J. (2007) 'Ten roles for teacher leaders' in *Educational Leadership*, 65(1): 74–7: http://www.ascd.org/publications/educational_leadership/sept07/vol65/num01/Ten_Roles_for_Teacher_Leaders.aspx

HMIe (2007) *Leadership for Learning*. Edinburgh: Her Majesty's Inspectors in Education: www.hmie.gov.uk/documents/publication/lflcltc.pdf

National College for Leadership of Schools and Children's Services (2008) *Everyone a Leader*: http://www.nationalcollege.org.uk/docinfo?id=21820&filename=everyone-a-leader.pdf

Teacher Leaders Network (2010) *Teacher Leadership Today*, Centre for Teaching Quality, USA: http://teacherleaders.typepad.com/teacher_leadership_today/

CHAPTER 13

INTERPROFESSIONAL APPROACHES TO PRACTICE

Margaret McCulloch

Key ideas explored in this chapter are:

- The discourse of 'joined-up working'
- Working with other professionals
- Collaboration
- Teachers' professional knowledge and identity

Over the past two decades the discourse of partnership and collaboration has become increasingly evident in all areas of public and professional life. Working together is seen as 'a good thing' and statements of professional standards for teachers and other professionals at all levels include references to the expectation that they will engage in both collegial and inter-professional practice (for example, GTCNI, 2007; GTCS, 2006; GTCW, 2009; TDA, 2007). Earlier chapters in this book examine how the role of the teacher involves working collaboratively with other teachers to support children's learning; working across interprofessional boundaries is another aspect of joint working to be considered. This chapter explores, first, the origins of the discourse of service integration. It then considers the implications for teachers' practice of interprofessional collaboration with others with potentially different perspectives on the purpose and relative value of different aspects of children's services. We return to the issue of identity explored in Chapter 10 and argue that the teacher's personal and professional identity is an important factor in developing and sustaining effective relationships with partners in learning.

The developing discourse of 'joined up working'

Historically teachers have worked as a separate profession with a focus almost exclusively on learning and teaching within the school context. Issues related to welfare, health and well-being, poverty and crime were the concerns of other professions; teachers became involved only intermittently at times of extreme crisis. However, education and social policy, as we have seen in Section 1, have become increasingly aligned and education now sits within a nexus of other social, health and welfare services. Recent educational policies have emphasised the importance of supporting the holistic development of the child or young person, with an emphasis on targeting support. The local authority structural context of 'Children's Services' has brought together, at organisational and delivery level, different services that support children, young people and their families.

However, in order fully to understand the current policy discourse, it is necessary to look briefly at recent political history to identify the key issues of ideology involved.

Market forces in education

Marketisation of the public sector, with the accompanying cultures of audit and performativity, was at the heart of the Conservatives' commitment to reducing what they saw as the inefficiencies of the welfare state when they came to power in 1979. Within education, increasing levels of parental choice and the consequent need for schools to 'sell' themselves to clients, were accompanied by a new public focus on standards and targets which have become an integral part of the public accountability of schools and teachers.

However, these developments in the 1980s had a significant impact on the goal of ensuring equal opportunities for all learners in school. An ideology based on a free-market approach to education involves an implicit acceptance of the inequalities which result from this approach. The acceptance that there would be winners and losers within the education system did not sit easily with the national and international agendas which were developing at the same time in relation to human rights, equality and anti-discrimination, based on equity of provision and opportunity, notably the *Convention on the Rights of the Child* (OHCHR, 1989) and *The Salamanca Statement* (UNESCO, 1994) with its focus on equity in educational provision for children with special educational needs (SEN). By the late 1990s, the tensions between the 'market' approach to allocating scarce resources and concern for groups of vulnerable young people, including those who required additional support in their learning, were clearly evident (Rouse and Florian, 1997).

New Labour and 'social inclusion'

The Labour government came to power in 1997 with a new discourse of 'social inclusion/exclusion' based on concerns for social cohesion and the aspiration to have a society made up of a 'strong and active community of citizens' (Blair, 1997), as opposed to the individualisation agenda pursued by the Conservatives. The Labour government's ongoing reform of the welfare state was framed around the pursuit of social justice, although key elements of new managerialism continued, with goals 'expressed in terms of targets, milestones and performance indicators' (Riddell and Tett, 2001: 2).

Fundamental to the aim of achieving social justice was the concept of 'joined-up government', with expectations of partnership working at all levels of service planning and delivery, and moving towards a client-centred approach. So joined-up working among agencies and departments involved in the lives of children and families, alongside the parents and young people themselves, can be conceptualised as one of the key ways by which the ideological and policy aims of social inclusion and social justice can be achieved.

By implication, the population most in need of support through joined-up working will include the most vulnerable families and young people in society and the tension noted earlier between attainment and inclusion remains, since even under Labour governance, interprofessional working remained fundamentally linked to concepts of raising attainment and 'maximising potential' and to 'the improvement agenda'. While the discourse of 'failing schools' may have receded, the replacement notion of 'school improvement' remains and may be in danger of overshadowing the goals of integrating children's services, unless achievement of these goals is itself seen as an indicator of a school's success (McConkey, 2009).

> **Thinking point 13.1**
>
> - What are some of the tensions in linking strategies to support the wider needs of children and young people and the demand for high attainment?
> - How might schools work to reconcile these issues?

Service integration

The move to service integration is evident in each education system in the UK. The Children Act 2004 led to the creation of a children's services department within local authorities in England under a single Director of Children's Services and in Wales a Lead Director for Children and Young People's Services. In England, changes arising from the publication of *Every Child Matters* (DfES, 2004a,), which established Children's Trusts, and the subsequent report *The Children's Plan* (DCSF, 2007) which extended the range of services working together, have led to schools being seen as the central point for accessing other services such as health, social care and support for parents, with areas of youth justice and mental health being added to the services to be delivered in an integrated way. A similar approach is demonstrated in the Welsh initiative *Children and Young People: Rights to Action* (WAG, 2004) and the subsequent formation of 'Young People's Partnerships' which are focused on improving facilities, information and opportunities for young people in a 'joined-up' way.

The holistic development of children and young people is central to this approach: thus the focus of these services is to collaborate in service provision within children and young people's own contexts, working with parents, families and communities in ensuring that needs, whether health, welfare, justice or educational, are met.

Planning for outcomes

A key element in policy development across the UK is that of joint planning for outcomes for young people both collectively and individually (for example, DCSF, 2007; OFMDFM, 2006; SE, 2001a; WAG, 2004). Different departments within children's services, including culture and leisure services, are required collaboratively to produce children's service plans at a local level (SE, 2001b). At an individual level, policies such as *Getting It Right for Every Child* (SE, 2007) recommend that shared plans should be established for

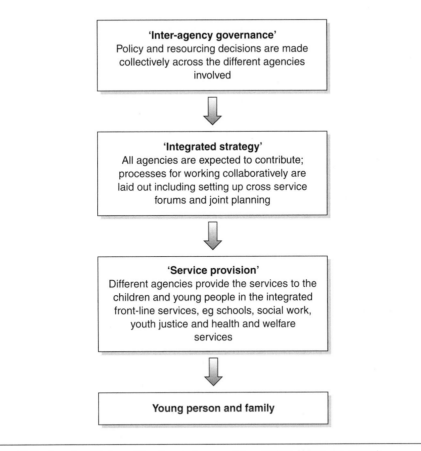

Figure 13.1   Levels of integration in service provision (DfES, 2004; SE, 2007)

young people with whom more than one agency is involved, particularly when a child or young person is at significant risk or presents a significant risk to others.

The 'joined-up' approach, which conceptualises children and young people at the centre of comprehensive, holistic support through integration at all levels of service provision, is illustrated in Figure 13.1.

The role of the teacher

Teachers must be aware that decisions about children's education are likely increasingly to be taken jointly with other professionals, including social workers, health workers and those involved with the youth justice system. In some cases, the child's learning may be the focus; in others, his or her life outside school may be the driver for the joint planning. This necessitates not only an understanding of the different perspectives on children's lives held by other childcare professionals, but also a much clearer awareness of the teacher's own professional knowledge about how learning works and of his or her role in emerging partnerships. Teachers must now conceptualise themselves as professionals working within an integrated services framework.

☁ Thinking point 13.2

- What will it mean for me to be one professional of many who may be part of a child's life?
- For which elements of the child's world do I think I have a core responsibility?

Working with other professionals

Structural contexts for joint working

In all areas of the United Kingdom, programmes have been established which reconceptualise schools as bases for hosting community resources with integration of the services being provided as a core element of the structures. Programmes established early in the first term of the Labour government have been subsumed into the new, more integrated structures demanded by the reports mentioned earlier. In England, the experiences and evaluations of the Sure Start programme, which established around 250 local programmes reaching 150,000 young children living in the most disadvantaged areas, are being used as the basis for the current development of children's centres across the country. Education, social care and health staff from both statutory and voluntary sectors worked together with parents towards improving health and the ability to learn, while strengthening families and community. Evaluations suggested that some areas dealt more effectively than others with those who were most in need of support; good practice guidelines were established for the children's centres which have followed (DfES, 2006a). Key factors identified for success were outreach and home visiting, underlining the importance of establishing and maintaining contact with families.

In Scotland, New Community Schools (NCS) were set up in the early days of Labour's first term in government. Their remit was to focus on the needs of all pupils in the school, engage with families and the wider community and provide all aspects of school education, health services and social work input with integrated management and delivery of services. Multi-disciplinary training and staff development were seen to be important. Effective interagency working was expected to result in improved levels of attainment (Scottish Office, 1998).

This philosophy has become the basis for the development of 'extended schools' in Northern Ireland and England and of 'community focused schools' in Wales.

Early evaluations of impact on attainment showed mixed results, but high-lighted that while co-location of services in the school was helpful in establish-ing formal and informal interprofessional relationships and for increasing accessibility of services to pupils and families, one of the most difficult prob-lems that NCS faced was joint working. A range of barriers was identified, including structural issues of different working hours and holiday arrange-ments, cultural issues such as levels of formality and dress codes, and profes-sional issues, for example, of confidentiality (Sammons et al., 2002). We return to these issues below.

Thinking point 13.3

- How might locating community services in schools impact on the perspectives of other professionals on collaborative working?

Practical contexts for joint working

Although the drivers noted above have given interprofessional working a new emphasis over the past decade, there is a long history in schools of 'working together' to support the learning of children who require additional support. Effective educational inclusion requires all those involved with the child/young person to work together towards shared outcomes.

To address the requirements of some pupils, collaboration at school/education authority level is sufficient. Policies regarding joint planning and delivery of services for children requiring different levels of support are well established through legislation relating to special educational needs (now known as addi-tional support for learning needs in Scotland). Some children, however, may require support from professionals from beyond education services, or may be involved with other professionals in their lives outside school without edu-cation services being aware of this, and it is at this point that ongoing develop-ments in 'joined-up working' should enhance effective collaboration.

In an 'extended school', access to certain other professionals may be more easily arranged. One of the key issues for authorities moving to develop more integrated services has been how to allocate scarce resources equitably. This may necessitate restructuring of traditional patterns of deployment to take account of the changing proportions of children in special and mainstream provision who may require access to health and other professionals.

At national level, account has been taken of the requirements for support for some particular groups of children and young people, and documents based on good practice are available to help staff, which suggest ways in which collaborative relationships can be developed with professionals and parents; for example, for pupils from gypsy/traveller families (DfES, 2006b; HMIe, 2005); for looked after children (DfES, 2007; HMIe, 2009a); for children arriving from overseas (HMIe, 2009b). In some cases support materials have been produced through interprofessional working; for instance in relation to supporting pupils with autism (DfES, 2004b).

With whom might a teacher collaborate?

Figure 13.2 suggests some of the other professionals and paraprofessionals who may be involved in the life and thus in the learning of a pupil and with whom it may be appropriate for a teacher to collaborate. Clearly this list is not exhaustive.

While teachers are aware that all aspects of a child's life will impact on his or her ability to learn, they must also recognise that in any collaborative situation with other professionals they have a particular area of responsibility in relation to assessment of and planning for the child's educational achievement. In the next section we consider the process of collaboration and the teacher's role in this.

Thinking point 13.4

- In what ways might professionals working with children within other public services have a different perspective on education from teachers?

Collaboration

While the principle of 'joined-up working', particularly in relation to children and families, may seem both to professionals and non-professionals to be sensible and, indeed, obvious, notions of 'partnership' and 'collaboration' should not be thought of as unproblematic, particularly when these relationships involve issues of power, culture and identity.

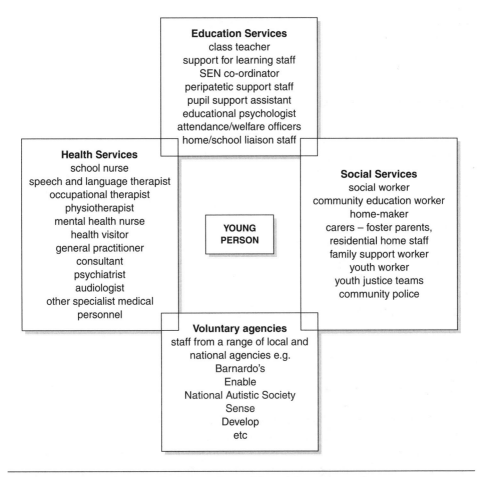

Figure 13.2   Some of the staff who may be working with young people

The terminology of co-working

McCartney (2009: 26) presents a useful summary of some of the types of co-working which have been identified as taking place among professionals. In some cases, targets are agreed separately and activities are delivered by professionals working separately. These models could be described as 'multi disciplinary' or 'consultancy'. In other situations, targets are agreed jointly and activities are carried out, either by professionals working separately (inter-disciplinary) or together (transdisciplinary, or cooperation). While it is generally assumed that joint planning and delivery of support would be preferable, different models may be successful depending on the context. Although there is a strong sense in professional literature that closer working relationships among staff are desirable, McCartney (2009: 27) suggests that this is more to do with professional satisfaction than impact on pupil learning. Nevertheless, it could be presumed that increased professional satisfaction would be likely to encourage individuals to engage in joint working.

Collaboration: functional or effective

Head (2003) suggests that there are functional elements of collaboration, including, for example, coordinating, consulting, communicating and cooperating. However, he argues that effective, deep collaboration takes place when individuals within the group recognise that they are developing a collective knowledge of the work which they are doing which is different from and greater than their existing personal knowledge. Learning from colleagues, whether within the same profession or from another background, is a powerful way of both affirming and extending one's own professional knowledge and recognising other perspectives on issues such as child development, policy and values.

The following case studies describe two different collaborative situations involving teachers.

Case study 13.1

As deputy head responsible for Year 9 in a comprehensive school in an area of socio-economic deprivation, Alison was concerned about six boys who were developing a pattern of regular exclusions, and who were coming to the attention of the community police officer. Following discussions at the school's Joint Assessment Team meeting, attended by education, health and social work staff, a small team was established: Alison, as class teacher of the boys in one curricular area, Carol, a member of the local peripatetic support for learning team, and Andy, a social worker from the community development team. The three planned a range of strategies and approaches involving both individual and team working with the pupils. Carol taught collaboratively with Alison in her class twice a week, and accompanied the boys once a week to the community centre where Andy led sessions with them on solution-focused approaches to dealing with challenging situations in school. Alison took part in these sessions occasionally. Carol and Andy visited the boys' homes and encouraged parents to sign the learning agreement established with the boys. Carol also saw the boys once a week in school, when specific school issues could be addressed as they arose, and Andy came to these sessions when possible. The three met weekly, after school hours, to review progress and to plan responsively. Over the 12-week intervention, the number of exclusions was significantly reduced.

Case study 13.2

Laura's Year 5 class included a pupil, Sean, with significant speech and communi-cation difficulties. Although referred for speech and language therapy (SLT) at the local health centre, he had attended few appointments and his increasing frustra-tion arising from his inability to communicate effectively with peers and adults was leading to outbursts in the classroom. Arrangements were made through the edu-cational psychologist for a speech and language therapist, Jackie, to come to the school once a week to work with Sean there. Jackie assessed Sean and drew up an eight-week plan, then worked with him individually in the medical room once a week. At the end of the initial input Jackie met with Laura to discuss Sean's progress. Jackie gave Laura some suggestions of how she could back up the SLT sessions in class. The input continued for a number of months until Jackie was sure that Sean had made as much progress with them as he could. Although Laura remained concerned that Sean still had noticeable difficulties with his speech, she understood from discussions with Jackie that SLT resources have to be prioritised.

These two examples illustrate different 'levels' of collaboration.

Thinking point 13.5

- What interprofessional issues might have had to be dealt with in order to ensure the most effective support for the young people concerned?
- In what ways were professionals able to share different perspectives on young people's learning?

Teachers' professional knowledge and identity

How teachers respond to collaborative opportunities with colleagues from other professions depends to a large extent on their own perceptions of their role and responsibilities as teachers. These are strongly related to their own personal and professional identities and to their confidence in their professional knowledge.

One of the key features of a 'profession', in addition to the skills and values which are embodied in codes and standards of practice, is the idea of a spe-cific body of knowledge which is possessed by that professional group. In the case of teachers, this would include knowledge of both subject content and pedagogy. We would argue, however, that teachers often find it problematic to recognise and articulate the body of knowledge which they possess; some teachers may identify themselves with a particular body of disciplinary knowledge, but the subject of 'education' may sometimes be reduced to a superficial competence view of practice. Placed in a room with other professionals who, they perceive, have acquired a body of knowledge in the medical, social work or youth justice field, teachers may not immediately position themselves as 'experts' in education, particularly when they recognise that the others all have personal experience of schooling which they may feel gives them some insight into the field of education in addition to their particular area of professional expertise. For collaborative working to be successful, it is crucial that all members of the group recognise each other's areas of professional knowledge and draw on these to plan effectively for the young person involved. Thus a significant part of professional identity development for teachers must be the establishment of a clear sense of the professional knowledge that they bring to interprofessional working.

So while colleagues from the health professions will have in-depth knowledge of, for example, the physical and emotional issues relating to a speech and language difficulty, teachers should also be aware of their own professional knowledge of language development, of social and emotional development and how to support this through classroom organisation and strategies, and of pedagogical issues relating to the social and cultural structures which affect learning. This knowledge is as important when planning support as the speech and language therapist's specialist knowledge. Similarly, when working with a vulnerable child, the teacher's knowledge of what are appropriately challenging targets for educational achievement and how to support the child to reach these in the classroom environment, and the social worker's knowledge of the support which is available and appropriate to get the child to school in the first place, are equally important.

On the other hand, it is also vital that the teacher's clear sense of professional identity must be balanced with an awareness of the different perspectives and cultures of other professionals. As noted earlier in the chapter, the major barriers to effective interprofessional working relate to competing priorities among professionals, linked sometimes to differing fundamental ideologies which underpin practice. Mutual respect for the insights that each brings to the context of the young person is crucial for effective interprofessional working.

Thinking point 13.6

- How would I articulate my understanding of my 'professional body of knowledge' as a teacher?
- How might I find out more about the perspectives of colleagues from other professional backgrounds?

If the purpose of working together with other professionals is to enhance the life chances of the child at the centre of the process, then a key responsibility of each individual must be to ensure that the process itself does not become more important than the outcome.

Summary

This chapter has outlined some of the issues involved in inter-professional working in children's services. It considers the ideology of social inclusion which underpins the most recent policy developments establishing 'service integration' as a key aim for local authorities. However, it also suggests that the competing priority of 'school improvement' might reduce the focus on integrating services.

Some of the specific policies establishing contexts for 'joined-up working' and the implications for teachers have been discussed. Structural contexts, such as 'extended schools' and 'new community schools' have been noted, and some of the professionals with whom teachers are likely to be working are identified.

A range of models of collaborative working has been identified and it was suggested that effective collaboration is likely to occur when members of a team actively learn from each other and improve their practice during the process of joint working.

Finally, it is suggested that, in order to work effectively as part of an inter-professional team, teachers must have a clear sense of their professional identity and of the professional knowledge which they bring to any collaborative process, while recognising the different perspectives and expertise of colleagues, and remembering that the focus must always be the best interests of the young person involved.

 Key questions for reflection and discussion

- How would you describe the key advantages for children/young people of interprofessional working?
- Can you suggest ways in which teachers and other professionals could be supported in developing interprofessional practice?
- How might the barriers to interprofessional working identified by Sammons et al. (2002) be addressed?
- Think of the models of collaborative working mentioned above. When might functional collaboration be appropriate?
- How would you articulate your values and beliefs about education to a colleague from a different professional background?

Further reading

Cheminais, R. (2009) *Effective Multi-Agency Partnerships: Putting Every Child Matters into Practice*. London: Sage. This is a helpful resource which, although aimed at those responsible for coordinating multi-agency partnership working, contains useful information about best practice in and evaluation of team working.

Flores, M.A. and Day, C. (2006) 'Contexts which shape and reshape new teachers' identities: a multi-perspective study', *Teaching and Teacher Education*, 22: 219–32. This article reports the findings of a two-year study into the development of new teachers' professional identities and the impact of these on practice.

Forbes J. and Watson C. (eds) (2009) *Service Integration in Schools: Research and Policy Discourses, Practices and Future Prospects*. Rotterdam: Sense Publishers. This is a collection of papers relating to policy and practice in children's service integration with a particular focus on implications for education in different areas of the UK.

Sachs, J. (2005) *The Activist Teaching Profession*. Buckingham: Open University Press. This is a book which challenges teachers to reclaim professionalism and to consider professional identity as a complex concept which develops as teachers make sense of the social and political contexts in which they work.

Web resources

Department for Children, Schools and Families, *Every Child Matters*: http://www.dcsf.gov.uk/everychildmatters/

Scottish Government, *Getting It Right for Every Child*: http://www.scotland.gov.uk/Topics/People/Young-People/childrensservices/girfec

Scottish Government, *Exploring the Evidence Base for Integrated Children's Services*: http://www.scotland.gov.uk/Publications/2006/01/24120649/0

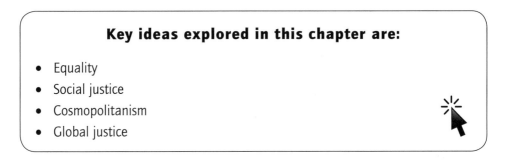

CHAPTER 14

CONCLUSION – THE FUTURE OF EDUCATION

Penny Enslin

Key ideas explored in this chapter are:

- Equality
- Social justice
- Cosmopolitanism
- Global justice

An assumption underlying the chapters in this book on contemporary issues in learning and teaching has been that education's fundamental purpose is to promote social justice, which David Miller describes as being roughly about 'how the good and bad things in life should be distributed among members of a human society' (Miller, 1999: 1). We have also suggested that this distributive goal should be pursued in a range of interrelated spheres: the classroom, the school, local community, national educational systems and in the wider global context. So, for example, in Chapter 2 Doherty emphasises how questions about *who* gets *what* in education are contested at all levels of the policy process and argues that policy should address the burdens of disadvantage among young people. Those defending the principle of equality in education claim that the 'who' refers to all members of a society and answering the 'what' question in a democracy should lead us to a principle of equal provision so that all benefit from education and can enjoy the social goods that follow from it, including fulfilling work and leisure as well as a say in how their society is run. We will return later to the question of how broadly we should define the who and the what.

Even fairly young children have a strong sense of justice, that it is fair for all to enjoy their share of whatever goods are in question, from access to toys, to even-handed treatment by their teachers. In a wider context, most of us share the intuition that a good society is one in which all citizens have fair access to goods and facilities, including education and jobs. Yet the report of the National Equality Panel (2010: 11) concludes that 'Britain is an unequal country, more so than many other countries and more so than a generation ago', showing an overall picture of considerable differences in the distribution of advantages and disadvantages and a decline in the position of young people in the labour market. For some, the report observes, the extent of the inequalities that characterise British society, for example, in educational outcomes and in incomes, is so great that it threatens social cohesion.

How does the idea of equality relate to that of social justice? For Brian Barry (2005: 10), 'Social justice is about the treatment of inequalities of all kinds'. Barry locates education at the heart of what needs to be done to counter social injustice:

> The first demand of social justice is to change the environment in which children are born and grow up so as to make them as equal as possible, and this includes (though it is by no means confined to) approximate material equality among families. The second demand – which is more pressing the further society fails to meet the first demand – is that the entire system of social intervention, starting as early as is feasible, should be devoted to compensating as far as possible, for environmental disadvantages. (2005: 58)

Clearly, education is one of many factors that both reflect and can contribute to inequality and hence to social injustice, although wider inequalities cannot be blamed on the education system alone, nor can the education system be expected to correct them single-handedly. But the authors of this collection share the conviction that there is much that teachers and schools can do to promote equality and hence foster greater social justice, whether in their attention to the purposes of education and so an understanding of educational policy (Section 1), having an understanding of what it means to be a teacher in the twenty-first century, especially in one's knowledge about learning (Section 2), or the professional context and evolving practice of teachers (Section 3).

As we now draw together the themes of this book, the central challenge for the future of education is how to promote education for social justice in spite of the prevailing influence of neoliberal policy's imperative to produce skilled workers for a competitive global economy, which has encouraged managerialist practices and the marketisation of education. We begin by exploring the idea of social justice and how it relates to equality, considering especially John Rawls's landmark approach to thinking about justice and its implications for education. Turning then to the idea that globalisation requires a cosmopolitan approach to education, we consider the meaning of cosmopolitanism and the demands and opportunities it offers to teachers and schools. Finally, we ask what justice in education might require if examined beyond the big picture of inequalities in Britain to the even bigger global frame beyond the nation state that applies the principle of inclusion to all of humanity in a cosmopolitan conception of justice.

Thinking about justice and social justice

One common, more everyday view of justice is that it is about making and applying laws, including punishing those who disobey them. But in this book we focus on 'justice' as a wider feature of societies that looks beyond law enforcement to the principles that underpin the ways in which they treat their citizens in general. As we will see, theorists writing about social justice have different approaches to explaining what they mean by this complex concept and for our purposes here we will assume that 'justice' and 'social justice' can be treated as largely interchangeable. David Miller's suggestion (2007: 12) that when we talk about social justice we are concerned with the distribution of 'rights, opportunities, and resources among the members of large societies', with complex institutions capable of regulating and delivering these goods, can be fruitfully linked to examples discussed in earlier chapters in our book's treatment of contemporary issues in learning and teaching. For example, in Chapter 5 Head's discussion of inclusion points to the roots of 'inclusion' as lying in the principle that all children have the *right* to be educated alongside their peers, and Chapter 9 notes that article 26 of the United Nations Declaration of Human Rights recognises that 'Everyone has the right to education'.

Recognition of equal *rights* to education has implications for our understanding of *opportunities* in education. A social justice perspective, as against one that sees the purpose of education as the fostering of a competitive economy, will be sensitive to the need to allocate *resources* including educational effort differentially if necessary to ensure fair educational opportunities for all. This could preclude, say, allowing class inequalities to be reproduced from generation to generation by permitting 'choice' in selection of their children's schools to wealthier parents. Similarly, in Chapter 9 Stack and Sutherland's discussion of gifted and talented pupils shows the complexity of deciding how to make a fair allocation of educational resources and the dangers of crude assumptions about whose needs are most deserving. Social justice requires careful reflection on how to match provision to ability alongside other competing imperatives. Taking inclusion seriously may require differential allocation of resources, for example, for complementary pedagogies. The pursuit of social justice does not demand that we address inequalities by treating all pupils in the same way.

Different theorists have taken their own approaches to addressing the question: what is justice? The most famous of these is put forward by John Rawls (1971) in a 'thought experiment' in his definitive book *A Theory of Justice*.

John Rawls invited us to imagine that a group of citizens who represent the members of a democratic society meet behind a 'veil of ignorance' to consider what principles of justice should underpin a fair allocation of basic rights and advantages. Behind this imaginary veil of ignorance, none of the participants knows who they are or the identities of those they represent, that is their abilities, beliefs, gender, ethnicity or religion. As a result, they would need to ensure that the principles of justice they devised together would not favour a particular group, such as men, whites, or the most wealthy.

Thinking point 14.1

Imagine that you are one of those participating in Rawls's thought experiment. You do not know who you would be in the society whose basic institutions and principles you are negotiating; you could be rich or poor, male or female, back or white. What principles of justice would you propose if you were one of the participants in Rawls's thought experiment; in other words, what would we need to agree to in order to ensure that we live in a fair society?

Rawls himself went on to propose two principles of justice as fairness.

The first principle, which is called the *liberty principle*, provides for a set of basic liberties for all citizens, such as freedom of conscience and freedom of speech.

The second principle is called the *difference principle*, which allows that there could be some inequalities, but they would have to be arranged so that they would benefit the least well-off members of society. For example, a doctor might earn more money than a factory worker, because she has spent more years studying to qualify and, if nobody did so, we would all suffer because there would be no doctors sufficiently well qualified to treat the rest of us when we are ill.

Applying these principles to education, fair opportunity for Rawls requires that to ensure equality of opportunity we ought to pay more attention to those who are 'born into the less favourable social positions' and to those whose 'native assets' (that is, those capacities they bring to their educational experience) are fewer (Rawls, 1971: 100). Applying the difference principle to the allocation of resources in education would need to be done in a way that improves the long-term prospects and opportunities of those most disadvantaged (1971: 101). Significantly, given our stance in favour of a broad set of educational goals, Rawls adds that education also has the benefit of enriching citizens' lives. In his theory of justice the value of education lies not merely in its economic or even in its social welfare benefits. 'Equally if not more important is the role of education in enabling a person to enjoy the culture of his society and to take part in its affairs, and in this way to provide for each individual a secure sense of his own worth' (Rawls, 1971: 101).

Although Rawls's approach has been very influential, it has also been strongly criticised. For example, because of their emphasis on seeing human beings as connected with others rather than as individuals acting in their own interests, feminists have objected to the very idea in Rawls's thought experiment of individuals with no attachments being able to negotiate principles of justice without reference to a social context. A prominent feminist theorist, Iris Marion Young (1990), criticised what she saw as a tendency to interpret justice in a way that overemphasises the distribution of resources, including education. Young preferred in her approach to justice to emphasise social relations like the exercise of power, as well as problems of institutionalised domination and oppression. In her preferred approach to justice, Young shares with others the opinion that issues like cultural oppression should be included in our concerns about justice. So for some, recognition has become as important a matter of justice as redistribution of educational resources. One can see how such an understanding of justice in education would approach the what and the who of social justice by emphasising the population movements that are a feature of globalisation, and so that multiculturalism must receive special attention in schools with ethically and religiously diverse pupil populations. Yet having acknowledged this, we should remind ourselves of the report of the National Equality Panel's (2010) warning that social cohesion can be threatened by extremes of poverty as well as by cultural oppression.

Cosmopolitanism and education

Until the late twentieth century, theories of justice tended to focus only on issues of justice in the distribution of goods like education within individual societies. So, for example, John Rawls made it clear that his theory was supposed to be about justice in a liberal democracy like the USA (though he did write a book about relations between states – Rawls, 1999). In a well-known article, Martha Nussbaum (1996) revived the ancient Greek ideal of cosmopolitanism: the idea that one's first allegiance is not to fellow members of a nation state, but to 'the worldwide community of human beings' (1996: 4). She has a strong educational interest in defending cosmopolitanism, arguing that it is not enough for pupils and students to learn only about the country of which they are citizens, for two reasons: first, that they should respect the human rights of citizens of other countries as well as their own; and secondly that as well as needing to learn about their own country students need to learn about the history and current situations of the rest of the world.

Emphasising that cosmopolitanism does not require that being a citizen of the world means giving up local identities and affiliations, Nussbaum (1996: 11–14) suggests several features of cosmopolitan education that are relevant to our purposes:

1. By studying other countries cosmopolitan education enables us to look at ourselves differently, through the eyes of others, and so to learn more about ourselves.
2. Cosmopolitan education will better enable us to solve problems like environmental degradation by fostering international cooperation, persuading children that our nation shares its future with others, with whom we need to cooperate if the planet is to continue to support human life.
3. Cosmopolitan education encourages children to recognise their obligations to citizens in the rest of the world, especially to developing countries with much lower standards of living than their own.

☁ Thinking point 14.2

Consider the Stoic idea, which Nussbaum discusses (1996: 9), of thinking of one's self as located within a set of widening concentric circles. Around the first circle placing you at the centre would usually be: immediate family, extended family (or friends?), neighbourhood, city, nation and other possible affiliations like church, ethnic group or fellow professionals, with humanity as a whole the largest, outside circle.

- How would you draw the circles of affiliation that define your identity?
- Do you agree with the cosmopolitan idea that while the citizen of the world is not expected to give up her local affiliations she should try to make all human beings part of her community of attention and concern?
- How do you think your pupils might draw such circles of affiliation around themselves?

Nussbaum's account of education for cosmopolitan citizenship, in which we are encouraged to see all human beings as belonging to a common community of concern, engaging in dialogue about shared problems, is one of the new directions our thinking about the future of education in a globalised world might take our thinking and actions as teachers in the twenty-first century. In a later book Nussbaum (1997) adds to the features of cosmopolitan education a fourth capacity by which education can enable us to 'recognize the worth of human life wherever it occurs and see ourselves as bound by common human abilities and problems to people who lie at a great distance from us' (1997: 9): the ability to exercise the 'narrative imagination', to imagine what it might be like to find oneself in a situation experienced by others whose circumstances are very different.

Cosmopolitan teaching, schools and curricula could take education in quite different directions from current preoccupations with preparation for work in a national economy directed at the competitiveness of a nation state pitted against others in a global contest for wealth, in which the power of large transnational corporations is often greater than the governments of smaller and poorer countries. Recent theories of cosmopolitanism challenge our thinking about justice in education in an international context (we invite you to explore possibilities for cosmopolitan education below). But there are further – perhaps more radical – implications of a cosmopolitan vision for an education of the future, to which we now turn.

From social justice to cosmopolitan justice?

We have argued that social justice, as the central aim of education, is about a complex set of questions to do with ensuring that the right to education is acknowledged in the ways in which educational opportunities are provided, largely through the distribution of resources, while noting that recognition of cultural factors is also significant. So far we have confined our focus to *who* gets *what* in a single country like the United Kingdom. But this does not yet take into account the full implications of globalisation which, some observers have argued, requires that we redraw traditionally assumed boundaries of justice. As the effects of time and space on human lives have been shifted by globalisation – through easier and faster travel as well as the proliferation of information and communication technologies and the rapid movement of people, ideas and commodities – the idea that nation states are separate and independent political and social communities is brought into question. Scheuerman (2006), for example, argues that globalisation has far-reaching implications for our most basic commitments, like justice and democracy, which we can no longer pursue in a meaningful way if we confine our understanding of them to the domestic, national sphere. If the cosmopolitanism in education that we have described is appropriate to a globalised world, does this not imply that the *who* applies to all people, internationally? As we now consider the idea of cosmopolitan justice, we will see that this controversial idea could have radical implications for our roles, identities and resources as educators.

Some argue that if duties of justice are owed to all those with whom we are associated (Moellendorf, 2002: 32) and global trade as well as the associations created by travel and international sport connect us with distant others, then duties of justice can no longer be confined to others within the borders of single nation states. Reading the work of Thomas Pogge (1989), for example, suggests that our duties of justice require that we assist not only those among our fellow nationals who suffer the consequences of poverty but also those in much poorer countries than the UK, which is one of the world's richest countries, notwithstanding its own growing domestic inequalities. Seen in this light, the neoliberal goals of education policy that regard international competitiveness as a national priority become a pressing problem of global justice. If we are committed to justice for all of humanity, is it not unjust that poorer countries are able to allocate far fewer resources per child to schooling than the UK does? This inequality in turn makes the economies of developing countries less competitive because their citizens have fewer opportunities to develop the skills required to compete with the world's most developed economies. It should, however, be noted that a theorist of social justice like Miller (2008) rejects the suggestion that global justice could be interpreted as social justice on a global scale. While acknowledging that standards of living (and, we would add, of education) vary enormously between developed Western countries and many in Africa, Asia and Latin America, Miller emphasises the importance of national communities living by their own beliefs and rules, taking responsibility for their own destinies.

Thinking point 14.3

- Should we understand social justice in education to be solely about the distribution of education in individual countries like the UK or should we interpret it as a global issue requiring international distribution of access to education?

- Try Rawls's thought experiment by applying it to an imaginary situation in which representatives of rich and poor countries meet to decide on the allocation of educational rights, opportunities and resources in a just global educational system. How would you approach such an imaginary situation if you were from, say, the USA or from Haiti?

Summary

Social justice is not only taken to be the central aim of education in this collection's exploration of contemporary issues in learning and teaching. It is also fundamental to the pursuit of a good society, especially in the face of growing inequalities in British society, and in contrast to the prevailing neoliberal imperatives that drive the provision of schooling.

After considering what is meant by social justice in education in relation to rights, opportunities and resources, we have noted John Rawls's approach to justice and how his principles of justice can be applied in education. His difference principle requires that resources be allocated so as to improve the opportunities of the least advantaged. And education is also crucially for the enrichment of human lives.

After noting Nussbaum's account of cosmopolitanism and its educational implications, we widened our focus to consider globalisation and the controversial idea of social justice as global justice, concluding by posing the question of whether justice in education demands the equal distribution of educational resources across national boundaries, on a global scale.

Key questions for reflection and discussion

- What forms of inequality have you observed in your own practice as a teacher and what steps would be required to achieve social justice by addressing them?
- How might your practice as a teacher reflect Nussbaum's ideas for cosmopolitan education?
- How might we reconcile the perceived need to educate for a globally competitive economy with demands for equalising educational opportunities across the globe?

Further reading

Barry, B. (2005) *Why Social Justice Matters*. Cambridge: Polity Press. In this book-length treatment of social justice, Barry develops a critique of the kind of market capitalism that underpins neoliberal policies in education. Setting out to put people ahead of profit, Barry attacks economic inequality and defends policies that promote social justice, including education and the global sphere in his focus.

Enslin, P. and Hedge, N. (2010) 'A good global neighbour: Scotland, Malawi and global citizenship', *Citizenship Teaching and Learning*. Special issue: 6(1): 91–105. Taking a cosmopolitan position, the authors develop a critical but sympathetic account of how globalisation's consequences are addressed in the idea of Scotland as a good global neighbour to Malawi and explore implications for citizenship education.

Nussbaum, M. (1996) 'Patriotism and cosmopolitanism', in J. Cohen (ed.), *For Love of Country: Debating the Limits of Patriotism*. Boston, MA: Beacon Press. Nussbaum's passionate and very readable defence of cosmopolitanism provoked a debate involving critical responses from a wide range of positions, published as short essays in this accessible collection.

Peters, M., Britton, A. and Blee, H. (2008) *Global Citizenship Education: Philosophy, Theory and Pedagogy*. Rotterdam: Sense Publishers. A collection whose authors take varying critical positions that explore the consequences of globalisation, this future-oriented book includes theoretical chapters on the meaning of concepts like cosmopolitanism and global citizenship, as well as some on pedagogy and professional practice.

Web resource

Education for All, UNESCO: http://www.unesco.org/education/efa/ed_for_all/

GLOSSARY

Assessment for Learning Assessment for learning focuses on the gap between where a learner is in their learning, and where they need to be – the desired goal. This can be achieved through processes such as sharing criteria with learners, effective questioning and feedback.

Attachment A bond between a child and a significant other which allows the child to learn the fundamental principles which underlie the human ability to form relationships.

Autonomy The ability of a professional to make decisions and take actions based on his or her expertise and experience.

Child Centred Approaches A set of approaches to education that start with the needs of the child when forming curriculum and pedagogy. These approaches are based on understandings about the ways in which children 'naturally' learn.

Coaching A process similar to mentoring but one that tends to have a more specific skills-based focus.

Collaborative learning An umbrella term describing a variety of approaches that involve students and teachers working together. In collaborative learning environments students engage in a common task in which each individual depends on and is accountable to each other. The students' task is both to create a product and to participate in a process that will help develop them as learners.

Communities of Practice Where staff in schools and other organisations work together to explore and develop their practice both individually and collectively.

Cosmopolitanism The view that all human beings belong to one worldwide community.

Distributed Leadership   An approach to leadership which actively supports the development of leadership in all members of a school community including teachers, support staff and pupils.

Entity theory of intelligence   Intelligence is depicted as an entity within us and is something we cannot change.

Extended schools   Schools which offer a range of additional services for children and for parents and families including access to health, housing and social care advice, and facilities for community use.

Giftedness   'Gifted' refers to pupils who are working or who could be working ahead of their age peers in one or more than one curricular area.

Globalisation   Global movement of people, commodities and ideas. Though globalisation has tended to be associated with the world economy, it impacts on the world community in political and cultural ways as well.

Holistic approach   An approach to education that emphasises the importance of the development of the whole person – the development of cognitive, affective, social, physical and spiritual aspects.

Ideology   An ideology is a set of beliefs that provide a basis for organised political action. Ideologies tend to offer a worldview or account of the existing social order, a model of the desired future (the Good Society), and a programme for bringing about political change.

Inclusive education   An approach to education which recognises the diversity of individuals' experiences, perceptions and backgrounds and values all students and staff equally. This approach requires consistent reflection on and changes in institutional structures, policies, practices and cultures to ensure that barriers to participation and learning are reduced for **all** students.

Incremental theory of intelligence   Intelligence is depicted as something that can be increased through effort.

Interconnectedness   Links and partnerships across the globe that occur from a macro to a micro level, for example, agreements between nation states or cooperation between cities, schools, communities and so on.

Interprofessional working   When teachers work with, for example, health, social work and other education professionals to ensure effective support for children, prosocial behaviour and action which results in a positive outcome for another/others.

Joined up working A term used to describe members of different organisations or professions working collaboratively to deal with common issues.

Knowledge economy/knowledge driven economy Used to describe the shift from traditional economies (for example, those based on heavy industry) to one where knowledge, skill acquisition and technical advantage have become drivers for and products of the economy.

Marketisation The process of changing public sector organisations, such as education, to function like private sector, profit-oriented companies.

Mentoring A process where a more experienced colleague supports another person in order to help them develop skills and knowledge in specific areas to enhance overall professional development.

Meta-analysis The combined analysis of several studies investigating the same, or similar, research questions.

Methodologies Different teaching strategies or strategies used by leaders to ensure good learning opportunities.

Neo-liberalism A political ideology which emphasises the predominance of market forces (i.e., a free market economy) and a limited role for the state.

Nurture group A class within a mainstream provision which endeavours to support children with social, emotional, or behavioural difficulties to remain within their mainstream setting with an expectation that they will be reintegrated into their class within 2/4 school terms.

Pedagogy The theory and practice of teaching.

Peer observation A way of gaining feedback on particular elements of your professional activities or to inform your own practice. For example, one teacher may observe how another teacher involves pupils in cooperative learning in groups, either to give feedback on how to further improve the practice of that teacher, or to enhance their own practice (if it is a method they are not familiar with).

Peer review Processes designed to assess the practice of a colleague. This process can be constructive and supportive but can often lead to anxiety where it is used as part of a performance management system.

Professional enquiry A form of professional learning and development where practitioners seek to develop their practice by undertaking systematic 'enquiries' or investigations into an aspect of that practice, using the principles of practitioner enquiry.

Professional learning community (PLC) A PLC is a way of working in a school. There are essentially three crucial elements: supportive and shared leadership, a clear focus on enquiry into the pupil learning experience and collaborative approaches to learning for teachers and pupils.

Professional practice The work undertaken by a professional in the context of their job.

Professional reflection An approach to professional learning and development where a professional reflects on their practice with the aim of improving aspects of it.

Prosocial behaviour Behaviour which has a positive effect on another person(s).

Resilience The ability to cope with change and develop positive relationships despite changing or unpredictable events in life.

Schools networks An approach where technology and other strategies are used to build collaboration between schools and school staff in order to break down isolation and build expertise.

Schools partnerships Agreements between schools to collaborate together on particular initiatives, usually supported by funding from a government agency such as the British Council or the Department for Foreign Investment (DFID).

Social inclusion A concept based on working towards policies and practices which ensure that all, regardless of background and social position, have opportunities to take part fully in society.

Social justice The principle that goods like education and health care should be fairly distributed among all members of society.

Social learning Social learning theory: where the learner learns through observing and modelling. Social learning (more generally): where learners learn through interacting and collaborating with others in order to deepen knowledge and understanding.

Special advisors Leading politicians, both in and out of office, appoint advisors who are specialists or have expert knowledge on areas of policy, for example, education, health or the economy.

Stage theory A theory of development which assumes that individuals progress through a universal series of stages.

Teacher leader Teachers who develop areas of expertise and work collaboratively with other teachers to develop teaching and learning in this area.

Teacher leadership   Teachers leading initiatives in teaching and learning which contribute to the school's development agenda.

Think-tanks   A think-tank is a privately funded organisation that looks to achieve certain aims or promote a particular set of values and ideas; often set or supported by its funders. Think-tanks are often aligned to political parties or have an ideological orientation. Think-tanks aim to influence and look to develop and advocate ideas and policy options.

Thought experiment   An imagined example that illustrates a problem or concept by analogy, commonly used by philosophers.

BIBLIOGRAPHY

Adams, K., Hean, S., Sturgis, P. and Macleod Clarke, J. (2006) 'Investigating the factors influencing professional identity of first-year health and social care students', *Learning in Health and Social Care*, 5(2): 55–68.

Allan, J. (2005) 'Inclusive learning experiences: learning from children and young people', in M. Nind, J. Rix, K. Sheehy and S. Sommons (eds), *Curriculum and Pedagogy in Inclusive Education: Values into Practice*. London: RoutledgeFalmer.

Archer, M.S. (1979) *Social Origins of Educational Systems*. London: Sage.

Archer, M.S. (1984) *Social Origins of Educational Systems*. University edn. London: Sage.

Arsenio, W. and Fleiss, K. (1996) 'Typical and behaviourally disruptive children's understanding of the emotional consequences of sociomoral events', *British Journal of Developmental Psychology*, 14: 173–86.

Ball, S. (1994) *Education Reform: A Critical and Post-Structural Approach*. Milton Keynes: Open University Press.

Barber, M. (2001) 'The Very Big Picture', *School Effectiveness and School Improvement*, 12(2), 213–28.

Barry, B. (2005) *Why Social Justice Matters*. Cambridge: Polity Press.

Baumfield, V., Hall, E. and Wall, K. (2008) *Action Research in the Classroom*. London: Sage.

Bayliss, V. (2001) 'Work in the knowledge-driven economy', *Industry and Higher Education*, 15(1): 13–18.

Bennathan, M. (2004) *Supporting Parents, Supporting Education: What Nurture Groups Achieve*. London: The Nurture Group Network.

Bennathan, M. and Boxall, M. (1998) *The Boxall Profile: Handbook for Teachers*. London: The Nurture Group Network.

Bennathan, M. and Boxall M. (2000) *Effective Intervention in Primary Schools*. London: David Fulton.

Bills, D.B. (2004) *The Sociology of Education and Work*. Oxford: Blackwell.

Bishop, S. (2008) *Running a Nurture Group*. London: Paul Chapman Publishing.

Blair, T. (1997) *Speech given on Monday 8 December 1997, at the Stockwell Park School, Lambeth, regarding the launch of the Government's new Social Exclusion Unit*, from http://www.cabinetoffice.gov.uk/media/cabinetoffice/social_exclusion_task_force/assets/publications_1997_to_2006/pm_speech_seu.pdf (accessed 8 October 2009).

Black-Hawkins, K., Florian, L. and Rouse, M. (2007) *Achievement and Inclusion in Schools*. London: Routledge.

Blasé, J.R and Blasé, J. (1998) *Handbook of Instructional Leadership: How Really Good Principals Promote Teaching and Learning*. Thousand Oaks, CA: Corwin Press.

Borland, J.H. (2005) 'Gifted education without gifted children: the case for no conceptions of giftedness', in R.J. Sternberg and J.E. Davidson (eds), *Conceptions of Giftedness*. 2nd edn. Cambridge: Cambridge University Press.

Bourdieu, P. and Passeron, J.C. (1990) *Reproduction in Education, Society and Culture*. London: Sage.

Bowlby, J. (1969) *Attachment and Loss: Vol. 1. Attachment.* New York: Basic Books.

Boxall M. (2002) *Nurture Groups In School: Principles and Practice*. London: Sage.

British Irish Council (2008) http://www3.british-irishcouncil.org/ (accessed 14 February 2010).

Bronfenbrenner, U. (1981) *On Making Human Beings Human*. London: Sage.

Brookfield, S.D. (1995) *Becoming a Critically Reflective Teacher*. San Francisco, CA: Jossey-Bass.

Brooks, R. and Goldstein S. (2002) *Nurturing Resilience in Our Children*. New York: McGraw-Hill.

Brown, A.L., Metz, K.E. and Campione, J.C. (1996) 'Social interaction and individual understanding in a community of learners: the influence of Piaget and Vygotsky', in A. Tryphon and J. Vonèche (eds), *Piaget–Vygotsky: The Social Genesis of Thought*. Hove: Psychology Press.

Bruner, J. (1996) *The Culture of Education*. Cambridge, MA: Harvard University Press.

Bryan, J.H. (1971). 'Model affect and children's imitative altruism', *Child Development*, 42, 2061–5.

Carr, M. and Kurtz Costes, B.E. (1994) 'Is being smart everything? The influence of student achievement on teachers' perceptions', *British Journal of Educational Psychology*, 64: 263–76.

Carroll, M. (2009) 'Chartered Teachers and the process of professional enquiry: the experience of five Scottish teachers', *Professional Development in Education*, 35 (1), 23-42.

CCEA (2007) *The Northern Ireland Primary Curriculum*. Belfast: CCEA. http://www.nicurriculum.org.uk/docs/key_stages_1_and_2/northern_ireland_curriculum_primary.pdf (accessed 19 June 2010).

Choh, Ssu Yee and Quay, May Ling (2001) 'Special educators' implicit theories of intelligence'. http://www.minds.org.sg/papers/mms40.htm (accessed 2004).

Claxton, G. and Meadows, S. (2008) 'Brightening up: how children learn to be gifted', in T. Balchin, B. Hymer and D. Matthews (eds), *The Routledge Companion to Gifted Education*. London: Routledge.

Cobb, R.W. and Elder, C. (1972). *Participation in American Politics: The Dynamics of Agenda-Building*. Baltimore, MD and London: Johns Hopkins University Press.

Colley, H., James, D. and Diment, K. (2007) 'Unbecoming teachers: towards a more dynamic notion of professional participation', *Journal of Education Policy*, 22 (2): 173–93.

Continuing Intercultural Professional Development in Europe (CIPDE) (2008–09) EU funded project. http://www.gla.ac.uk/departments/cipde/ (accessed 19 June 2010).

Cook, C., Yeomansb, J. and Parkesc, J. (2008) 'The Oasis: nurture group provision for Key Stage 3 pupils', *Emotional and Behavioural Difficulties*, 13 (4), 291–303.

Cooper, P. and Tiknaz, Y. (2007) *Nurture Groups in School and at Home*. London: Jessica Kingsley.

Cordingley, P. and Bell, M. (2002) *Literature and Evidence Search: Teachers' Use of Research and Evidence as They Learn to Teach and Improve their Teaching*. London: TTA.

Cordingley, P., Bell, M., Thomason, S. and Firth, A. (2005) *The Impact of Collaborative Continuing Professional Development (CPD) on Classroom Teaching and Learning. Review: How Do Collaborative and Sustained CPD and Sustained but Not Collaborative CPD Affect Teaching and Learning?* In Research Evidence in Education Library. London: EPPI-Centre, Social Science Research Unit, Institute of Education, University of London.

Corson, D. (1993) 'Introduction: the meaning and place of work', in D. Corson (ed.), *Education for Work. Background to Policy and Curriculum*, Clevedon: Multilingual Matters.

Coulby, D. (2006) 'Intercultural education: theory and practice', *Intercultural Education*, 17(3): 245–7.

Crick, N.R. and Dodge, K.A. (1994) 'A review and reformulation of social information-processing mechanisms in children's social adjustment', *Psychological Bulletin*, 115: 74–101.

Crowther, F., Ferguson, M. and Hann, L. (2009) *Developing Teacher Leaders: How Teacher Leadership Enhances School Success*. 2nd edn. Thousand Oaks, CA: Corwin Press.

Dadds, M. (1997) 'Continuing professional development: nurturing the expert within', *British Journal of In-service Education*, 23 (1): 31–8.

Daniels, H. (2001) *Vygotsky and Pedagogy*. London: RoutledgeFalmer.

Darder, A., Baltodano, M.P. and Torres, R.D. (eds) (2009) *The Critical Pedagogy Reader*. New York and London: Routledge.

Davies, B. (2006) *Leading the Strategically Focused School: Success and Sustainability*. London: Paul Chapman Publishing.

Day, C. and Harris, A. (2002) 'Teacher leadership, reflective practice and school improvement,' in K. Leithwood and P. Halliger (eds), *Second International Handbook of Educational Leadership and Administration Part Two*. Dordrecht: Kluwer Academic. pp. 957–77.

De Castro, B.O., Slot, N.W., Bosch, J.D., Koops, W. and Veerman, J. (2003) 'Negative feelings exacerbate hostile attributions of intent in highly aggressive boys', *Journal of Clinical Child and Adolescent Psychology*, 32: 56–65.

Delors, J. (2006) *Learning: The Treasure Within*. Report to UNESCO of the International Commission on Education for the Twenty-first Century. Paris: UNESCO. http://www.unesco.org/delors/ (accessed 13 September 2009).

Denham, A. (1996) *Think-tanks of the New Right*. Aldershot: Dartmouth.

Department for Children, Schools and Families (2007) *The Children's Plan: Building Brighter Futures*. http://www.dcsf.gov.uk/childrensplan/downloads/The_Childrens_Plan.pdf (accessed 14 February 2010).

Department for Children, Education, Lifelong Learning and Skills, Welsh Assembly Government (2008a) *Education for Sustainable Development and Global Citizenship*. Cardiff: WAG. http://www.esd-wales.org.uk/english/ESDreports/pdf/reports%204/ESDGC%20strategy-updates%20(e).pdf (accessed 19 June 2010).

Department for Children, Education, Lifelong Learning and Skills, Welsh Assembly Government (2008b) *Education for Sustainable Development and Global Citizenship: A Common Formats for Schools.* Cardiff: WAG. http://wales.gov.uk/docs/dcells/publications/081204commonunderstschoolsen.pdf (accessed 19 June 2010).

Department for Education and Skills (DfES) (2003) *Raising Standards and Tackling Workload: A National Agreement*. London: DfES.

Department for Education and Skills (2004a) *Every Child Matters: Change for Children*. http://publications.everychildmatters.gov.uk/eOrderingDownload/DfES10812004.pdf (accessed 14 February 2010).

Department for Education and Skills (2004b) *Every Child Matters: Change For Children: Autism*. http://publications.everychildmatters.gov.uk/eOrderingDownload/Autism-Exemplar.pdf.pdf (accessed 14 February 2010).

Department for Education and Skills (2006a) *Sure Start Children's Centres: Practice Guidance*. http://www.dcsf.gov.uk/everychildmatters/research/publications/surestartpublications/1854/ (accessed 14 February 2010).

Department for Education and Skills (2006b) *Raising the Achievement of Gypsy Traveller Pupils: A Guide to Good Practice*. http://publications.teachernet.gov.uk/eOrderingDownload/0443%202003MIG1977.pdf (accessed 14 February 2010).

Department for Education and Skills (2007) *Care Matters: Time for Change*. http://www.commissioningsupport.org.uk/pdf/1_Care%20matters%20white%20paper.pdf (accessed 14 February 2010).

Department for International Development (DFID) http://www.dfid.gov.uk/About-DFID/Our-organisation1/DFID-Directory/International-Divisions/United-Nations-Conflict-and-Humanitarian-Division/ (accessed 14 February 2010).

Dewey, J. (1933) *How We Think: A Re-Statement of the Relationship of Reflective Thinking to Learning*. New York: D.C. Heath.

Dobrow, S.R. and Higgins, M. (2005) 'Developmental networks and professional identity: a longitudinal study', *Career Development International*, 10(6/7): 567–83.

Dodge, K.A. and Frame, C.L. (1982) 'Social cognitive biases and deficits in aggressive boys', *Child Development*, 53: 620–35.

DuFour, R., Eaker, R. and Many, T. (2006) *Learning by Doing: A Handbook for Professional Learning Communities at Work*. Bloomington, IN: Solution Tree.

Dweck, C.S. (1999) *Self-Theories: Their Role in Motivation, Personality and Development*. Philadelphia, PA: Psychology Press.

Earl, L.M., Katz, S. and Fullan, M. (2006) *Leading Schools in a Data Rich World*. Thousand Oaks, CA: Corwin Press.

Education (Additional Support for Learning) (Scotland) Act (2004) Office of Public Sector Information. http://www.opsi.gov.uk/legislation/scotland/acts2004/asp_20040004_en_1 (accessed 16 February 2010).

Eisenberg, N. (1986) *Altruistic Emotion, Cognition, and Behavior*. Hillsdale, NJ: Erlbaum.

Eisenberg, N. and Fabes, R.A. (1998) 'Prosocial development', in W. Damon and N. Eisenberg (eds), *Handbook of Child Psychology*. 5th edn. Vol. 4, New York: Wiley. pp. 701–78.

Eisenberg, N. and Mussen, P. (1989) *The Roots of Prosocial Behavior in Children*. Cambridge: Cambridge University Press.

'Emotional well-being and learning'. http://www.caspari.org.uk/ (accessed 16 February 2010).

Enslin, P. and Tjiattas, M. (2008) 'Cosmopolitan justice: education and global citizenship', in M. Peters, A. Britton, and H. Blee (eds), *Global Citizenship Education: Philosophy, Theory and Pedagogy*. Rotterdam: Sense Publishers.

Erdley, C.A. and Asher, S.R. (1996) 'Children's social goals and self-efficacy perceptions as influences on their responses to ambiguous provocation', *Child Development*, 67: 1329–44.

Eyre, D., Coates, D., Fitzpatrick, M., Higgins, C., McClure, L., Wilson, H. and Chamberlin, R. (2002) 'Effective teaching of able pupils in the primary school: the findings of the Oxfordshire effective teachers of able pupils project', *Gifted Education International*, 16: 158–69.

European Union. http://europa.eu/index_en.htm (accessed 14 February 2010).

Fabes, R.A. and Eisenberg, N. (1996) 'An examination of age and sex differences in prosocial behaviour and empathy', unpublished data, Arizona State University.

Fagan, C. (2006) 'Three Es for teachers: economics, enterprise and entrepreneurship', *Teacher Development*, 10 (3):275–91.

Fisher J. (1996) *Starting From the Child?* Buckingham: Open University Press.

Flores, M. and Day, C. (2006) 'Contexts which shape and reshape teachers' identities: a multi-perspective study', *Teachers and Teacher Education*, 22 (2): 219–32.

Florian, L. (2008) 'Special or inclusive education: future trends', *British Journal of Special Education*, 35 (4): 202–8.

Ford, D.Y. (1996) *Reversing Underachievement among Gifted Black Students: Promising Practices and Programs*. New York: Teachers College Press.

Forde, C., McMahon, M., McPhee, A.D. and Patrick, F. (2006) *Professional Development, Reflection and Enquiry*. London: Sage.

Freeman, J. (1998) *Educating the Very Able: Current International Research*. London: The Stationery Office.

Freeman, J. (2001) 'Mentoring gifted pupils', *Educating Able Children*, 5: 6–12.

Freeman, J. (2008) *Gifted Children Growing Up*. London: David Fulton.

Frost, D., Durrant, J., Head, M. and Holden, G. (2000) *Teacher-Led School Improvement*. London: RoutledgeFalmer.

Furlong, J. (2008) 'Making teaching a 21st century profession: Tony Blair's big prize', *Oxford Review of Education*, 34 (6): 727–39.

General Teaching Council for Northern Ireland (n.d.) *Professional Competences*. http://www.gtcni.org.uk/index.cfm/area/information/page/ProfStandard (accessed 8 February 2010).

General Teaching Council for Northern Ireland (GTCNI) (2007) *Teaching: The Reflective Profession*. http://www.gtcni.org.uk/uploads/docs/GTCNI_Comp_Bmrk%20%20Aug%2007.pdf (accessed 14 February 2010).

General Teaching Council for Scotland (GTCS) (2006) *The Standard for Full Registration*. http://www.gtcs.org.uk/Publications/StandardsandRegulations/The_Standard_for_Full_Registration.aspx (accessed 14 February 2010).

General Teaching Council for Wales (GTCW) (2009) *Chartered Teacher Standards*. http://www.gtcw.org.uk/gtcw/images/stories/downloads/chartered_teacher_standards/GTCW%20Chartered%20Teacher%20Standards%20English.pdf (accessed 14 February 2010).

Goodman, R. (1997) 'The strengths and difficulties questionnaire: a research note', *Journal of Child Psychiatry and Psychology*, 38 (8): 581–5.

Greener, S.G. and Crick, N.R. (1999) 'Normative beliefs about prosocial behaviour in middle childhood: what does it mean to be nice?', *Social Development*, 8: 350–63.

Greenleaf, R.K. (1998) *The Power of Servant-Leadership*, San Francisco, CA: Berrett-Koehler.

Gronn, P. (2000) 'Distributed properties: a new architecture for leadership', *Educational Management Administration and Leadership*, 28 (3): 317–38.

Gronn, P. (2002) 'Distributed leadership', in K.A. Leithwood and P. Hallinzer (eds), *Second International Handbook of Educational Leadership and Administration, Part Two*. Dordrecht, Netherlands: Kluwer Academic Press.

Gronn, P. (2003) *The New Work of Educational Leaders*. London: Paul Chapman Publishing.

Groundwater-Smith, S. (2007) 'Questions of quality in practitioner research', in P. Ponte and B.H.J. Smit (eds), *The Quality Of Practitioner Research: Reflections on the Position of the Researcher and the Researched*. Rotterdam: Sense Publishers. pp. 57–64.

Grusec, J.E., Davidov, M. and Lundell, L. (2002) 'Prosocial and helping behaviour', in P. K. Smith and C. Hart (eds), *Blackwell Handbook of Childhood Social Development*. Oxford: Blackwell. pp. 457–90.

Guile, D. (2003) 'From "Credentialism" to the "Practice of Learning": reconceptualising learning for the knowledge economy', *Policy Futures in Education*, 1(1): 83–105.

Hargreaves, A. and Fink, D. (2006) *Sustainable Leadership*. Chichester: John Wiley and Sons.

Hargreaves, D.H. (2003) *Education Epidemic Transforming Secondary Schools through Innovation Networks*. London: Demos.

Harris, A. (2003) 'Teacher leadership as distributed leadership: heresy, fantasy or possibility?' *School Leadership and Management*, 23(3): 313–24.

Harris, A. (2008) *Distributed School Leadership: Developing Tomorrow's Leaders*. London: Routledge.

Harris, A. and Muijs, D. (2005) *Improving Schools through Teacher Leadership*. Maidenhead: Open University Press.

Hay, D.F., Castle, J., Davies, L., Demetriou, H. and Stimson, C.A. (1999) 'Prosocial action in very early childhood' *Journal of Child Psychology and Psychiatry*, (40)6: 905–16.

Head, G. (2003) 'Effective collaboration: deep collaboration as an essential element of the learning process', *Journal of Educational Enquiry*, 4(2), 47–62.

Head, G. and Pirrie, A. (2007) 'The place of special schools in a policy climate of inclusion', *Journal of Research in Special Educational Needs*, 7(2), 90–6.

Heclo, H. (1972) 'Review article: policy analysis', *British Journal of Political Science*, 2: 83–108.

Held, D. (2004) *A Globalizing World? Culture, Economics, Politics*. 2nd edn. London: Routledge.

Held, D. and McGrew, A. (eds) (2003) *The Global Transformations Reader. An Introduction to the Globalization Debate*. 2nd edn. Cambridge: Polity Press.

HMIe (2005) *How Good Is Our School? Taking a Closer Look At: Inclusion and Equality – Meeting the Needs of Gypsies and Travellers*. www.hmie.gov.uk/documents/publication/hgiosmnog.doc (accessed 14 February 2010).

HMIe (2009a) *Count Us In: Improving the Education of Our Looked After Children*. http://www.hmie.gov.uk/documents/publication/cuimnnus.pdf (accessed 14 February 2010).

HMIe (2009b) *Count Us In: A Sense of Belonging*. http://www.hmie.gov.uk/documents/publication/cuiielac.pdf (accessed 14 February 2010).

Hord, S.M. (2004) *Learning Together, Leading Together: Changing Schools Through Professional Learning Communities*. New York: Teachers College Press.

Huffman J.B. and Hipp, K.K. (2003) *Reculturing Schools as Professional Learning Communities*. Lanham, MD: Scarecrow Education.

Huffman, J.B. (2003) 'Perceptions of professional learning communities', *Leadership in Education*, 6(3): 239–50.

Hume, D. (1957) *An Inquiry Concerning the Principles of Morals*. Vol. 4. New York: Liberal Arts Press. (Originally published in 1751.)

International Monetary Fund (IMF). http://www.imf.org/external/index.htm (accessed 14 February 2010).

Jackson, D. and Street, H. (2005) 'What does "collaborative enquiry" look like?', in H. Street and J. Temperley (eds), *Improving Schools Through Collaborative Enquiry*. London: Continuum. pp. 41–70.

James, K. (2005) 'International education: the concept and its relationship to intercultural education', *Journal of Research in International Education*, 4(3): 313–32.

Jarvis, P., (2007) *Globalisation, Lifelong Learning and the Learning Society*. London: Routledge.

Jenkins, W. I. (1978) *Policy Analysis: A Political and Organisational Perspective*. London: Martin Robertson.

Jones, S. (2008) 'Treat us like infants and you'll get deskilled staff', *Times Educational Supplement*. http://www.tes.co.uk/article.aspx?storycode=6006281 (accessed 8 February 2010).

Joyce, B.R. and Showers, B. (1995) *Student Development through Staff Development: Fundamentals of School Renewal*. London: Longman.

Kant, I. (1895) *Fundamental Principles of the Metaphysics of Ethics*. London: Longmans Green.

Kennedy, J.F. (1963) Civil rights address delivered 11 June.

Kincheloe, J.L. (2008) *Knowledge and Critical Pedagogy*. New York: Springer.

Kohlberg, L. (1969) 'Stage and sequence: the cognitive-developmental approach to socialization', in D. A. Goslin (ed.), *Handbook of Socialization Theory and Research*. New York: Rand McNally. pp. 325–480.

Kohlberg, L. (1981) *The Philosophy of Moral Development: Moral Stages and the Idea of Justice*. San Francisco, CA: Harper and Row.

Kostogriz, A. and Peeler, J. (2007) 'Professional identity and pedagogical space: negotiating difference in teacher workplaces', *Teaching Education*, 18(2): 107–22.

Lauder, H., Brown, P., Dillahough, J. and Halsey, A. (2006) *Education, Globalization and Social Change*. Oxford: Oxford University Press.

Lave, J. and Wenger, E. (1991) *Situated Learning: Legitimate Peripheral Participation*. Cambridge: Cambridge University Press.

Lawton, D. (2005) *Education and Labour Party Ideologies, 1900–2001 and Beyond*. London: RoutledgeFalmer.

Leithwood, K., Harris, A. and Hopkins, D. (2008) 'Seven strong claims about successful school leadership', *School Leadership and Management*, 28(1): 27–42.

Lemerise, E.A. and Arsenio, W. (2000) 'An integrated model of emotion processes and cognition in social information processing', *Child Development*, 71: 107–18.

Leyden, S. (1998) *Supporting Children of Exceptional Ability*. London: Fulton.

Louis, K.S. and Kruse, S.D. (1995) *Professionalism and Community: Perspectives on Reforming Urban Schools*. Thousand Oaks, CA: Corwin Press.

Lucas, S., Insley, K. and Buckland, G. (2006) *Nurture Group Principles and Curriculum Guidelines*. London: The Nurture Group Network.

Macbeath, J. (2005) 'Leadership as distributed: a matter of practice', *School Leadership and Management*, 25(4): 349–66.

MacGilchrist, B., Myers, K. and Reed, J. (2004) *The Intelligent School*. London: Sage.

McCartney, E. (2009) 'Joined up working: terms, types and tensions', in J. Forbes and C. Watson (eds), *Service Integration in Schools: Research and Policy Discourses, Practices and Future Prospects*. Rotterdam: Sense Publishers. pp. 23–36.

McConkey, R. (2009) 'Creative tensions in service integration', in J. Forbes and C. Watson (eds), *Service Integration in Schools: Research and Policy Discourses, Practices and Future Prospects*. Rotterdam: Sense Publishers. pp. 51–3.

McLaren, P. (2009) 'Critical pedagogy: a look at the major concepts', in A. Darder, M.P. Baltodano and R.D. Torres (eds), *The Critical Pedagogy Reader*. London: Routledge.

McLean, A. (2003) *The Motivated School*. London: Paul Chapman Publishing.

Menesini, E, Sanchez, V., Fonzi, A., Ortega, R., Costabile, A. and Lo Feudo, G. (2003) 'Moral emotions and bullying: a cross-national comparison of differences between bullies, victims, and outsiders', *Aggressive Behavior*, 29: 515–30.

Middlewood, D. (2005) *Creating a Learning School*. London: Paul Chapman Publishing.

Miller, D. (1999) *Principles of Social Justice*. Cambridge, MA and London: Harvard University Press.

Miller, D. (2007) *National Responsibility and Global Justice*. Oxford: Oxford University Press.

Miller, D. (2008) 'National responsibility and global justice', *Critical Review of International Social and Political Philosophy*, 11(4): 383–98.

Moellendorf, D. (2002) *Cosmopolitan Justice*. Boulder, CO: Westview Press.

Molina Y., Garcia, S. and Alban-Metcalfe, J. (2005) 'The need for a new model', in M. Nind, J. Rix, K. Sheehy and S. Sommons (eds), *Curriculum and Pedagogy in Inclusive Education: Values into Practice*. London: RoutledgeFalmer.

Molzten, R. (1996) 'Underachievement', in D. McAlpine and R. Moltzen (eds), *Gifted and Talented: New Zealand Perspectives*. Palmerston North: Massey University ERDC Press. pp. 407–26.

Moore, S.A. and Mitchell, R.C. (2008) *Power, Pedagogy and Praxis*. Rotterdam: Sense Publishers.

Moran, J.J. (2001) *Collaborative Professional Development for Teachers and Adults*. Malabar, FL: Krieger.

Moutious, S. (2009) 'International organizations and transnational education policy', *Compare*, 39(4): 469–81.

Murk, C. (2006) *Self-Esteem Research, Theory and Practice: Toward a Positive Psychology of Self-Esteem*. New York: Springer.

National Equality Panel (2010) *An Anatomy of Economic Inequality in the UK: Report of the National Equality Panel*. London: Government Equalities Office.

Nelson, D.A. and Crick, N.R. (1999) 'Rose-colored glasses: examining the social information-processing of prosocial young adolescents', *Journal of Early Adolescence*, 19(1): 17–38.

Noddings, N. (2007) 'The one-caring as teacher', in R. Curren (ed.), *Philosophy of Education: An Anthology*. Oxford: Blackwell.

Northern Ireland Assembly (n.d.) *Northern Ireland's Statistics*. http://www.deni.gov.uk/index/21-pupils_parents-pg/pupils_parents-suspensions_and_expulsions_pg.htm (accessed 16 February 2010).

Northern Ireland Council on the Curriculum, Examinations and Assessment (NICCEA). http://www.ccea.org.uk/ (accessed 14 February 2010).

Nurture Network. http://www.nurturegroups.org/ (accessed 16 February 2010).

Nussbaum, M. (1996) 'Patriotism and cosmopolitanism', in J. Cohen (ed.), *For Love of Country: Debating the Limits of Patriotism*. Boston, MA: Beacon Press.

Nussbaum, M. (1997) *Cultivating Humanity: a Classical Defense of Reform in Liberal Education*. Cambridge, MA: Harvard University Press.

Nussbaum, M. (2006) *Frontiers of Justice: Disability, Nationality, Species Membership.* London: The Belknap Press of Harvard University Press.

O'Connor, K. (2008) '"You choose to Care"; Teachers, emotions and professional identity', *Teaching and Teacher Education*, 24(1): 117–26.

Office of the First Minister and Deputy First Minister (OFMDFM) (2006) *Our Children and Young People – Our Pledge. A Ten Year Strategy for Children and Young People in Northern Ireland 2006-2016*. http://www.allchildrenni.gov.uk/ten-year-strategy.pdf (accessed 14 February 2010).

Office of the High Commissioner for Human Rights (OHCHR) (1989) *Convention on the Rights of the Child*. http://www2.ohchr.org/english/law/crc.htm (accessed 14 February 2010).

Olssen, M., Codd, J.A. and O'Neill, A.M. (2004) *Education Policy: Globalization, Citizenship and Democracy*. London: Sage.

Ozga, J. (2005) 'Modernizing the workforce: a perspective from Scotland', *Educational Review*, 57(2): 207–19.

Palmer, P. J. (1998) *The Courage to Teach*. San Francisco, CA: Jossey-Bass.

Pedder, D., James, M. and MacBeath, J. (2005) 'How teachers value and practise professional learning', *Research Papers in Education*, 20(3): 209–43.

Peters, M.A. (2000) 'National education policy constructions of the "Knowledge Economy": a review and critique', research paper presented to Educational Studies Seminar Programme, autumn term, 12 December, University of Dundee.

Piaget, J. (1965) *The Moral Judgment of the Child*. Trans. M. Gabain. London: Routledge. (Originally published in 1932.)

Pring, R. (1995) *Closing the Gap*. London: Hodder and Stoughton.

Pogge, T. (1989) *Realizing Rawls*. Ithaca, NY: Cornell University Press.

Prunty, J. (1985) 'Signposts for a critical educational policy analysis', *Australian Journal of Education*, 29(2): 133–40.

QCA (2004) *Framework for Work Related Learning*.

QCA (2008) *Every Child Matters at the Heart of the Curriculum*. http://www.qcda.gov.uk/15299.aspx

QCDA (2008) *Framework for Economic Wellbeing 11–19: Career, Work-Related Learning and Enterprise*. Coventry: Qualification and Curriculum Development Agency.

Radke-Yarrow, M., Zahn-Waxler, C. and Chapman, M. (1983) 'Children's proso-cial dispositions and behavior', in P.H. Mussen (ed.), *Handbook of Child Psychology*. 4th edn. Vol. 4. *Socialization and Social Development*. New York: Wiley. pp. 465–545.

Rawls, J. (1971) *A Theory of Justice*. Oxford: Oxford University Press.

Rawls, J. (1999) *The Law of Peoples*. Cambridge: Harvard University Press.

Reeves, J., Forde, C., O'Brien, J., Smith, P. and Tomlinson, H. (2002) *Performance Management in Education: Improving Practice*. London: Paul Chapman Publishing.

Reeves, J., Turner, E., Morris, B. and Forde, C. (2003) 'Culture and concepts of school leadership and management: exploring the impact of CPD on aspiring headteachers', *School Leadership and Management*, 23(1): 5–24.

Reeves, J., Turner, E., Morris, B. and Forde, C. (2005) 'Changing their minds: the social dynamics of school leaders' learning', *Cambridge Journal of Education*, 35(2): 255–73.

Reid, K. (1986) *Disaffection from School*. London: Methuen.

Renzulli, J. (1998) 'A rising tide lifts all ships: developing the gifts and talents of all pupils', *Phi Delta Kappan*, 80(2): 105–11.

Riddell, S. and Tett, L. (eds) (2001) *Education, Social Justice and Inter-Agency Working: Joined Up or Fractured Policy?* London: Routledge.

Rix, J. (2005) 'Creating and using inclusive materials, collaboratively and reflectively', in M. Nind, J. Rix, K. Sheehy and S. Sommons (eds), *Curriculum and Pedagogy in Inclusive Education: Values into Practice*. London: RoutledgeFalmer.

Rogoff, B. (1990) *Apprenticeship in Thinking: Cognitive Development in Social Context*. Oxford: Oxford University Press.

Rosenthal, R. and Jacobson, L. (1966) 'Teachers' expectancies: determinates of pupils' IQ gains', *Psychological Reports*, 19: 115–18.

Rouse, M. and Florian, L. (1997) 'Inclusive education in the marketplace', *International Journal of Inclusive Education*, 1(4): 323–36.

Sachs, J. (2003) *The Activist Teaching Profession*. Buckingham: Open University Press.

Sammons, P., Power, S., Robertson, P., Elliot, K., Campbell, C. and Whitty, G. (2002) *National Evaluation of the New Community Schools Pilot Programme in Scotland: Phase 1 (1999–2002) Interim Findings and Emerging Issues for Policy and Practice*. http://www.scotland.gov.uk/Publications/2002/08/15194/9565 (accessed 14 February 2010).

Sapon-Shevin, M. (1994) *Playing Favorites: Gifted Education and the Disruption of the Community*. New York: State University of New York Press.

Scheuerman, W. (2006) 'Globalization', in E. Zalta (ed.), *The Stanford Encyclopedia of Philosophy*, Fall edn. http://plato.stanford.edu/archives/fall2008/entries/globalization/ (accessed 7 December 2009).

Scottish Executive (SE) (2001a) *For Scotland's Children: Better Integrated Children's Services.* http://www.scotland.gov.uk/library3/education/fcsr-00. asp (accessed 14 February 2010).

Scottish Executive (SE) (2001b) *A Teaching Profession for the 21st Century: Agreement reached Following Recommendations Made in the McCrone Report.* Edinburgh: Scottish Executive. http://www.scotland.gov.uk/library3/education/tp21a.pdf

Scottish Executive (SE) (2004) *A Curriculum for Excellence.* Edinburgh: Scottish Executive.

Scottish Executive (SE) (2007) *Getting It Right for Every Child: Guidance on the Child's or Young Person's Plan.* http://www.scotland.gov.uk/Resource/Doc/163531/0044420.pdf (accessed 14 February 2010).

Scottish Executive Education Department (SEED) (2002) *Determined to Succeed: A Review of Enterprise in Education.* Edinburgh: The Stationery Office.

Scottish Government (2008a) *The Guide to Getting It Right for Every Child.* http://www.scotland.gov.uk/Publications/2008/09/22091734/0 (accessed 14 February 2010).

Scottish Government (2008b) *National Statistics Publication.* http://www.scotland.gov.uk/Resource/Doc/210491/0055658.pdf (accessed 16 February 2010).

Scottish Office (1998) *New Community Schools Prospectus.* http://www.scotland.gov.uk/library/documents-w3/ncsp-00.htm (accessed 14 February 2010).

Sergiovanni, T.J. (1994) *Building Communities in Schools.* San Francisco, CA: Jossey-Bass.

Servage, L. (2008) 'Critical and transformative practices in professional learning communities', *Teacher Education Quarterly*, 6(1): 63–77.

Seymour, D. (2009) *Convention Brings Progress on Child Rights, but Challenges Remain.* http://www.unicef.org/rightsite/237_241.htm (accessed 27 October 2009).

Shawlands Academy (n.d.) *Shawlands Academy.* http://www.shawlandsacademy.glasgow.sch.uk/default.aspx

Shayer, M. and Adey, P. (2002) *Learning Intelligence.* Buckingham: Open University Press.

Skilbeck, M. (1993) 'Vocational education at the OECD', *Broadcast, Journal of the Scottish Further Education Unit*, 13(April): 13–15.

Smith, A. (1853) *The Theory of Moral Sentiments.* London: Henry G. Bohn. (Originally published in 1759.)

Smith, C. (2005) *Teaching Gifted and Talented Pupils in the Primary School: A Practical Guide.* London: Paul Chapman Publishing.

Smith, C. (2006) *Including the Gifted and Talented: Making Inclusion Work for More Able Learners.* London: Routledge.

Smith, M. (2008) 'Educational outcomes and social justice in Scottish residential care', in S.A. Moore and R.C. Mitchell (eds), *Power, Pedagogy and Praxis*. Rotterdam: Sense Publishers.

Social, Emotional and Behavioural Difficulties (SEBD). http://www.digitald-esk.org/external/behaviour/sebd.html (accessed 16 February 2010).

Solomon, D., Watson, M.S. and Battistich, V.A. (2001) 'Teaching and schooling effects on moral/prosocial development', in V. Richardson (ed.), *Handbook of Research on Teaching*. 4th edn. Washington, DC: American Educational Research Association.

Søreide, G.E. (2006) 'Narrative construction of teacher identity: positioning and negotiation', *Teachers and Teaching: Theory and Practice*, 12(5): 527–47.

Special Educational Needs and Disability Act (2001) Office of Public Sector Information. http://www.opsi.gov.uk/acts/acts2001/ukpga_20010010_en_1 (accessed 16 February 2010).

Special Educational Needs and Disability (Northern Ireland) Order 2005. Office of Public Sector Information. http://www.opsi.gov.uk/si/si2005/20051117.htm (accessed 16 February 2010).

Spillane, J.P. (2006) *Distributed Leadership*. San Fransisco, CA: Jossey-Bass.

Stoll, L. (2003) 'School culture and improvement', in M. Preedy, R. Glatter and C. Wise (eds), *Strategic Leadership and Educational Improvement*. London: Paul Chapman Publishing.

Stoll, L. and Louis, K.S. (eds) (2007) *Professional Learning Communities*. Maidenhead: Open University Press.

Sutherland, M. (2005) *Gifted and Talented in the Early Years: A Practical Guide for 3–5 Year Olds*. London: David Fulton.

Sutherland, M. (2008) *Developing the Gifted and Talented Young Learner*. London: Sage.

Tomlinson, S. (1994) *Educational Reform and Its Consequences*. London: IPPR/Rivers Oram Press.

Topping, K. and Maloney, S. (eds) (2005) *Inclusive Education*. London and New York: RoutledgeFalmer.

Torrance, H. and Pryor, J. (2001) 'Developing formative assessment in the classroom: using action research to explore and modify theory', *British Educational Research Journal*, 27(5): 667–83.

Training and Development Agency for Schools (TDA) (n.d.) *Early Professional Development*. http://www.tda.gov.uk/partners/cpd/epd.aspx (accessed 8 February 2010).

Training and Development Agency for Schools (TDA) (2007) *Professional Standards for Teachers: Qualified Teacher Status*. http://www.tda.gov.uk/upload/resources/pdf/s/standards_qts.pdf (accessed 14 February 2010).

Tuomi-Gröhm, T. (2003) 'Development transfer as a goal of internship in practical nursing', in T. Tuomi-Gröhm and Y. Engeström (eds), *Between School and Work: New Perspectives on Transfer and Boundary Crossing*. Oxford: Pergamon. pp. 199–232.

UK Mission to the UN. http://ukun.fco.gov.uk/en/uk-at-un/thematic-issues/post-conflict/peacekeeping/

UNESCO (1994) *The Salamanca Statement and Framework for Action on Special Needs Education*. http://www.unesco.org/education/pdf/SALAMA_E.PDF (accessed 14 February 2010).

UNESCO *World Heritage Sites*. http://whc.unesco.org/en/about/

United Nations. http://www.un.org/en/aboutun/index.shtml (accessed 14 February 2010).

UNICEF. http://rrsa.unicef.org.uk/?nodeid=rrsa&section=6 (accessed 14 February 2010).

Warden, D. and Mackinnon, S. (2003) 'Prosocial children, bullies and victims: an investigation of their sociometric status, empathy and social problem-solving strategies', *British Journal of Developmental Psychology*, 21: 367–85.

Wardle, G.A. (2007) 'Children's perceptions of peer prosocial behaviours and motives: Why are children nice to each other?'. Unpublished PhD thesis, University of Strathclyde.

Watson, C. (2006) 'Narratives of practice and the construction of teaching identity', *Teachers and Teaching: Theory and Practice*, 12(5): 509–26.

Welsh Assembly Government (n.d.) *World Class Wales – Transforming Learning for Success in a Globalised World*. http://wales.gov.uk/docs/dcells/publications/090619worldclasswalesen.pdf (accessed 14 February 2010).

Welsh Assembly Government (WAG) (2004) *Children and Young People: Rights to Action*. http://wales.gov.uk/docs/caecd/publications/090415rightstoactionen.pdf (accessed 14 February 2010).

Welsh Assembly Government (2006) *The Learning Country, Vision into Action*. http://new.wales.gov.uk/topics/educationandskills/publications/guidance/learningcountry/?lang=en (accessed 14 February 2010).

Welsh Assembly Government (WAG) (2006) *Inclusion and Pupil Support* (Wales) Welsh Assembly Government. http://wales.gov.uk/topics/educationandskills/publications/circulars/2463797/?lang=en (accessed 16 February 2010).

Welsh Assembly Government (WAG) (2008) *Making the Most of Learning*. Cardiff: WAG. http://wales.gov.uk/dcells/publications/curriculum_and_assessment/arevisedcurriculumforwales/nationalcurriculum/makingthemostoflearningnc/Making_Standard_WEB_(E).pdf?lang=en (accessed 19 June 2010).

Welsh Assembly Government (WAG) (2009a) *Schools in Wales General Statistics 2009 Attendance and Exclusions*. http://wales.gov.uk/topics/statistics/publications/schoolsgen09/?lang=en (accessed 15 February 2010).

Welsh Assembly Government (WAG) (2009b) *Wales, Europe and the World – A Framework for 14- to 19-year-old Learners in Wales*. Cardiff: WAG. http://wales.gov.uk/docs/dcells/publications/091019frameworken.pdf (accessed 19 June 2010).

Wenger, E. (1999) *Communities of Practice: Learning, Meaning and Identity*. Cambridge: Cambridge University Press.

Wilson, V., Hall, J., Davidson, J. and Lewin, J. (2006) *Developing Teachers: A Review of Early Professional Learning*. Glasgow: University of Glasgow, SCRE Centre.

Winch, C., (2000) *Education, Work and Social Capital. Towards A New Conception of Vocational Education*. London and New York: Routledge.

Wolf, A. (2005) *Does Education Matter? Myths about Education And Economic Growth*. London: Penguin Books.

Woolfolk, A., Hughes, M. and Walkup, V. (2008) *Psychology in Education*. Harlow: Pearson.

Woolhouse, M. (2005) 'You can't do it on your own: gardening as an analogy for personal learning from a collaborative action research group', *Educational Action Research*, 13(1): 27–41.

Young, I.M. (1990) *Justice and the Politics of Difference*. Princeton, NJ: Princeton University Press.

Zembylas, M. (2005) 'A pedagogy of unknowing: witnessing unknowability in teaching and learning', *Studies in Philosophy and Education*, 24(2): 139–60.

Zembylas, M. (2007) *Five Pedagogies, a Thousand Possibilities*. Rotterdam: Sense Publishers.

INDEX

Added to a page number 'f' denotes a figure, 'n' denotes a note and 'g' denotes glossary.